AF709921

MAKING SOCIAL SECURITY LAW

This book is dedicated to
Trevor, David and Roy's respective partners:
Barbara, Frances and Claire

Making Social Security Law

The Role and Work of the Social Security and Child Support Commissioners

TREVOR BUCK
DAVID BONNER
University of Leicester, UK

ROY SAINSBURY
University of York, UK

ASHGATE

© Trevor Buck, David Bonner and Roy Sainsbury 2005

All rights reserved. No part of this publication may be reproduced, stored in a retrieval system, or transmitted in any form or by any means, electronic, mechanical, photocopying, recording or otherwise without the prior permission of the publisher.

Trevor Buck, David Bonner and Roy Sainsbury have asserted their right under the Copyright, Designs and Patents Act, 1988, to be identified as the authors of this work.

Published by

Ashgate Publishing Limited
Gower House
Croft Road
Aldershot
Hampshire GU11 3HR
England

Ashgate Publishing Company
Suite 420
101 Cherry Street
Burlington, VT 05401-4405
USA

Ashgate website: http://www.ashgate.com

British Library Cataloguing in Publication Data
Buck, Trevor
Making social security law : the role and work of the Social Security and Child Support Commissioners
1. Great Britain. Social Security and Child Support Commissioners 2. Social security - Law and legislation - Great Britain 3. Child support - Law and legislation - Great Britain 4. Administrative remedies - Great Britain 5. Independent regulatory commissions - Great Britain
I. Title II. Bonner, David III. Sainsbury, Roy
344.4'1032'0269

Library of Congress Cataloging-in-Publication Data
Buck, Trevor.
Making social security law : the role and work of the social security and child support commissioners / by Trevor Buck, David Bonner, and Roy Sainsbury.
p. cm.
Includes bibliographical references and index.
ISBN 0-7546-4381-6
1. Great Britain. Social Security and Child Support Commissioner. 2. Social security courts--Great Britain. 3. Administrative remedies--Great Britain. 4. Examiners (Administrative procedure) --Great Britain. 5. Child support--Law and legislation--Great Britain. I. Bonner, David. II. Sainsbury, Roy. III. Title.

KD3199.B83 2005
344.4102'3--dc22

2005015265

ISBN-10: 0 7546 4381 6

Printed and bound by Athenaeum Press, Ltd.
Gateshead, Tyne & Wear.

Contents

List of Tables and Figures

Preface

The aim of this book is to provide a comprehensive and critical account of the role and work of the Social Security and Child Support Commissioners of the United Kingdom ('the Commissioners'). The work has been based on an empirical research project funded by the Nuffield Foundation.

In our early formulation of this project (in 1999) we realised that there was a significant gap in the scholarly literature about the Commissioners. The last attempt to provide a full account was Sir Robert Micklethwait's *Hamlyn Lectures* in 1976. This is an intriguing account, but of course relates to a social security system that is now less recognisable and was written from a standpoint vulnerable to claims of subjectivity – Sir Robert was appointed a Commissioner in 1959 and was the Chief Commissioner from 1961 until his retirement in 1975.

We were also attracted to this research because it has always been a challenging prospect for researchers to obtain access to members of the judiciary. We got to experience later some of the reasons why that is so. Moreover, as the idea developed and Trevor Buck enlisted David Bonner (three doors away on the same corridor at Leicester) and Roy Sainsbury (rather further away in York) to form the research team, there were two public interventions that were to have a profound impact on the Commissioners; a Select Committee inquiry in 2000 and the Leggatt review of tribunals in 2001.

The data collection stage of the project occurred just after the Select Committee had reported and just before the publication of the Leggatt report. A number of assumptions and beliefs about the Commissioners were therefore being challenged from several directions; a state of affairs that was conducive to an interesting research environment. The Leggatt proposals for reforming the whole tribunal system have, after some delay, been taken up by the government. Their main thrust was formally accepted in 2003 and a White Paper followed in July 2004 setting out the government's plans that included the introduction of legislation in 2005 to take forward a new unified *Tribunals Service.*

The Commissioners are a long-standing example of a 'second-tier' appellate authority in the tribunal sector. They take applications for leave and appeals from the Appeals Service tribunals. The government's White Paper has proposed that a generic second-tier appellate body in the tribunal sector, called an 'Administrative Appeal Tribunal', is established. We believe therefore, that our study is not only relevant to those who have an interest in the subject matter of the Commissioners' jurisdictions, but also to anyone with an interest in the future of the entire tribunal system and the development of administrative justice generally.

The intention of this project has also been to combine socio-legal, academic law and social policy scholarship in order to better analyse and inform this work. At various times, different members of the research team have provided important contributions to the overall project: Trevor Buck's initiative in obtaining research funding and general management of the project, David Bonner's historical work on the provenance of Commissioners and contribution to creating an overall structure for the book, and Roy Sainsbury's confident grasp on methodological issues and invaluable assistance with helping to negotiate 'access' in the early stages of the project, to name but a few. We hope that this combined effort is reflected in this work.

Academics, like the Commissioners, are now also audited in a number of ways. Increasingly we have to account for ourselves, in particular in relation to research output for the purposes of the Higher Education Funding Council for England's 'research assessment exercise' which is applied to all University departments. Consequently, while recognising that such a judgement is not an exact science, we have agreed that responsibility for the authorship of this book cannot be delineated by chapter responsibility but should rest as follows: Trevor Buck (65 per cent), David Bonner (25 per cent) and Roy Sainsbury (10 per cent).

Trevor Buck
David Bonner
Roy Sainsbury

3 May 2005

Acknowledgements

We are delighted to be able to acknowledge the assistance and encouragement of a number of individuals who have contributed to this research project. However, particular thanks must go to the Nuffield Foundation for funding this research and to Judge Kenneth Machin QC who, as Chief Commissioner (1990-2001) during the time we were making our applications for research funding, warmly welcomed our enterprise and contributed to the practical arrangements that had to be made for the purposes of interviewing a sample of appellants and all the full-time Commissioners in the United Kingdom.

Thanks are also due to Judge Machin's successors, Judge Harris (2001-2003) and Judge Hickinbottom (2003-present) who have also co-operated with our research project and agreed to be interviewed by us. A collective thanks must also be made to all the Commissioners, Deputy Commissioners and legal officers whom we interviewed at the London, Edinburgh and Belfast offices, and a special thanks to Jennifer Fowler, and Chris Smith, the senior legal officers in the London and Edinburgh offices respectively. We also received evidence, information and assistance from a number of other professionals in this field; particular thanks are due to Stewart Wright (CPAG) and Stephen Cooper (DWP Solicitor's branch). In addition, particular thanks must go to Commissioner Mark Rowland who provided some useful additional factual information in respect of one of the chapters.

Over the last five years there have been a number of administrative support staff within the three offices of the Commissioners who have given us much needed assistance, in particular we would like to thank Lesley Armes, Marisa Baldini, Debbie Joy, Bhu Mistry, Susan Niven, Lincoln Pereira, and Claire Zubler. In the early stages of this research project we received some very helpful research assistance from Barbara Bogusz. We must also record our thanks to the research associate, Sarah Scott, employed under the Nuffield grant, for her contribution, in particular in assisting with the practical arrangements required to interview the Commissioners, access appellants' files and to undertake telephone interviews. A number of Trevor Buck's students helped with the transcription of the interview tapes – Helen, Matthew, Rosa and Shamila. Further secretarial assistance was also provided by Dorothy Tomlinson and Mary McCormack at Leicester. Roy Sainsbury would like to thank the secretarial and administrative support staff at the Social Policy Research Unit (SPRU), particularly Sally Pulleyn and Teresa Frank. Thanks also to Jane Sowler at Leicester who assisted with proof reading the text of the book. Of course, any remaining errors belong to the authors.

Finally, we would like to express our gratitude to the two anonymous referees of the book proposal; both provided enthusiastic support and one encouraged us to explore further the theoretical dimensions, which we have attempted to do.

List of Abbreviations

ACIB	Adjudication and Constitutional Issues Branch
ADR	Alternative Dispute Resolution
AO	Adjudication Officer
AS	Appeals Service
CAB	Citizens Advice Bureau
CAT	Central Appeal Tribunal
CBJSA	Contribution-based Job Seekers Allowance
CICAP	Criminal Injuries Compensation Appeal Panel
CPAG	Child Poverty Action Group
CSA	Child Support Agency
DCA	Department for Constitutional Affairs
DLA	Disability Living Allowance
DM	Decision-Maker
DMA	Decision Making and Appeals
DMG	Decision Makers' Guide
DSS	Department of Social Security
DWP	Department of Work and Pensions
ECJ	European Court of Justice
IAA	Immigration Appellate Authorities
IAT	Immigration Appeals Tribunal
IB	Incapacity Benefit
IBJSA	Income-based Job Seekers Allowance
ICLR	Incorporated Council of Law Reporting
IRS	Independent Review Service
IS	Income Support
JSA	Job Seekers Allowance
LCD	Lord Chancellor's Department
NACAB	National Association of Citizens' Advice Bureaux
NILT	National Insurance Local Tribunal
OSSCSC	Office of the Social Security and Child Support Commissioners
PAA	Privileged access agreement
QR	'Query Reporting'
SBAT	Supplementary Benefit Appeals Tribunal
SENDIST	Special Educational Needs and Disability Tribunal
SSA	Social Security Act
SSAA	Social Security Administration Act
SSAC	Social Security Advisory Committee
SSAT	Social Security Appeals Tribunal
SSCBA	Social Security Contributions and Benefits Act
TSP	Tribunal Service Programme

Chapter 1

Introduction and Overview

Introduction

Based squarely on a Nuffield-funded empirical research project outlined below, this book examines and appraises the work of the Social Security and Child Support Commissioners, a specialist body of judges exercising statutory appellate jurisdiction throughout Great Britain on a point of law from the decisions of first-tier appeals tribunals in respect of the range of cash transfer payments we know as social security administered by the Department for Work and Pensions (DWP), the Inland Revenue, and by local authorities; and in respect of child support payments administered by the Child Support Agency (CSA). It also examines and appraises the comparable work done by the Commissioners' Northern Ireland counterparts.

Chapter 2 explores the creation of the Commissioners and subsequent changes both in title and in jurisdiction. Outlining the range of social security benefits, tax credits and child support matters that Commissioners consider, it notes the changing patterns by types of benefit/issue in their workload in the period surveyed by the research project (2000-2004). Finally, it examines just who the Commissioners are, particularly in terms of legal and professional background and how the Commissioners consider that background may have impacted on their work as Commissioners.

Chapter 3 examines and evaluates the Commissioners' role in the decision-making and appellate process. The Commissioners' work can be seen as primarily a paper-based jurisdiction with Commissioners exercising an inquisitorial role. This chapter provides, in particular, an account of the Commissioners' own views about some of the significant features of their appellate functions. It also examines the role of the 'legal officers' a unique resource in this jurisdiction. The chapter gives details of developments in the appeal work caseload and the impact of the decision-making and appeals (DMA) reform processes on the work of the Commissioners.

Chapter 4 analyses a range of other key concerns about the work of the Commissioners, centring on access to justice issues. It primarily consists of an analysis of the qualitative data from our interview work with participants in the process: the claimants, representatives and Commissioners. The analysis is set within a model of justice that identifies 'rights', 'needs' and 'deserts' (Miller, 1976). The chapter analyses the claimants' motivations in appealing, the perception of the Commissioners' independence, the impact of delay, questions relating to users' participation and the importance of the dignity factor in users' experiences of the appeal process. Finally, it explores the appellants' and Commissioners' views about representation and self-representation, the latter being a significant element in the 'Leggatt-style' reforms the government is currently considering.

Chapter 5 considers the Commissioners' crucial law-ascertaining and law-creating roles in 'making' law, and in constructing case law. It deals further with those concerns about access to justice which focus on the availability of Commissioners' decisions which 'make' law and with issues about the process of identifying the 'authoritative' decision from amongst that mass of, possibly inconsistent, decisions. This involves both the consideration of the formal legal rules to identify the hierarchy of authority, but more importantly it explores in detail the process whereby a small body of Commissioners (usually chaired by the Chief Commissioner) decides which Commissioners' decisions are to have the higher authoritative status of a 'reported' decision. It argues that the formal legal rules, though appropriate enough when there were only a few Commissioners, now raise new difficulties not least consequent upon the increased numbers of Commissioners in post and in the range of their jurisdictions. It evaluates the extent to which the Commissioners' process of reporting can be a viable model for the reformed tribunal system likely to be established in the near future.

Chapter 6 looks to matters of accountability of the Commissioners. This flows out of an examination of one aspect of this in Chapter 5: the requirement that they make reasoned decisions which are then available for public and professional critique. Chapter 6 explores the structured and informal arrangements for accountability and supervision while preserving the judicial independence of the Commissioners. In particular, it analyses the supervision provided by the courts by means of further appeals and/or judicial review; the nature of the role of the Lord Chancellor/Secretary of State for Constitutional Affairs; the scrutiny afforded by the Council on Tribunals, the inquiry by the House of Commons Select Committee on Social Security and of the Leggatt review of Tribunals; the element of 'collegiality' amongst Commissioners and the role played by the user group.

Finally, Chapter 7 seeks to bring together findings from the other chapters to evaluate the role of the Commissioners, their response to the concerns identified by a number of reviews and commentators, and their place as a formative model for the second-tier appellate level in the reformed tribunal structure. Broadly, it concludes that the response to concerns has generally been successful, sometimes not. Notable successes include major reductions in the time needed expeditiously to process cases and in creating markedly improved access to Commissioners' decisions, making good use of modern technology in electronic publishing. Problems still exist, however, in clearly defining the criteria for the selection of decisions to be given the more authoritative 'reported' status and in securing appropriate representation for individuals whose cases are being dealt with by the Commissioners in these complicated areas of law. More fundamentally, but perhaps inevitably, given the Commissioners' more court-like status than first-tier tribunals, there are problems resulting from perceptions of the process as being too complex and remote from the needs of lay users as they see them.

Within that purpose and structure, this chapter first provides, for the reader new to all this, a brief introduction to the Commissioners and their core functions, and seeks to place them and their work in a number of perspectives: that of comparable appellate bodies; that of a court structure aimed at ensuring a degree of accountability. The chapter then outlines the unique empirical research project undertaken by the authors over the period 2000-2004, on which this work draws. An overview of the context of this research is then given.

During the research period there were a number of public examinations of the work of the Commissioners raising a variety of issues, ranging from detailed administrative arrangements to wider policy and structural issues. Since we began writing this book, the Department for Constitutional Affairs (DCA) produced recommendations (White Paper, 2004) in response to the radical proposals advanced in the Leggatt report on tribunals (Leggatt, 2001) and the government is planning to introduce a Courts and Tribunals Bill at the end of 2005 (see Appendix 6 for the government's timetable of reform). The Commissioners are a significant second-tier appellate body within the wider tribunal environment. This book is, therefore, a timely contribution to the consideration of how best to organise a reformed tribunal service. But we hope that it will also shed light on the problem of adjudication, not only in the important social security field in particular, but also in administrative law generally. Finally, this chapter briefly introduces the reader to some general theories of adjudication, specialised and bureaucratic justice that are referred to in later chapters to shed light on the role and work of the Commissioners.

Who are the Commissioners and what do they do?

The Commissioners were established in 1948 and have played a central role in social security adjudication in the United Kingdom since then. Chapter 2 charts the development of and changes in their jurisdiction (see Appendix 4 which sets out the main categories of benefit currently dealt with by the Commissioners). For the moment, we focus on more general points.

The Commissioners – all senior lawyers of at least 10 years standing – are members of the senior judiciary (a Commissioner in terms of salary and protection against removal is the equivalent of a circuit judge), and they are independent in the exercise of their judicial functions. There are (currently) also 17 deputy Commissioners; assisting with the workload and providing a pool of expertise from which future Commissioners can be drawn. All Commissioners in Great Britain fall under the jurisdiction of the Lord Chancellor. Twelve legal officers exercising significant quasi-judicial functions aid the work of all Commissioners and deputies. They are further assisted by some 60 court staff. Their administrative arm, the Office of the Social Security and Child Support Commissioners (OSSCSC), falls under the auspices of the Lord Chancellor's Department (LCD) in England and Wales, (and, in Scotland, that of the Justice Department of the Scottish Executive).

In Northern Ireland, there are comparable appeal rights to (two) Northern Ireland Commissioners, including a Chief Commissioner, but under separate legislation.[1] Appeals arise from decisions of officials in the Northern Ireland Social Security Agency constituted under the supervision of the Department for Social Development. It is formally a distinct legal jurisdiction to that of Great Britain. However, in practice, the two Commissioners in Northern Ireland liaise with the GB Commissioners on a range of matters.

There are, at the time of writing, 20 full-time Commissioners in the United Kingdom, including the Chief Commissioner for Great Britain, currently HH Judge Hickinbottom, appointed in September 2003, and a Chief Commissioner for Northern Ireland, currently HH Judge Martin, appointed in 1997. There are currently two Commissioners sitting permanently in Scotland under the Great Britain jurisdiction. Mr May QC is the Senior Commissioner for Scotland. Each Commissioner constitutes in law a separate tribunal. A full list of the current Commissioners and past Commissioners retiring from 1997 is given in Appendix 3.

Their jurisdiction is entirely statutory and almost exclusively appellate. All aspects of it are civil rather than criminal. It embraces: a range of means tested and non-means tested social security benefits dealing with unemployment, incapacity for work, and disability administered by the DWP; child benefit, guardian's allowance and a variety of tax credits administered by the Inland Revenue; the child support scheme operated by the CSA; pensions (and soon to include war and armed forces pensions); the regulated (but not the discretionary) social fund; housing benefit and council tax benefit administered by local authorities; and recovery of social security benefits from compensation. They have original jurisdiction with respect to denial of social security benefits on the basis of the forfeiture rule. Their work thus covers primarily areas of state–citizen dispute, but child support takes them into an area at the interface of public and private law, since there the dispute involves not only the state but also disputes between parents. The area of compensation recovery places Commissioners at the interface of social security and personal injury litigation, having in reality if not in precise legal form, insurance companies as one of the parties to the proceedings.

Most of the rules they apply emanate from statute, whether Acts or Statutory Instruments, and from case law of themselves and the courts. Inevitably there has been, since 1973, a European Union law dimension and, in the Human Rights Act era, a Convention rights dimension. Moreover, they also deal with appeals on points of law arising from the bilateral social security agreements between the UK and other countries. The Commissioners hear cases from all parts of Great Britain (England, Scotland and Wales). Northern Ireland has virtually identical systems in these areas, and its own Commissioners. In this book, 'Commissioners' refers to those in both the GB and Northern Ireland jurisdictions unless the context indicates otherwise.

---

[1] See the Social Security (Northern Ireland) Order 1998, SI 1998/1506 (NI 10) and the Justice (Northern Ireland) Act 2002.

The Commissioners and other large tribunals

The Commissioners' caseload is best considered in comparison with the appeal work performed by the other large tribunals connected with the work of central government. It is by no means the smallest. But nor is it the largest, being dwarfed by immigration, tax, and mental health areas.

Table 1.1 Number of appeals to the largest tribunals

Tribunal	Received
Mental Health Review Tribunals	20,408
Criminal Injuries Compensation Appeal Panel	4,434
Special Educational Needs and Disability Tribunal	3,638
General & Special Commissioners of Income Tax	29,498
VAT & Duties Tribunal	2,496
Social Security and Child Support Commissioners	6,364
Pensions Appeals	3,372
Immigration Adjudicators	91,945
Immigration Appeal Tribunal	41,889

Source: White Paper (2004:15). The Social Security and Child Support Commissioner figures are for April 2003 – March 2004.

The Commissioners: accountability within the court structure

The Commissioners, since 1948, despite attempts to render their decisions 'final' and minimise court intervention for reasons examined in Chapter 2, have been subject to the scrutiny of the courts. Initially this was by way of judicial review in the Divisional Court, but the courts generally deferred to the Commissioners' specialist expertise (see Chapter 6). There was some public concern, as detailed in Chapter 2, about the dislocation occurring generally between the tribunal system and the courts. Receding fears of 'judicial sabotage' and the need for legal consistency were factors in ensuring that, in 1980, the decisions of the Commissioners were appealable, with leave of Commissioner or Court, on a point of law, to the Court of Appeal (Court of Session in Scotland, Court of Appeal in Northern Ireland). But most appeals do not progress beyond the level of the Commissioners (see Chapter 6), meaning that in reality they are the court of final instance on appeals of great importance to the more vulnerable sectors of our society. Moreover, Commissioners' decisions establish points of law to be followed by all below them and generally by other Commissioners. The binding and law making nature of decisions is examined in Chapter 5. The extent to which the

Commissioners' decisions are in fact accountable to the higher court control is examined in further detail in Chapter 6.

The research project methods

The research project, which informs much of this work, was conceived in 1999 and received a small pump-priming grant from the University of Leicester in that year, followed by an award from the Nuffield Foundation in 2001. The former helped to initiate some original historical research on the origin and development of the jurisdiction: see Bonner (2002). The latter enabled the employment of a research associate for one year and the collation of statistical and interview data. In brief, the empirical research involved interviewing all the full-time Commissioners (23) in the United Kingdom, other professionals in the field, for example some of the 'legal officers' within OSSCSC, a representative from the Child Poverty Action Group (CPAG) and a structured sample of appellants' for their views on the process. Finally, we were also given observational status over a two-year period to meetings of a small group of Commissioners, chaired by the Chief Commissioner, who decide which decisions will be 'reported' and thus carry greater authority.

The overall aims of the research[2] were to (i) chart the development of the role of the Commissioners since 1975 and (ii) to evaluate the utility of the Commissioners' appeal work for claimants and their advisers. The project focussed on three principal research sites: face to face interviews with all the full-time Commissioners; tracking a sample of appellants' cases and examining the documentation followed by telephone interviews; and the observation of Commissioners' meetings to discuss the reporting of Commissioners' decisions.

Interviewing the Commissioners

Researchers have in the past often found difficulty in obtaining research access to the senior judiciary (Baldwin and McConville, 1977), though some are on record as having encountered less difficulty (Paterson, 1982:5 n26). However, the Commissioners, under the then leadership of Chief Commissioner Judge Machin QC and the former Senior Commissioner for Scotland, Mr William Walker QC, proved to be very co-operative[3] in our enterprise and willing to be interviewed, subject to meeting concerns about confidentiality. The Commissioners would not agree, however, to questions being put about *individual* cases on the basis that any 'extra judicial' pronouncements on specific cases, however anonymised, might

---

[2] The research questions are explored in an earlier article: Bonner, Buck and Sainsbury (2001).

[3] The Chief Commissioner was shown an extract from Paterson (1982:4-8) which provided a welcome reassurance that if the Law Lords could be interviewed by an academic it would probably be all right if the Commissioners submitted to similar treatment!

compromise their judicial function. We also experienced delays in getting the final permission (from the then Lord Chancellor, Lord Irvine) to undertake this work and to agree the terms and conditions on which the interviewing would take place, even though 'in principle' agreement had been obtained from the Chief Commissioner and officials of the Lord Chancellor's Department at a meeting back in February 1999.

All the full-time Commissioners (23) then in post, including three Commissioners in Edinburgh and two in Belfast, were interviewed between October 2001 and November 2002.[4] The Commissioners were interviewed by at least one of the senior research team members (Trevor Buck, David Bonner or Roy Sainsbury) and our research associate also assisted with these interviews. Each (tape-recorded) interview lasted about one and a half to two hours and was later transcribed for analysis. The research team used a short questionnaire (see Appendix 1) that had been sent to each individual Commissioner prior to the interview. It was designed to include some general questions on the professional background of the Commissioners and their perceptions of how this had informed their work. It also included some more specific questions relating to the work of the Commissioners, for example, the value of oral hearings. Finally, each interview concluded with another set of general questions relating to the Commissioners' perceptions of the reporting arrangements, the issue of delay and their general contribution to developing the social security jurisdiction. During the period of interviewing, the Commissioners were also acutely aware of the activities of the Leggatt review team and were in the process of writing their response to the Leggatt report: see Machin (2001) (London office Commissioners), Walker (2001) (Edinburgh office Commissioners) and Martin (2001) (Belfast office Commissioners). They were also mindful of the Select Committee (2000) inquiry into their work that had reported the year before. The thoughts of the Commissioners on these two external interventions were fresh at the time of the interviews and consequently, though it does not appear on the interview topic guide, questions about various aspects of Leggatt and the Select Committee and Commissioner 'collegiality' were either put into the verbal questioning or naturally arose in the course of the interviews.

Tracking appellants' cases and interviewing

This took longer than anticipated in setting up due to the concerns raised by the Commissioners about confidentiality issues relating to the appellants and the technical difficulties in extracting the information we wanted from OSSCSC's operating system. The OSSCSC was accommodated in a split site in London: the Commissioners were accommodated at Harp House while the administrative support staff were accommodated at Newspaper House. This had caused a number

[4] In addition, the newly appointed Chief Commissioner, Judge Hickinbottom, was interviewed by Trevor Buck on 5 March 2004.

of administrative difficulties in the Commissioners' operation. In May 2004, the administrative support staff were moved into a new office: Procession House in London. However, the Commissioners remain at Harp House.

We had to manage some delicate negotiations to achieve the desired access to an appropriate data set of appellants and access to their documentation. Once this had been settled with the Chief Commissioner and officials from OSSCSC and the LCD, the latter issued a 'privileged access agreement' to the research team.[5] A key concern by all involved was to ensure that the appellants were clearly informed that the research was independent and would have no bearing on the outcome of their appeals. Guarantees of the appellants' anonymity in any subsequent research were given. The procedures, explained below, which were developed in consultation with the Chief Commissioner and officials from OSSCSC, in effect provided a 'double-lock' of an opt-out and opt-in procedure to ensure that appellants had clearly and freely consented to being approached by the researchers. An opt-out or opt-in procedure has become a standard procedure in DWP research contracts,[6] but it was not known how respondents would react to both procedures being used consecutively. The research team were, frankly, concerned that such caution might leave us with few appellants to interview, but, as will be seen, we had a healthy response rate from a good number of respondents who did not opt out at the initial stage of our procedure and who positively opted in at the second stage to indicate agreement to participate in the research.

One of the central objectives of the research project was to track a sample of cases selected from applications and appeals received by the Commissioners' office for a one-year period (from April 2000 to March 2001). The intention was to use this data set of cases as a baseline to assess the nature and make-up of the volume of cases received by OSSCSC. Once the consents had been obtained from the appellants we would then examine the documentation of some of these cases and, following that examination, we would select a smaller set of appellants for telephone interview.

An initial trawl of 650 cases was undertaken for the research team by OSSCSC administrative staff from their electronic database.[7] These were selected, under guidance from the research team, to ensure a reasonable spread over the calendar year was achieved and that there would be sufficient representation of disability living allowance (DLA) and incapacity benefit cases (which constitute a higher percentage of cases received by OSSCSC: see Chapter 3, Table 3.7) in addition to a

---

[5] Privileged access agreements (PAA) have been refined and developed by the LCD and now the DCA. 'If the research will involve looking at court files or recording other restricted information a PAA will be issued by the Court Service Record Management Service. This is a binding agreement between the researchers and the department that the research will fully anonymise all information collected, and that certain other safeguards will be met. It is to protect sensitive information under the terms of the Data Protection Act.' See http://www.dca.gov.uk/research/access.htm

[6] See Department of Social Security, *Research Guidance Manual*, paras 7.2.1-2.

[7] 'ERIC' (Every Record Is Casetracked). The initial trawl could not be undertaken by members of the research team who did not at that stage have consent from the appellants.

range of other benefits. In order to ensure that the appellants' consents were properly obtained, OSSCSC wrote to all 650 appellants explaining what the research was about, introducing the independent research team and making available an 'opt-out' slip to be returned to OSSCSC in the event the respondent did not wish to participate further. The list of respondents (who had not opted out) and their contact details and OSSCSC reference number were then handed over to the research team. There were 460 such cases.

These 460 appellants were then contacted directly by the research team and given a further opportunity to opt-out of the research. The appellants were sent a letter enclosing an 'opt-in' slip to confirm their consent in writing. 290 appellants returned completed consent slips and of these we accessed the files held at Harp House of 160 appellants. Notes were taken of key points contained in the documentation detailing the progression of the case, the core 'point of law' at issue and any other features of the case of particular interest and relevance to the work of the Commissioners.

We then interviewed 26 appellants by telephone and (with their further oral consent) tape-recorded and transcribed these interviews. A similar procedure, adapted to the manual filing system still in existence, was adopted for the Edinburgh office, resulting in eight telephone interviews. The selection process to identify the telephone interviewees was intended to maintain the broad representation of different benefit types used at our initial identification of the appellant data set. We also had regard to the regional location of each appellant. The interviews with appellants were conducted using a brief interview schedule (see Appendix 2). The schedule was used by the researchers as an *aide memoire* to ensure that each appellant was asked broadly the same questions around the following themes: the main issues raised by the appeal; appellants' perceptions of the independence of appeal tribunals and the Commissioners; their views about representation before the Commissioners; the timescale of appeals; perceptions about the choice between oral and paper hearings; and a number of open questions to sweep up any residual information about the users' experiences of the appeal process as a whole.

Observation of 'Star Chamber' meetings

Prior to undertaking our research we were aware that a small group of Commissioners met regularly under the chairmanship of the Chief Commissioner to select decisions for 'starring' and then subsequently to decide which of these 'starred' decisions ought to be formally 'reported'. The Commissioners colloquially referred to these meetings as the meeting of the 'Star Chamber', an appellation no doubt reflecting some awareness of the lack of wider accountability in the reporting process.[8] We had not foreseen in our original applications for

[8] The 'Star Chamber' is a reference to the arcane system of 'starring' Commissioners' decisions, as explained below, but it is also remindful of the 'Court of Star Chamber'

research funding that we would obtain access to these meetings and had intended merely to perform a desk-based review of this rather unique system of reporting. However, the then Chief Commissioner, HH Judge Machin QC, afforded Trevor Buck and David Bonner unprecedented observer status at these quarterly meetings. We observed a total of eight meetings, the first on 9 January 2001 and the last on 13 May 2002. These included meetings chaired by Judge Machin and then his successor as Chief Commissioner, Judge Harris. We were provided with the minutes and agenda papers in advance of the meetings. The research team typed up the written notes of these observations.

All Commissioners' decisions are formally binding on Appeals Service (AS) tribunals and are normally followed by other Commissioners, but 'reported' decisions have an added authority, the details of which are explained in Chapter 5. In undertaking this aspect of the research project therefore we were observing the Commissioners, quite literally, 'making social security law'.

In addition to the three main research sites, outlined above, the project also involved a smaller number of interviews with other professionals in the field: the legal officer of CPAG, Deputy Commissioners, and two of the Commissioners' legal officers (one in London and one in Edinburgh). There were also some observations of oral hearings at the Commissioner's office in London and of a Tribunal of Commissioners at the Royal Courts of Justice (the change of venue being necessitated because of the numbers of parties and lawyers in this compensation recovery case).

The context and importance of the research

We believe that this book is both timely and important, not only for its contribution to the debate about a reformed tribunal system and the Commissioners' place within it. There has also been no *comprehensive* appraisal of the role and function of the Commissioners since the account given by Sir Robert Micklethwait, who was himself a Commissioner (Micklethwait, 1976), though aspects of the Commissioners' operation have been commented upon from time to time (e.g. Harris, 1995; Roe, 1996; Machin, 1992). However, the context of their operation has changed substantially in the past 30 years. Their jurisdiction has grown. There have also been concerns about the delays in processing appeals, the costs associated with such appeals and the difficulties in producing a suitable system to make available the reported decisions of the Commissioners. Some of those

which had become a byword for the abuse of power by the Stuart Kings. Charles I used the Court of Star Chamber as a substitute for Parliament during the years 1628-40, when he refused to call Parliament. The Star Chamber was abolished by the Long Parliament in 1641 but the name still conjures up the spectre of arbitrary, secretive proceedings in opposition to personal rights and liberty.

concerns were highlighted by a Parliamentary inquiry into the Commissioners undertaken by the Select Committee on Social Security (Select Committee, 2000).

The Select Committee inquiry

That Committee undertook a 'short inquiry' into the work of the Social Security Commissioners. It took oral evidence at meetings on 16 February and 1 March 2000. The Committee reported in May 2000 (Select Committee, 2000) and the government's response to the report was issued in August of that year (Government Response, 2000). Four principal concerns emerged from the report: undue delay in getting appeals determined; inadequate arrangements made for the publication and availability of Commissioners' decisions; questions about the impact of the new DMA processes; and judicial independence.

The Committee concluded that 'there are substantial delays in determinations by the Commissioner, both in granting leave and in determining appeals' (Select Committee, 2000: para 10). They found that the average time between applications for and the granting of leave had been 23.7 weeks in 1997 and the average time between granting leave and a decision in 1998 had been 64.3 weeks. The Committee pointed to three causative factors: a split site office (then Newspaper House and Harp House); inadequacy of IT resources at OSSCSC; and the practice of cases not necessarily being dealt with by the same 'legal officer'.[9] It took the view that there was a 'culture of delay' and delays were cumulative in their detrimental effect.[10] However, the Committee conceded that some factors lay outside of the Commissioners' direct control and were the responsibility of the Appeals Service; for example, the delays in tribunal chairmen giving reasons for their decisions, the time it took for the Appeals Service to send the papers to OSSCSC, and the frequent requests by the Department for extensions of time to make written observations on cases going to the Commissioners. A 'test case' destined for the Court of Appeal or even the House of Lords would result in the 'stacking' of 'lookalike' cases at OSSCSC. The case of *Bate v Chief Adjudication Officer*[11] was a prime example. The House of Lords decided this case in May 1996, but prior to its final determination it resulted in about 5,000 'lookalike' cases frozen in the appeals system. On legal aid, the Committee, perhaps not unsurprisingly, concluded that 'the widespread use of legal aid [in social security

---

[9] The small team of legal officers are appointed by the Lord Chancellor and Secretary of State for Scotland. They have a number of delegated duties on procedural matters (e.g. determining requests for oral hearings, waiving irregularities, extending or abridging time, directing expedition): see SI 1999 No 1495, reg. 7.

[10] '[D]elay engenders further delay. The further away you get from the tribunal, the more difficult it becomes to recall the facts.' Simon Cox (barrister), Select Committee, 2000:Q.153, *Minutes of Evidence II.*

[11] [1996] 2 All ER 790. *Plummer and another v Chief Adjudication Officer*, 8 December 1998, (unreported) and *Cockburn v Chief Adjudication Officer and another*; *Secretary of State for Social Security v Fairey* (*also known as Halliday*) [1997] 3 All ER 844 were cited in the Committee's evidence as further examples.

cases] would be unlikely to be acceptable to the Government', but recommended that consideration should be given to the availability of legal aid in complex cases.[12]

As regards the publication and availability of Commissioners' decisions, the Committee were astonished and alarmed at the chaotic and almost laughable situation which applied to the availability of Commissioners' decisions; their availability was in a woeful state, such as to amount, in conjunction with the legal aid problems, to a possible breach of the Human Rights Act 1998.

Some thought the Select Committee's inquiry premature; to the extent that the DMA changes would need more time before their impact on the appeals process could be fully realised. For example, amidst the Commissioners' caseload were a substantial number of 'supported appeals', that is, ones where the claimant's application for leave or appeal was made with the support of the Secretary of State. The new setting aside power contained in SSA 1998, s.14(7) removes a substantial number of supported appeals that 'should never have come to the Commissioners in the first place.'[13] Equivalent powers available at tribunal level[14] might further stem the flow of applications for leave and appeals to the Commissioners.[15] Finally, the generous powers (SSA 1998, ss.25-27) to defer decisions in 'lookalike' cases until the lead case had reached its final destination could mean that 'lookalike' cases would not even get as far as OSSCSC.[16] See generally, Chapter 3, Figure 3.2, for a diagrammatic illustration of what we term in this book as appeal 'filtering' tools.

The propriety of the Select Committee challenging a purely judicial authority was raised, though there was recognition that a number of administrative issues arising on appeal, for example, processing time, could rightfully be within the Committee's remit.[17] This is explored further in Chapter 6. Evidence from CPAG suggested that 'in general, the Commissioners are very well respected by welfare rights organisations, claimants, Government agencies and the Courts'[18] The views of the Commissioners are frequently referred to in favourable terms in both the Court of Appeal and in the House of Lords (see further, Chapter 6). The complexity of the decisions with which they must deal was also noted. However, the Select Committee identified unfavourably in its report a 'degree of contact' between the Commissioners and the Department for Social Security (DSS) including the holding of 'regular meetings and the pressing of issues both ways'. The Committee concluded, 'the present arrangements are too cozy' and recommended a 'more even-handed method of prioritising cases based on claimant hardship and/or the potential importance of the case'. It urged the Chief

[12] Select Committee, 2000:para. 21.
[13] *Ibid*: Q.191, *Minutes of Evidence II.*
[14] Social Security Act 1998, s.13(2) and (3).
[15] Select Committee, 2000:Q.201, *Minutes of Evidence II.*
[16] *Ibid*: Memorandum submitted by the Office of Social Security and Child Support Commissioners (APP 4), para. 7.
[17] *Ibid*: para. 3.2.
[18] Memorandum submitted by CPAG (APP 11), para. 2.1, *Minutes of Evidence I.*

Commissioner to meet regularly with user groups and consult more widely in relation to the reporting of decisions.[19]

The response to the Select Committee's report

The Committee's inquiry clearly had a strong influence, both in the course of the inquiry and, following the publication of its report, in concentrating the minds of policy makers and administrators in the DSS, LCD and OSSCSC on the issues raised. There had been some significant progress in the publication of Commissioners' decisions. The Government Response (2000) contained little more than an endorsement of those elements in the Select Committee's report consistent with their own policies on the modernisation of public services. It also recorded the practical, on-going developments in the appeals process since the inquiry had first been announced. It rejected any suggestion that legal aid be extended more generally for social security cases, though it noted the Lord Chancellor's special power to fund legal representation in 'exceptional' circumstances.[20] In essence, the government thought that the overall design of the appeal system was sufficiently attentive to claimants' interests to preclude the need for the general funding of legal representation. Proceedings before both the AS tribunals and the Commissioners were inquisitorial and DSS officers representing the Secretary of State in effect adopted the role of an *amicus curiae* while claimants' representative groups, such as Citizens Advice Bureaux (CABx) were in any case publicly funded.

The government's response on necessary timetable improvements set a target of 26 weeks from receipt of the claimant's appeal, to be achieved by April 2002. It further noted with approval OSSCSC's plans to have new management information systems in place from October 2000 to produce better quality statistics and to monitor and record the length of time at each stage. The Government disagreed with the suggestion that legal officers be allocated to particular cases throughout; such a move 'would result in a loss of flexibility and would impede our ability to speed up the end to end process and throughput in the more straightforward cases.' The government also approved the establishment of a forum 'to seek to identify particular trends and [test case] campaigns at an early stage', so that 'lookalike' cases could be held at the lowest possible level pending resolution of the lead case. The suggestion that sanctions might be applied to control administrative delays in appeal processing was also rejected. A sanction by means of payment of benefit throughout the appeal period was rejected on the basis that this would, in effect, be providing payment without legal entitlement; and an 'interest sanction' was rejected on the basis that the Parliamentary Ombudsman was available to remedy 'maladministration' (a concept encompassing delay).

---

19 Select Committee (2000: para. 42).

20 Legal Aid Act 1988, s.4(2) and (4). These powers have now been carried over into the Access to Justice Act 1999, section 6(8). See further, the Select Committee, 2000: 'Supplementary memorandum submitted by CPAG' (APP 11A), *Minutes of Evidence I.*

The government's report also noted that there had been some necessary degree of contact between the Commissioners and the DSS; for example, to agree that certain cases be prioritised according to the claimant's hardship and/or potential importance of the case. The Chief Commissioner had also established and had an initial meeting of a Commissioners' 'user group' in order to produce the more even-handed approach indicated by the Committee (see further Chapter 6). Finally, the government stated there would be a review of the working of the whole appeal process but would 'consider its scope and timing'.

The Leggatt review of tribunals

Sir Andrew Leggatt, a retired Court of Appeal judge, was appointed by the Lord Chancellor on 18 May 2000 to undertake a review of tribunals. The report was published on 16 August 2001. The review team's terms of reference focussed on the administrative arrangements that could be made to provide an overall coherent, accessible, human rights-compliant, and efficiently managed and monitored system of tribunals. The Leggatt report (Leggatt, 2001) contained some quite radical recommendations to provide greater coherence in the system of administrative justice. There were some far-reaching proposals relating to the administrative and legal structure of the tribunal system. There were also some significant proposals to change or develop the overall culture and ethos of the tribunal sector.

As regards the administrative and legal structure, the report recommended the creation of a unified, overarching structure; a new 'Tribunal Service' giving access to all tribunals and placed under the departmental authority of the Lord Chancellor, who would make all tribunal appointments. The existing system of having some of the tribunals under the administrative control of a 'sponsoring' department was criticised as fundamentally flawed.[21] Tribunals to be included in the new structure would include not only citizen *v* state (e.g. social security) but also party *v* party (e.g. employment) tribunals. The report advocated the adaptation of court-based civil justice reforms to tribunal litigation to ensure procedures were expeditious, proportionate and cost effective. The report envisaged a staged approach to the creation of a new Tribunal Service (to be an executive agency of the LCD) and separate from the Court Service. The tribunals themselves would be organised into a divisional structure 'by coherent areas of work'.

A first tier of (first instance) tribunals would be allocated into nine Divisions (one of these to be a party *v* party division). Procedure for citizen *v* state tribunals should be based on a suitably revised version of the Council on Tribunals' *Tribunal Model Rules*. Procedure for party *v* party tribunals procedure should approximate to modern court procedure. Employment tribunal rules could be re-worked to correspond more closely with the Civil Procedure Rules. Each Division should have a national training strategy. Decisions of first-tier tribunals would not set any

---

[21] 'There should be separation between the ministers and other authorities whose policies and decisions are tested by tribunals, and the minister who appoints and supports them'. Leggatt Report (2001: para 2.23).

precedent in law. There would be judicial Presidents for each of the nine divisions; normally Circuit judges or senior lawyers and provision for Regional Chairmen to assist with the largest first-tier tribunals. The Presidents would have statutory duties to provide training.

Second-tier (appellate) tribunals should be established in five generic areas: Immigration, Social Security and Pensions, Land and Valuation, Financial, and Employment. The system of precedent setting practised by the Social Security Commissioners and the Immigration Appeal authorities ought to be adopted across all second-tier tribunals. A judicial Senior President would lead these tribunals along with the other Presidents and some of these would be High Court judges. Finally, there should be a general appeal available from the second-tier tribunals to the Court of Appeal. The ground for an appeal both from first- to second-tier tribunals and from the latter to the Court of Appeal ought to be on the generic ground that the decision of the tribunal was 'unlawful'.

A common time limit for appealing to the second-tier of six weeks from the date of the first-tier tribunal's reasoned decision was recommended. Statutory provisions to limit cases leaking out of the tribunal system into the supervisory jurisdiction of the Administrative Court were recommended: an overall preclusion of judicial review of second-tier tribunal decisions and an exclusion of judicial review of first-tier tribunal decisions where rights of appeal had not been exhausted.

The report suggested, rather weakly, that the Council on Tribunals could monitor the development of the tribunal system during the first few years of the new system as it was settling down and check that the practices and procedures of government departments were human-rights compliant. The Council should 'champion users' causes as its primary duty' and in general become a more 'proactive' body, e.g. monitoring training needs. It should report to a relevant Minister and Parliamentary Select Committee. The report recommended the Council's powers should be strengthened to review primary as well as secondary legislation in relation to tribunal matters.

Of even less clarity, was the proposal for a 'Tribunals Board' to direct the system. This would be made up of the Senior President, Presidents of appellate tribunals (High Court judges) and Presidents of the first-tier Divisions plus the chair of the Council on Tribunals, the chair of the tribunals committee of the Judicial Studies Board, and the chief executive of the Tribunals Service. The Board would advise LCD on the qualifications for members and chairmen, it would oversee the appointment of tribunal members, co-ordinate training, investigate complaints and recommend changes in rules of procedure where necessary. However, much of the detail of how this Board would relate to the revised Council on Tribunals and its precise duties was not worked through in any detail in the Leggatt report.

Nevertheless, the message of the report in respect of the cultural changes expected, was quite clear, though again the report lacked any detailed discussion of how this might be achieved. The report stated that a reformed tribunal system should be a more 'user-friendly' system: there should be better information available, in particular to facilitate users to prepare and present cases themselves. 'User groups' would feed back information about how the tribunal system was working. Furthermore, tribunals should adopt an 'enabling approach' to give users confidence in their ability to participate; and tribunals should try to compensate for any lack of skill or knowledge of users.

The most disappointing recommendations of Leggatt were those concerned with the public funding of tribunal cases. The report places the support of users to 'understand their case and its merits' at the top of the priority order for state assistance. However, although it is recommended that the Community Legal Service contract scheme should be extended to a wider number of advice organisations, the report states that:

> The remit of the Community Legal Service should be extended to include representation in more tribunals, but on an exceptional basis by reference to specific cases or classes of case, rather than particular tribunals. (Leggatt, 2001: para 48)

In short, subject to some narrow exceptions, state funding of legal representation for tribunal work should not be widened, indeed quite the opposite. The philosophy of 'do-it-yourself' advocacy in Leggatt has attracted some criticism from policy analysts (Adler, 2002). Indeed, our exploration of the views of social security appellants gives some support to those concerns: see Chapter 4.

Finally, the Leggatt report contained a brief account of the work of the Commissioners. The report noted the general concern about delays in case handling. It also recorded that the Commissioners were attempting to decide cases themselves rather than remit them back to the local tribunals. On the question of legal representation, the report records the Commissioners' view that barristers from the Free Representation Unit were 'usually of high quality' and welfare organisations 'generally provided a good service', though there was some reservation about advisers who were not legally trained and therefore 'not always able to get to the heart of a case'. Likewise, unrepresented appellants could pose problems, often helped by the intervention of the Commissioners' legal officers at the preparatory stage. The report noted the prevalent view that legal aid was necessary for Commissioner cases, but rejected this proposition on the basis of its wider conclusion that the extension of legal aid would not be the right answer for advice and assistance in its vision of a reformed tribunal system.

The Leggatt report also noted the difficulties experienced in the liaison arrangements between OSSCSC administrative staff (from the Court Service under the auspices of the LCD) and AS administrative staff (DSS civil servants). These organisations had 'developed different cultures and processes'. It concluded that although some improvements had taken place 'there remains a good deal to be done'.

The report made some favourable comments about the Commissioners' legal officers. Their role 'was seen as helpful by all those to whom we spoke, members and users alike'. They 'often provide a more expert analysis of the merits of the case than can the parties themselves' and could enable the Commissioners to take a more inquisitorial approach where the claimant was unrepresented. More generally, the Leggatt report also saw a role for 'registrars' in a reformed tribunal structure, a role not dissimilar in certain respects to the legal officers at OSSCSC. See further Chapter 3.

Transforming public service: the Government's White Paper (2004)

The government announced in March 2003 that it had accepted at least some of the main recommendations of Leggatt. The new Tribunal Service would bring together the ten largest tribunals (including the Commissioners), with other tribunals joining later, and the new Service would be accountable to the Lord Chancellor.[22] The government's subsequent White Paper (2004) confirmed that plan and the creation of a unified Tribunal Service as an executive agency of the DCA. It also accepted the need for a coherent split between first- and second-tier tribunals but it rejected Leggatt's suggested 'divisional' structure. Instead, it has proposed the creation of a single judicial office of 'Tribunal Judge' for first-tier tribunal work and 'Appellate Tribunal Judge' for second-tier tribunals. Individual jurisdictions will continue to have Presidents, though it is proposed a number of jurisdictions will be combined in due course. The White Paper proposed that the Council on Tribunals be renamed the 'Administrative Justice Council' and it should take on a more strategic role in supervising administrative justice generally. Under these plans, central leadership will be provided, not by Leggatt's suggestion of a 'Tribunals Board' but by the joint efforts of a Chief Executive of the new DCA agency and a Senior President of Tribunals.

The White Paper also announced a five year strategy for the DCA around four key elements: the development of policies that empower citizens; moving out of courts and tribunals disputes that could be resolved elsewhere, by means of better information, advice and 'proportionate dispute resolution'; radical change in the way in which services are delivered; and re-shaping the DCA's organisation and structure. In certain respects, it has taken Leggatt's notion of greater user-friendliness a step further. The White Paper states:

> But we see this new [Tribunal Service] as much more than a federation of existing tribunals. This is a new organisation and a new type of organisation. It will have two central pillars: administrative justice appeals, and employment cases. Its task, together with a transformed Council on Tribunals, will not be just to process cases according to law. Its mission will be to help to prevent and resolve disputes, using any appropriate method and working with its partners in and out of government, and to help to improve administrative justice and justice in the workplace, so that the need for disputes is reduced. (White Paper, 2004: para 1.14)

---

[22] Lord Chancellor's Department, 'Government Announces Modernised Tribunals Service' *Press Release, 106/03*, 11 March 2003.

Lord Filkin, a Parliamentary Under-Secretary of State at the DCA, declared similarly:

> I expect the tribunals, judiciary and staff to work together to provide a range of established and innovative services to tribunal users and to those who currently do not seek redress from the system. The approach to proportionate dispute resolution is the first manifestation of the department's new strategy for helping users of the justice system resolve issues without recourse to formal hearings.[23]

The timetable for reform (see Appendix 6) includes the introduction of a Courts and Tribunals Bill in Parliament later in 2005, the formal launch of the Tribunals Service agency and the creation of the Administrative Justice Council in April 2006. The Appeals Service is due to join the new Service in April 2007 and a new 'Administrative Appeals Tribunal' (the second-tier appellate body) will be operational on this date. The mental health tribunals and the Criminal Injuries Compensation Appeal Panel (CICAP) will join the new Service in April 2008 and remaining central government tribunals will join the new Service in 2009 (White Paper, 2004: 55).

In November 2004, the Lord Chancellor, Lord Falconer, announced the appointment of a Chief Executive (Peter Handcock) for the new executive agency of the DCA and the Lord Chief Justice, with the agreement of the Lord President of the Court of Session and the Lord Chief Justice of Northern Ireland, appointed Sir Robert Carnwath (a Lord Justice of Appeal) to act as the Senior President-designate of Tribunals.[24]

Informative theories of dispute resolution and adjudication

The Commissioners can be seen as a sophisticated example of administrative law adjudication at an appellate level. It is, therefore, important, the better to approach analysing and evaluating the role(s) and functions of the Commissioners, to outline some of the theoretical understandings about dispute resolution and adjudication, as a number of these perspectives and models inform this work. We should emphasise that the following section provides only a very brief and selective account of these theoretical perspectives in a wide field of scholarship in this area.

---

[23] Department for Constitutional Affairs, *Press Release,* 15 July 2004, Government News Network, London.

[24] *Ibid*, *Press Release*, 25 November 2004, Government News Network, London.

General theories of dispute settlement and adjudication

Legal theorists have always had an interest in why disputes arise in society and how to deal with them. There is an impressive literature of legal anthropology, which examines the processes in different societies of dispute resolution. There has also been substantial philosophical enquiry into theories of adjudication, i.e. the resolution of a dispute by judicial pronouncement.

Natural law proponents assert there are self-evident principles for human action and 'law' can be identified only if it is a product of reason, it is aimed at promoting general well being, and must be made publicly known. Ultimately, natural law is conceived as a higher order of ethical standard which mere human laws must conform to in order to be valid. Arguably, a modern version of this perspective is contained in Dworkin's theory of adjudication which he calls 'Law as Integrity':

> Judges who accept the interpretive ideal of integrity decide hard cases by trying to find, in some coherent set of principles about people's rights and duties, the best constructive interpretation of the political structure and legal doctrine of their community. They try to make that complex structure and record the best these can be. (Dworkin, 1986: 255)

Classical doctrinal legal theory, by contrast, regarded law in isolation from morality or policy. An inductive process of reasoning from reading the cases could identify the fundamental principles, or legal doctrines, from which rules of law could be derived. The concern of this school of thought is with certainty of outcome rather than moral content. This results in the interpretative exercise being conceived as constrained to the 'text' of the law, i.e. the case rule and/or statutory provision, with no room for external sources of validation.

The American 'Legal Realist' school definitively rejected this approach. This school of thought advocated that judges do not really gather their decisions from natural or doctrinal law principles, but in fact from a series of hunches about what is right in the particular case affected by their own biases and rationalised through the medium of any convenient rule. In short, adjudication is a rationalisation of policy decisions.

The exposure of this more multi-faceted understanding of what judges do by the American realists has been prevalent with most contemporary theorists of dispute resolution and adjudication. Posner (1993), for example, argues that 'law is an activity rather than a concept or a group of concepts'. Laws are not abstractions but socially determined goals for shaping behaviour to conform to society's values. He argues that judges actually make difficult decisions by alighting upon a range of informal methods of what he terms 'pragmatic' reasoning. He asserts, in a later work that pragmatic decision-makers can consider the broad systemic effects of their decision making[25] in addition to case specific effects and that pragmatists

[25] Interestingly, the White Paper (2004: 11) approved of the 'systemic recommendations' forthcoming from independent complaint handlers in their survey of dispute resolution methods.

should focus on empirical evidence of effectiveness rather than 'abstract moral and political theory' (Posner, 2003).

The modern development of 'critical legal studies' and 'economic analysis of the law' can be regarded as derived from the Legal Realist school. The economic analysis approach produced the argument that judges ought to choose the legal rule that maximised the ratio of benefits to costs as measured by society's willingness to pay, i.e. a welfarist theory of adjudication. However, there are difficulties in this analysis. One might construct a theory of adjudication at two levels. Firstly, one might take as given the general structure of adjudication within a particular legal system and simply ask what obligations judges have within that system. Secondly, one could more radically pose the question of how to design the judicial system from scratch. Most theories of adjudication are of the first type. However, the second approach will bring in more information about the institutional environment within which the judge operates in addition to the evaluation of the judges' obligations within the system.

The American jurist, Lon L. Fuller also attempted to find the essence of adjudication (Fuller, 1978). Fuller thought there were essentially two forms of social ordering: organisation by common aims and organisation by reciprocity. He argued that contract was an archetypal application of the latter and elections an application of the former. Adjudication, contract and elections, he argued were 'three ways of reaching decisions, of settling disputes, of defining men's relations to one another', but the characteristic linking feature of each form lay in the manner in which the affected party *participated* in the decision reached. As regards adjudication he stated:

> This whole analysis will derive from one simple proposition, namely, that the distinguishing characteristic of adjudication lies in the fact that it confers on the affected party a peculiar form of participation in the decision, that of presenting proofs and reasoned arguments for a decision in his favour. Whatever heightens the significance of this participation lifts adjudication towards its optimum expression. Whatever destroys the meaning of that participation destroys the integrity of adjudication itself. Thus, participation through reasoned argument loses its meaning if the arbiter of the dispute is inaccessible to reason… (Fuller, 1978: 364)

Adjudication therefore gives formal expression to reasoned argument. Fuller argued that behind 'reasoned argument' there must be some underlying principle from which to rationalise. In civil cases the issues would therefore come down to a claim of a 'right' or in criminal cases, accusations of fault. Whatever one's view on Fuller's concept of adjudication, he does at least remind us of the need to identify and support the 'rational core' of the adjudication process. The Fullerian analysis is also a useful reminder of the conceptual differences between *adjudication* and *mediation*. When a judge diverts from the reasoned task of rights discourse and steps down to suggest a 'deal' between the parties s/he steps out of the role of adjudicator into a mediator's role. This debate is a poignant one in the light of the present government's increasing desire to find 'robust' alternative dispute resolution (ADR) methods to formal court and tribunal adjudication.

Of particular relevance too in the Commissioners' case and in the context of state welfare benefits and adjudication machinery, are theories of 'specialised justice' and 'bureaucratic justice'. Consequently these warrant more detailed treatment.

Theories of specialised justice

Legomsky noted that the few available studies, which have addressed the subject of specialised adjudication, have often merely described the respective advantages and disadvantages of specialist adjudication:

> They have not proceeded to what strikes me as the logical next question: For which groups of cases will the benefits of specialized adjudication outweigh the costs? By what criteria can such cases be identified? (Legomsky, 1990: 4)

Legomsky formulated a general theory containing practical criteria capable of identifying cases in which the benefits of specialised justice would outweigh the disadvantages. He proposed the following 12 criteria (Legomsky 1990: 22-32).

- *Mix of law, fact and discretion* – a high proportion of law questions would generally weigh against specialist adjudication; fact questions are conducive to specialisation, particularly at the initial stages of adjudication; and discretionary questions, to which there is a wide range of possible answers, lend themselves to specialised scrutiny.
- *Technical complexity* – the specialist forum will know the overall programme and how the detail fits in.
- *Degree of isolation* – how discrete or unique is the area of law? If it does not affect analogous areas then a specialist forum is more appropriate.
- *Cohesiveness* – a high degree of internal consistency within a particular area favours specialisation.
- *Degree of repetition* – a high number of similar cases raises the importance of consistency and favours specialisation.
- *Degree of controversy* – the greater degree of controversy favours a generalist approach to ensure legitimacy.
- *Clannishness* – where there is a close network of professionals in a particular field a generalist arrangement should be preferred.
- *Peculiar importance of consistency* – specialised adjudication can enhance consistency within the given field.
- *Dynamism* – a rapidly changing subject matter favours specialisation.
- *Logistics: volume, time per case, and geographic distribution* – a high volume of (like) cases can be more efficiently dealt with by a specialist

body, especially where such cases are time consuming and geographically dispersed.

- *Special need for prompt resolution* – specialists will take less time to clear cases and be better equipped to filter out unmeritorious cases.
- *Unique procedural needs* – the procedure can be customised to the attributes of type of case, e.g. giving the adjudicator an active role in areas where advocacy is weak, developing informal procedures where the claimant is vulnerable and/or unrepresented.

It should be noted that these criteria are advanced with the qualification that none of them are necessary or sufficient conditions for specialisation. They are factors that may conflict and may be of varying weight and will therefore require careful balancing. The model Legomsky (1990: 38-42) preferred is what he called 'multiple-speciality adjudication'. Interestingly, this is arguably the general model implicit in the Leggatt reform proposals that envisaged a divisional structure of grouped tribunal jurisdictions (see above). Although, Legomsky conceded that a single speciality model would have the advantage of greater expertise, nevertheless the merits of multiple speciality are convincing. He argued that the advantages existed to some extent at the initial decision-making stage but were greater at the appellate stage. At the appellate stage 'the incremental value of expertise becomes marginal once the threshold level of familiarity has been achieved.'

> [T]his marginal sacrifice of specific expertise permits the purchase of substantially all the benefits of legal generalism. The members are exposed to a diverse case-load. The benefits of a generalist perspective lie principally in the value of analogy; the multiple-speciality model would seem at least as likely as the general jurisdiction model to expose the adjudicators to analogous cases. It might even be argued that, if anything, the multiple-speciality approach is more likely to sprout productive analogies because the specialities that are combined can be deliberately selected with an eye toward that goal. (Legomsky, 1990: 40)

Further advantages put forward for this model were that it reduced the quality-related dangers of specialised justice, e.g. reducing the monotony that might otherwise hinder recruitment of able individuals. This approach, it is claimed, could also promote the efficient use of scarce resources.

Ultimately, the issue of specialised justice is a constitutional one touching upon political decisions regarding the preferred institutional balance to be achieved in particular policy areas. Different national legal orders, even within the same 'family' of legal system, have alighted upon different solutions to the problem. In South Africa, for example, the government identified in 1997 court specialisation as one of the key strategies for the provision of 'an adequate network of accessible and service-oriented courts and other judicial and quasi-judicial institutions for all communities' (Altbeker, 2003). It listed, in particular, family law, sexual offences and juvenile justice as areas particularly ripe for specialist court treatment. In the UK in the post-war era, as explained in Chapter 2, administrative tribunals were in part established to deal with the large numbers of appeals expected from the establishment of more comprehensive social welfare systems but were also the chosen format, as some senior Labour politicians of the day simply mistrusted the political neutrality of the judiciary in the general court system. Prior to the Franks Report (1957) the policy was to isolate tribunals from the regular court system, in part because of the 'judicial sabotage of socialist legislation' that judges might apply to welfare state institutions.[26] Although later British governments did not develop those concerns further, the courts developed judicial review as a remedy that eventually pervaded the tribunal sector. It also became accepted that there ought to be a right of appeal from tribunals back to the courts. This was achieved for some tribunals by separate legislative amendment (e.g. in the social security field). A general provision applying to a number of tribunals was inserted into the Tribunals and Inquiries Act 1992, thus in effect developing this integration with the court system.

Bureaucratic justice: Mashaw and the social/public administration perspective

Mashaw (1983) has provided perhaps the most intriguing and relevant analysis of models of justice in the social security context. In reviewing the critical literature concerning the administration of disability benefits in the United States, he delineated three strands of commentary. One strand focussed on the failure to manage the adjudication of claims in ways that produced predictable and consistent outcomes. In other words, a concern that the system was out of control and further objective criteria should be provided for the exercise of adjudicatory discretion. The system was viewed in bureaucratic terms and criticised for 'its inadequate management controls'. Another strand was that the disability programme failed to provide adequate service to claimants. The failure of the decision making process to emphasise the role of professional judgment and to adopt an appropriate service orientation was seen as the programme's major deficiency. A third strand was primarily concerned with the individual claimant's capacity to assert and defend his or her rights to disability benefits. This literature was concerned with, for example, the need for representation, the lack of adversarial testing of evidence. In short, the concern was with the failure of the decision making process 'to provide the essential ingredients of judicial trials'.

He hypothesised that there were elements that unified each of these three perspectives, and each of the 'models of justice' he asserted could be utilised for the evaluation of administrative adjudication *generally*. He suggested the three perspectives in the literature produced three types of justice arguments:

(i) that decisions should be accurate and efficient concrete realisations of the legislative will;
(ii) that decisions should provide appropriate support or therapy from the perspective of the relevant professional cultures; and

[26] *Hansard*, HC Debs. vol 425, 1983 (27 July 1946, Mr Aneurin Bevan MP).

(iii) that decisions should be fairly arrived at when assessed in the light of traditional processes for determining individual entitlements. (Mashaw, 1983: 25).

He labelled these models of justice respectively: *bureaucratic rationality*, *professional treatment*, and *moral judgment*. From the perspective of bureaucratic rationality, administrative justice requires pre-eminently processes that are suitably rationalised to take account of costs. The classic techniques of decision-making are information retrieval and processing. The model is legitimated on the basis that it seeks to accurately implement, within any one field, pre-established social goals, while conserving social resources for other programmes. The primary goal of professional treatment, on the other hand, is to serve the client. An administrative system, therefore, to administer welfare benefits would be client-oriented. Such services to the client would of course be constrained by cost considerations. In the professional treatment model 'the incompleteness of facts, the singularity of individual contexts, and the ultimately intuitive nature of judgment are recognized, if not exalted.' In an administrative justice system under this model, substantive and procedural rules, hierarchical controls and efficiency considerations 'would all be subordinated to the norms of the professional culture' (Mashaw, 1983: 27). Finally, the paradigm adjudicatory situations in moral judgment are those of the civil and criminal trial. On the surface it may seem that if this approach is mainly about getting the facts right so as to correctly apply legal rules it is little different to bureaucratic rationality. However, Mashaw states that the moral judgment perspective should be viewed as 'value defining'. 'The question is not just who did what, but who is to be preferred, all things considered, when interests and the values to which they can be relevantly connected conflict' (Mashaw, 1983: 29-30). In short, the moral judgment model has the goal of awarding entitlements on the basis of a notion of the deservingness of the parties in the particular context, giving rise to a claim for a right. Mashaw argues that this model implies a just process of proof and decision.

It is certainly the case that looking at the decision-making and appellate process within social security as a whole one can detect elements of all three of Mashaw's typology (see Chapter 3). The initial benefit decision making by departmental officials is probably best characterised as an exercise in bureaucratic rationality. The increasing technocratic approach, in particular to disability benefits, is arguably a good example of this approach. The way in which the medical profession is utilised in relation to disability decision-making is a good example of aspects of the professional treatment model. However, the appeal hearing function of the Commissioners probably corresponds most closely, at least on an initial analysis, with moral judgment. Its legitimating value is fairness, its primary goal is conflict resolution, and it requires an independent adjudicator and employs the classic technique of contextual interpretation (see further Chapter 6). Mashaw's typology of the three justice models (see Table 1.2 below) remains a useful analytical tool for our purposes and will be revisited again in the following chapters of the book. Chapter 7 attempts to apply the Mashaw analysis specifically to the Commissioner system.

Table 1.2 Features of the three justice models (Mashaw)

Dimension/ Model	Legitimising Value	Primary Goal	Structure or Organization	Cognitive Technique
Bureaucratic Rationality	Accuracy and Efficiency	Programme Implementation	Hierarchical	Information Processing
Professional Treatment	Service	Client Satisfaction	Interpersonal	Clinical Application of Knowledge
Moral Judgment	Fairness	Conflict Resolution	Independent	Contextual Interpretation

Source: Mashaw (1983: 31).

The Commissioners and social justice

Miller's seminal study of social justice nearly 30 years ago offers a useful parallel analysis to Mashaw. Miller argues that the subdivision of the concept of justice has its roots in early Greek and Christian thought, and identifies one of the most important of these as 'social justice'. For Miller, social justice concerns:

> ...the distribution of benefits and burdens throughout a society, as it results from the major social institutions – property systems, public organisations, etc. It deals with such matters as the regulation of wages and ... profits, the protection of persons' rights through the legal system, the allocation of housing, medicine and welfare benefits etc. (Miller, 1976: 22)

From here he suggests that there are three principles by which the distribution of benefits and burdens in society can be made: on the basis of 'rights', 'needs' and 'deserts'. Miller acknowledges that these principles may at times come into conflict but what is useful from our perspective in the exploration of the Commissioners is that they seem to lie at the heart of Mashaw's models of administrative justice.

The model of bureaucratic rationality has as its legitimating value the accurate implementation of transparent rules. In relation to the British social security system these rules are principally enshrined in primary and secondary legislation that are legal rights that can be claimed and enforced by individual citizens. The bureaucratic rationality model therefore reflects a view of social justice based on rights. Mashaw's professional treatment model by contrast does not rely on a body of rules but a body of professional knowledge. Its practitioners seek to make decisions that apply that knowledge in the best interests of their clients. Professional treatment can therefore be seen as a means of distributing society's goods in response to people's needs. As explained earlier, the characteristic that distinguishes Mashaw's model of moral judgment from bureaucratic rationality and professional treatment is that is 'value-defining' and seeks to establish the deservingness of the parties to a dispute. Here we have echoes of Miller's third conceptualisation of social justice as the allocation of society's burdens and benefits on the basis of deserts.

This synthesis of Mashaw and Miller becomes a powerful theoretical basis for understanding the experiences and views of appellants whose cases are heard by the Commissioners, a matter that will be explored further in Chapter 4.

Chapter 2

The Commissioners and the Development and Nature of their Jurisdictions

Introduction

This chapter explores the creation of the Commissioners and subsequent changes both in title and in jurisdiction. Outlining the range of social security benefits, tax credits and child support matters that Commissioners consider, it notes the changing patterns by types of benefit/issue in the Commissioners' workload in the period surveyed by the research project. Finally, the chapter examines just who the Commissioners are, particularly in terms of legal and professional background and how that background may have impacted on what they do as Commissioners, and the ways in which they do it, using material from our interview work to convey the Commissioners' own perspectives on this matter.

Context is provided by first identifying ancestors of the Commissioners, enabling useful contrasts to be drawn between past and present adjudication systems, prefacing throughout the development of the jurisdictions with a consideration of the key features of the social security law with which the Commissioners – and their predecessors – had to deal. Just as the creation of the structures and benefits in the post-World War II social security system, based on the Beveridge blueprint, was a 'British revolution', building on and consolidating the best of the past, so too were its systems for redress of grievances.

Social security adjudication: the ancestry, and establishment, of the Commissioners in 1948

The period from 1897 sees a move from appeal as a complete re-hearing, covering both law and fact on title to benefit, to one on a point of law only. The end result is a more coherent, rational appellate structure than in the late Victorian/early Edwardian period. Other than hinting that the Unemployment Insurance Umpire was an influential model in the establishment of the Commissioners in 1946, Micklethwait (1976) does not look back at the process that led to their creation. This section of the chapter considers: how the Commissioner model of social security adjudication came to be established from the mélange of models in the pre-

1948 system; why the Umpire model was chosen as its base; the reasons for the change of title to Commissioner; and more fundamentally, why have Commissioners rather than the courts, and why no right of appeal to the courts was conceded?

Bonner (2002) suggests that the establishment of the National Insurance and Industrial Injuries Commissioners and the exclusion of the courts is in part the product of a degree of post-War difference in outlook between the Labour government and the Conservative/Liberal opposition on the exact scope of the welfare state and, more particularly, on welfare state adjudication and the role of the courts. The change to 'Commissioner' appears to be the result of a degree of division among the bodies and Ministers responsible for reconstruction and planning in the wartime Coalition Government over the composition and title of a judicial body rather than the courts as final arbiter. The most marked difference of opinion was that between two key Ministries – the Ministry of Labour and National Service (headed by Ernest Bevin) and the Home Office (with Herbert Morrison at its head), reflective of departmental reluctance to abandon their traditional, but differing, ways of doing things. The outcome is thus the product of a division of work between ministries resulting in compromises to get the job done, rather than a clear follow on from principles such as uniformity. It may also reflect a marked degree of personal and political rivalry between the two political heads of the key ministries concerned. Bonner (2002) clarifies how we arrived at Commissioners rather than courts and tells us why further recourse to courts was barred. Ultimately, the change from 'Umpire' was merely one of nomenclature rather than of real substance, since the 'Commissioner' model of adjudication proves merely to be the 'Umpire' model under another name.

Existing models of social security adjudication: the choice of 'Umpire'

Social Security Adjudication 1897 to 4 July 1948

Modern social security began when the Workmen's Compensation Act 1897 required employers to pay no-fault compensation to employees suffering personal injury by accident arising out of, and in the course of, their employment (Beveridge Report, 1942). Non-contributory, but means-tested, old age pensions followed in 1908 (Old Age Pensions Act 1908). The National Insurance Act 1911 brought in insurance-based sickness and medical benefits (Part I) and, for certain trades, insurance-based unemployment benefit as a temporary lifebelt to aid those thrown out of work while the new 'labour exchanges' helped them to find new employment (Part II). The unemployment scheme was later extended to a wider range of employments (National Insurance (Part II) (Munitions Workers) Act 1916; Unemployment Insurance Act 1920). Contributory retirement pensions and widows and orphans benefits followed in 1925 (Widows', Orphans' and Old Age Contributory Pensions Act 1925). Mass, long-term unemployment, saw a variety of extensions to the ostensibly temporary contribution-based unemployment benefit, culminating in the handling of long-term unemployment by a national body through means tested unemployment assistance (relief) in 1934, thus establishing 'the principle of a "national minimum"' (Bruce, 1968: 272; Unemployment Act 1934).[1] Throughout, the Poor Law, revised in terms of administration and nomenclature (a move to public assistance and public assistance committees rather than Boards of Guardians), remained the ultimate safety net. As the Beveridge Report (1942) noted, all this change and development was dealt with separately, with little or no reference to allied problems.

With a much narrower base of Departments of State than now, this radical Liberal-inspired venture into collectivism to ward off socialism,[2] was, inevitably in an experiment in social reform at odds with notions of a 'small' State, somewhat variegated in terms of bases and principles of entitlement and administrative structure. So were the adjudicatory aspects of the arrangements for redress of grievances:

> The method of adjudication adopted in connection with health insurance, unemployment insurance, widows', orphans' and contributory old age pensions, and unemployment assistance, disclosed no common principles regarding either the choice of the tribunal, its constitution, the powers conferred on it, the procedure it was required to follow, or the facilities for appeal. It was impossible to distinguish on logical or sociological grounds between the judicial functions which were allocated to individual ministers, to the court of referees and the umpire, to individual referees or to local committees. (Robson, 1951: 188)

Indeed, the dispute resolution scheme in the Workmen's Compensation Act 1897 was essentially a 'private law' model, albeit enforcing a statutory right. Negative perceptions of this scheme, allied to the respect Beveridge had for the (familiar to him) 'three tier plus' system of adjudication in unemployment insurance, produced the 'Umpire' model (albeit eventually under another name) as the preferred one for adjudication, so far as possible, throughout the national insurance system, and its adoption for the more extensive State-run industrial injuries system which replaced workmen's compensation from July 5, 1948. Beveridge had worked on the creation of the unemployment insurance scheme with Hubert Llewellyn-Smith, the Permanent Secretary at the Board of Trade who devised its novel adjudication machinery (Beveridge, 1953: 83). Beveridge aimed to convert workmen's compensation from a 'lawyers' paradise' to a 'social service'

---

1 Based on the Royal Commission on Unemployment Insurance (1932), this established what has become the standard distinction between insurance based-benefit, as of right but time-limited, and the availability, after its exhaustion, of means-tested assistance or relief. The Act also extended the range of industries covered. The 'household means test', discouraging family solidarity and encouraging evasion, was replaced in 1941 by the sort of 'personal means' test that has ever since governed social assistance in Great Britain.

2 Although the Workmen's Compensation Act 1897 was the product of a Unionist (Conservative) rather than a Liberal Government, it was steered to completion by Joseph Chamberlain, the Liberal Unionist, opposed to Home Rule, serving in that Government.

(Harris, 1997: 389). Griffiths, the Minister who piloted the 1946 national insurance and industrial injuries bills through the Commons, saw as a significant advantage 'the setting up of judicial tribunals to determine disputes, so removing one of the evils of the old system: the waste of vast sums of money in litigation.' (Griffiths, 1969: 83).

Workmen's compensation The scheme envisaged disputes between employer (or employer's insurers) and employees being settled by agreement or by specified forms of arbitration, or, in default, by the county court as arbitrator (Workmen's Compensation Act 1897, s.1(3) and Sched. 2). The scheme proved litigious and adversarial, a contest between unequal parties. Despite Joseph Chamberlain's hopes for resolution through an informal process of 'friendly arbitration', a sort of 'fireside chat', the default became the typical model, with disputes initially heard in the county court with onward appeal through the Court of Appeal to the Lords (Cornish and Clark 1989: 533-36). That spawned a vast array of House of Lords' decisions on the parameters of the scheme, still influential in today's fully public law industrial injuries scheme, e.g. *Chief Adjudication Officer v Faulds.*[3] The scheme failed to provide income security for the workman and was undermined by there being no obligation to insure except in the mining industry. It had not assisted the rehabilitation of workmen. Insofar as it covered industrial disease – a matter of gradual development rather than a single causative event – it made the pinning of responsibility on a single employer particularly inappropriate. Administrative costs were high (Beveridge Report 1942).

Non-contributory old age pensions Under the 1908 Act, claims and questions on entitlement to this non-contributory, means-tested pension for those aged 70 and over, subject to a 'good character' test, were determined initially by a Pensions Officer with further recourse to a local pensions committee, appointed by the borough or county council, and ultimately to the central pensions authority, a branch of the Local Government Board (the equivalent of a modern Department of State) (Old Age Pensions Act 1908, ss.7, 8). There was, thus, no independent 'judicial' element.

National Insurance: sickness, disablement, maternity and medical benefits These were the subject of a public-private partnership, administered by approved (often Friendly) societies (the self-help sector of Victorian and Edwardian provision against poverty) and insurance committees, the latter a mix of councillors and members appointed by the Insurance Commissioners. Medical benefit (medical treatment and attendance for the insured person) was effected by arrangements made by the insurance committees with doctors in accordance with regulations made by the Insurance Commissioners, the central administrative, rule-making and oversight element in the scheme, reflecting the standard administrative use of the term 'Commissioners' (*c.f.* Poor Law Commissioners, Commissioners for Sewers),

[3] [2000] 1 WLR 1035.

rather than an appellate ancestor of the Social Security and Child Support Commissioners. They also determined key questions on contributions, with a right of recourse to the County Court and from there, on a point of law only, to the High Court (National Insurance Act 1911, s. 66).

National Insurance: retirement, widows' and orphans' pensions Here, appeal lay from the administrative decision-maker to a senior lawyer, the Referee (Widows', Orphans' and Old Age Contributory Pensions Act 1925, s. 29). His decisions were not publicly reported. An ability to state a case for the High Court seems not to have been exercised (Ogus *et al*, 1995: 659).

National Insurance: unemployment benefit As with other areas of national insurance, this was influenced by the German model of using special tribunals in social insurance schemes, thus avoiding the formality of the ordinary courts. In unemployment insurance, this model – a 'novel feature of the scheme' (Beveridge Report, 1942) – was one of appeal from the departmental (Board of Trade) decision-maker (an 'independent' adjudicator, the insurance officer) to a three person tribunal (a generally legally qualified chairman, qualified to deal in a knowledgeable way with social and industrial questions, plus two 'wing' members, one from each side of industry) known as a court of referees, with further appeal to the Umpire, a Crown appointed lawyer of standing, some of whose decisions were reported by HMSO, and are still occasionally cited by the Social Security Commissioners.[4] The creation of this independent adjudication machinery was a

> ...means of relieving the President of the Board of Trade of constitutional responsibility for decision on individual claims of benefit; otherwise the President would have to spend most of his life in explaining why benefit had been refused to John Smith or withdrawn from him. (Beveridge, 1953: 83)

Most cases were resolved on the papers rather than by oral hearing. The Royal Commission on Unemployment Insurance (1932) considered the machinery to be working satisfactorily and suggested no major alterations but merely minor improvements, an approach contrasting markedly with Dicey's hostile reaction (Dicey, 1914: xxxii-xliv).

Unemployment assistance and assistance for the aged The 'relief' model of means-tested assistance to the long-term unemployed who had exhausted their insurance based benefit was deployed in 1940 also to deal with pensioners, the

---

[4] See, e.g., *CU66/1986(T)*, an unreported Tribunal of Commissioners' decision on the trade dispute disqualification, noted in Wood *et al* (2001: 98-99). A search of the 'Ferret' database of reported Commissioners decisions 1977 – date, and unreported decisions 1986 – date, revealed some 20 different cases, right across the social security spectrum in which reference was made either to a specific Umpire's decision or to the trend of Umpires' decisions on a particular matter, the latest reported decision being *R(U) 9/88* and the latest unreported one *CIS/14661/1996*.

Unemployment Assistance Board then becoming the Assistance Board. Both schemes removed important client groups from the rigours and stigma of the Poor Law. The appeals tribunals for the unemployed – the ancestors of national assistance and supplementary benefit appeal tribunals (SBATs) – were there less because it was thought important to have a right of appeal than to insulate the Ministry from political pressure on 'relief' decisions: as Lynes (1976: 7) put it, their creation

> ...was thus a deliberate political act, aimed at making an inherently unpopular reform more acceptable and at the same time protecting the Minister of Labour from the impact of parliamentary and public criticism of the actions of the Board and its officials. It had little to do with any abstract ideas of justice or legal rights. The judicial role of tribunals was from the start played down.

Their 'independence' has been described as 'clearly spurious for reasons of policy' (Fulbrook, 1978: 166). Their essentially administrative nature was reflected in one of its members being appointed by the Board and often being its district officer (Alder and Bradley 1976: 37). There was no right of appeal from the decision of the Unemployment Assistance Tribunal.

The Beveridge Report

Set up in June 1941, the interdepartmental Committee on Social Insurance and Allied Services had the remit of inquiring into the various anomalies which had come about as a result of the 'haphazard and piecemeal growth of the social security system' (Harris, 1997: 365), delineated above. Beveridge chaired it, and it was very much driven by him. His proposals – a revolution of sorts rather than merely patching, but nonetheless to some extent a rationalisation and extension of existing provision – sought to defeat his five 'giants': *want, disease, ignorance, squalor and idleness*. The proposals were founded on three prior assumptions: that government would maintain full employment, provide family allowances, and that there would be a comprehensive health service. His social insurance scheme to defeat *want* would not stifle personal initiative but would provide a base on which individuals could build. His plan,

> ...envisaged in return for a single weekly contribution a cradle-to-grave provision of sickness, medical, unemployment, widows', orphans', old-age, maternity, industrial injury and funeral benefits. It was universal in coverage of both risks and persons and would provide subsistence benefits for all. It was a well-organised scheme of *planned* social insurance based on the six components: flat-rate subsistence benefits, unification of administrative responsibility, adequacy of benefits, comprehensiveness and classification. (Fraser, 1984: 214)

While he saw in relation to disability that a 'complete solution' could only be found in a wholly unified scheme without distinguishing between causes of disability, his proposed scheme retained an 'industrial preference' (better provision for those disabled or incapacitated at and through their work) (Beveridge Report, 1942) but removed into State hands compensation for employment accidents and employment-related diseases, taking it out of the 'tortuous field of legal process' (*ibid*) which had tainted the workmen's compensation scheme.

Universal social insurance would be the mainstay of provision. For a declining residual category of cases, discretionary means-tested relief – national assistance – would provide the ultimate safety net.

Beveridge's proposals on appeals occupy only two paragraphs. Unsurprisingly given his background in unemployment insurance, the adjudicatory model there was to be applied, with some slight modification, across the board of social insurance, industrial injuries and national assistance. Appeals on benefit – whether on amount, conditions or period – would lie from an officer in the Ministry of Social Security to a local tribunal analogous to the existing Courts of Referees with further appeal to an Umpire appointed by the Crown, whose decision would be final. The Minister's decisions on liability to contributions, including the class in which contributions had to be made, were to be similarly appealable, save that the local tribunal would consist only of the chairmen of the Courts of Referees. As regards industrial injuries pensions and grant, the only modifications to this structure were that assessment would be undertaken in the Ministry by officers specialising in that work and that appeal would lie to special local tribunals composed of three regular members (in place of a chairman and assessors from a panel as with Courts of Referees).

A degree of uniformity was one priority with Beveridge as it was initially with those bodies in the executive branch of government charged with planning for reconstruction in this field; the Cabinet committee on reconstruction priorities during 1943 and that on reconstruction throughout 1944 and into 1945. Sectional departmental and other interests, practical politics and, perhaps, a small degree of 'fallout' from some deeper-seated antipathy between key ministers (Morrison at the Home Office and Bevin at the Ministry of Labour), produced a rather more variegated structure and a change in terminology, if not finally in terms of substance, at the 'Umpire' level of appeal.

From 'Umpire' to 'Commissioner'

The Beveridge Report met with an enthusiastic response from the governed, but a rather more lukewarm response from the Coalition government whose first task was victory in war and which was concerned at the overall cost (Donoghue and Jones, 1973: 314; Fraser, 1984: 218). Planning ahead was permissible, but implementation would have to await the results of a General Election. In marked contrast stood Churchill's lack of real interest (Gilbert, 1986: 292) and Morrison's enthusiasm (Donoghue and Jones, 1973: 314-15). In examining how, against an initially unpromising background, the Beveridge blueprint became concrete reality, the disparate responsibilities for social security of a range of government departments, must be borne in mind as in part explaining later divergences:

> In 1941, no less than seven government departments were directly or indirectly concerned with administering cash benefits for different kinds of need. Thus workmen's compensation was supervised by the Home Office, unemployment insurance by the Ministry of Labour, national health insurance by the Ministry of Health and the Department of Health for Scotland. Non-contributory old-age pensions were administered by the Customs and Excise, contributory old-age pensions by the Ministry of Health and 'supplementary pensions' by the Unemployment Assistance Board – which also dealt with the long-term unemployed. War victims and their dependants were relieved by the Ministry of Pensions, while the civilian disabled, widows and orphans were insured by the Ministry of Health. In addition there was a nation-wide network of local authority committees – the heirs of the old Poor Law guardians – which paid means-tested public assistance to persons in need. Benefits under these systems were financed in a number of different ways. Thus workmen's compensation was paid for by the employer; war pensions, non-contributory old-age pensions, and unemployment assistance by the taxpayer; public assistance by the ratepayer; and health, unemployment and old-age pensions insurance by tripartite contributions from employers, workers and the state. (Harris 1997: 365)

Reconstruction – planning for social and economic life after the war – began early in the war. The Minister for Reconstruction, Arthur Greenwood announced Beveridge's appointment in the House of Commons (Harris, 1997: 370). The nature of interests and forces in the Coalition Government meant that, despite being a minority, key Labour politicians (Attlee, Bevin and Morrison) proved the driving force behind their work on social security.

Bonner (2002) reveals that the term 'Umpire' was initially displaced in May 1944 in favour of the appellation 'Industrial Injuries Insurance Commissioner' in the industrial injuries scheme, hived off from the main scheme of social insurance, in part as a result of trade union representations, as being the subject of more consensus. Only at a much later stage, around the time the National Insurance Bill was introduced into Parliament in December 1945, does the term 'National Insurance Commissioner' appear.[5] But even after that some Cabinet documentation early in 1946 still refers to the 'Umpire' model. It would seem that the initial desire for uniformity, somewhat displaced when industrial injuries was allowed to take a different route, re-asserted itself in terms of replacing 'Umpire' with 'Commissioner' across both types of insurance-based schemes. While there were differences between departments over the composition of the second/final tier appellate body (the Home Office favouring a rather more grandiose body than the others), and over the scope of its jurisdiction (a full right of appeal or one confined only to law), the end result of the differences proves only to be one of nomenclature, since closer analysis than initial impression reveals the newly named 'Commissioner' model to be the 'Umpire' model by another name.

Independently of each other, both the Home Office (workmen's compensation/industrial injuries) and the other departments concerned with the

[5] The correspondence between Ministry and Parliamentary Counsel refers throughout most of 1945 to 'umpire': see Office of Parliamentary Counsel, *National Insurance Act 1946*, Vol V, pp 124-323.

broader social insurance scheme (the Ministries of Labour and National Service, of Health, and the Scottish Department of Health[6] considered more grandiose schemes. The Home Office wanted the final appeal on a point of law to go with leave, not to the Umpire, but to a specially constituted Central Appeal Tribunal (CAT), consisting of three legally qualified members, one of whom might be a High Court judge nominated by the Lord Chancellor. Medical questions – both assessments of disability and disputes – would be decided by special medical Boards able to co-opt specialist members when necessary, for example, in cases of industrial disease.

The other departments thought that an appeal might lie from the referee/local tribunal in a broad range of fields to an Umpire, or three Umpires sitting together, or replacing them with appeal on a point of law by way of case stated to a Social Insurance Tribunal, the decision of which would be final and conclusive, thus obviating any need for further recourse to the courts:

> …thus the [Tribunal] will not have to hear any witnesses of fact and the procedure would involve a minimum of disturbance. The advantages of having an expert and specialised Tribunal to deal with social insurance questions is [sic] considerable. A claimant with no means and legal backing can have his case heard. The Tribunal should sit in public and counsel and solicitors should have a right of audience.

If the similarity of this to the CAT was noticed, there is no record of this. And the social insurance model soon took a return track to Referee/local tribunal and Umpire, who would be a Crown appointment.

In 1944, the forum for consideration of these issues became the War Cabinet reconstruction committee, with two sub-committees: one on social insurance, the other on workmen's compensation. It was becoming clear on the social insurance side that complete uniformity of adjudication arrangements was not going to be possible given the different benefits' histories and accepted ways of doing things from very different departmental perspectives. The social insurance sub-committee, resolved that the draft white paper proposals on appeals be drawn up in such a way as not to preclude such modifications. The end result was the silence of the eventual white paper on appeals questions, and the legislation leaving so much detail to be embodied in secondary legislation (National Insurance Act 1946, s.43).

Morrison considered that the workmen's compensation scheme raised very complicated legal issues. He proposed instead the CAT scheme, described earlier. The CAT, dealing with appeals on a point of law only, would have jurisdiction throughout Great Britain. The CAT scheme for Great Britain as a whole was rejected as not acceptable to Scotland. The Committee instead endorsed a proposal that the unemployment insurance model of Umpire level appeal be used, with a deputy Umpire taking Scottish cases. The Umpire (or deputy) could sit with assessors where necessary. Morrison accepted this but to avoid confusion renamed the Umpire as the Industrial Injuries Insurance Commissioner. Matters of

---

[6] National Archives catalogue ref PIN 8/139.

insurability, as before, were for the Secretary of State and the High Court. Medical matters were to be dealt with by medical boards with a right of appeal to a medical appeal tribunal.

The proposals were embodied in the National Insurance (Industrial Injuries) Bill (Clauses 40–45). Introduced into the Commons after the Labour landslide in the General Election in 1945, in much the same form as an earlier one introduced by the Conservative caretaker government prior to the dissolution of Parliament for that election,[7] it received Royal Assent on 26 July 1946.

Industrial injuries and the wider national insurance scheme were proceeding on diverging tracks in terms of adjudication and appeals: Commissioner in the former, Umpire in the latter. They could have met had the ideas of the CAT and the Social Insurance Tribunal been merged, but did not. The less-controversial industrial injuries Bill was introduced first – in June 1945 by the Conservative government and then in August 1945 by the Labour government. The national insurance Bill did not appear until December that year. Disparity in nomenclature was not thought particularly important: in part the variety of terms used is attributable to the confusing pace of change in a hectic legislative programme and a tendency to be more comfortable talking in familiar terms.

The most plausible hypothesis, however, for the move from Umpire to National Insurance Commissioner, is that it represents a reassertion of a desire for uniformity and to avoid confusion with previous appellate structures by having a complete break with the historical terminology.

The exclusion of the courts

The issues of Commissioner or High Court and of a possible right of appeal on a point of law from the Commissioner to the High Court were also canvassed to a degree within those executive committees of the wartime Coalition government. Bevin was adamant that appeals within the state scheme should lie to a special tribunal rather than the courts.[8] His vehement repudiation of the courts, reflective of deep distrust of them in the labour movement, and perhaps his own experiences at their hands, is telling:

> If an appeal were allowed from the Umpire to the High Court there would be increased delay in reaching a final decision, over and above the delay which frequently occurs now, and legal costs would have to be incurred by the parties. Much more serious is the risk – I think the certainty – that the carefully constructed system of case-law would be wrecked by High Court decisions delivered with insufficient appreciation of the structure of industrial relations and with a total disregard of the effect of these decisions on those relations if the decisions are thought to be necessitated by strict legal logic. We have had bitter experience in the past of the way in which the High Court can 'throw a spanner' into the industrial machine, often with the result of compelling legislation

[7] National Archives catalogue ref PREM 4/87/8.
[8] National Archives catalogue ref CAB 87/12 – PR(43)12 and 87/13 – PR(43) 20.

remedies going much beyond the position which might otherwise have been satisfactory to all concerned. It is for this reason that I believe it would be a thoroughly retrograde and dangerous step to give the High Court any say in unemployment benefit law.[9]

This perspective looks back beyond workmen's compensation to reactionary decisions in relation to trades union and worker's rights, and was a strong current influencing the stance of the labour movement to courts in general in dealing with social and political issues, something which made the process of conversion to a Bill of Rights a very slow one (Wallington and McBride 1976: App 3; Greer 1999: 4-5). To keep out the courts, the Umpire should be a Crown appointment. Bevin's antipathy to court involvement was more general, but he insisted on its ouster only with respect to his own field of responsibility, unemployment benefit. He conceded that the position might be different with sickness benefits and pensions. He would, however, rather sacrifice uniformity than have courts deal with unemployment benefit. The Committee accepted that there should be no right of appeal to the courts in unemployment benefit cases. The matter was again broached when its 29th meeting considered (ultimately to reject) Morrison's proposal for the CAT scheme. Since, under that scheme, appeal would lie on law only, a question was raised as to why the matter could not instead go to the courts. The riposte was to note Trade Union Council opposition.[10]

These issues were also at the heart of the post-war parliamentary debates on both the industrial injuries and the national insurance bills, this time with the political differences between the Labour government and the Conservative and Liberal opposition much more starkly defined. Consideration of both the public and less public record also brings out a suspicion of 'administrative tribunals' with roots in Diceyan opposition to the National Insurance Act 1911, and in the related reactionary legal tradition that produced Lord Hewart CJ's, *The New Despotism*,[11] pressures from which led to the Donoughmore Committee (1932) on ministers' powers. The relatively clean bill of health produced by that committee is shown not to have erased the opposition to settlement of disputes outside courts.

The principal public airing of these issues was in the debates on the industrial injuries bill rather than the national insurance bill. During the Commons committee stage of the industrial injuries bill, concern initially focussed on whether tribunals with a membership appointed by the Minister could be said to be a better forum than the county courts, experienced in workmen's compensation issues.[12] The Minister of National Insurance spelled out clearly the reasons for preferring the tribunals:

---

[9] National Archives catalogue ref CAB 87/12 and 87/13 – PR(43)96.

[10] National Archives catalogue ref LCO 2/3776 – R(44) 29.

[11] Hewart (1929).

[12] House of Commons, Official Report, Debates of Standing Committee A on the National Insurance (Industrial Injuries) Bill, cols. 380-389, Thursday November 29, 1945 (Parliamentary Session 1945-1946).

> ...after careful consideration we came to the conclusion that the machinery set up in the Bill would be the best kind for settling these cases. This was decided with no sense of offence to the county court, nor were we disregarding the experience and knowledge of many of the county court judges, who were first class in dealing with cases of this kind. There was, however, a general desire that we should take this question of benefit for injuries out of the atmosphere of litigation and contention which had surrounded it, and which had created so many suspicions by giving a man the view that his compensation depended upon some legal argument between very skilled lawyers. It was for this reason that it was decided to make this change. It is our desire that these tribunals should be bodies which will do the job judiciously and do it well.[13]

The model had been proved to work well in unemployment insurance. Attention then turned to the final tier of appeal: the Commissioner and his deputies. Opposition members suggested two amendments. Similar justifications were advanced in support of their essence. The Commissioner was seen, essentially, as a *ministerial* tribunal, an emanation of the State in its executive capacity,[14] so that there should be a right of appeal to the courts.[15] Difficult questions of law would arise, not necessarily resolvable satisfactorily by the Commissioner himself, which should be the purview of courts composed of judges learned in the law, wholly impartial and unwilling to be influenced by the wishes of the executive.[16] The courts, moreover, had long experience with workmen's compensation of the types of issues that would arise. And its key terminology had been brought into the bill. One would get a more authoritative and clearer construction of statute from the High Court than from the Commissioner. There would be a better chance of finality and certainty, given the doctrine of binding precedent, with High Court decisions accessible to claimant and State alike in the Law Reports.[17]

The government, thought such a right of appeal to be an 'outrage', given that the objectives of the Bill were to move away from the excessive litigation surrounding workmen's compensation. The idea was to have, in words that presage those of the Franks Report (1957) on administrative tribunals, specialist resolution of disputes that would be speedier, cheaper and less formal, freer from excessive technicality, and more open to the 'little man'. The scheme in the Bill was fair and equitable. The Commissioner would have no list other than industrial injuries and national insurance cases. Where difficult factual questions arose, the Commissioner could sit with 'the assistance of people who understand what the facts are ... with two assessors, drawn from both sides of industry, who will guide and advise him'. When difficult questions of law arose, the Commissioner – 'a lawyer of high standing and experience' – would sit as a Tribunal with two deputy Commissioners. Decisions of the Commissioner would be 'completely reported'. Having either of the suggested rights of appeal was thought to render otiose having a Commissioner.

---

[13] *ibid*, at col 385.
[14] *ibid*, at cols 408 (Byers), 410 (Nield).
[15] *ibid*, at col 408.
[16] *ibid*, at cols 408-409 (Byers), 410-411 (Nield).
[17] *ibid*, at cols 414-415.

This drew the natural riposte of having an appeal direct to the High Court from the local tribunals, so that the issue (Commissioner or court) also came briefly into the debate.

What emerges is the idea of the Commissioner as an expert doing a similar job to the High Court. In the Lords, the Lord Chancellor also stressed the qualifications of the Commissioner who would be 'somebody of the status of a High Court judge, somebody from the class of people I should be considering if there was a vacancy on the [High Court] Bench.'[18] Commissioners and deputies would be 'lawyers of distinction', 'lawyers of first rate standing and the sort of people who are of the status of a High Court judge'. A right of appeal on a point of law from the Commissioner to the High Court would, be a 'profound mistake'. The right of appeal from tribunal to Commissioner (or Tribunal of Commissioner and two deputies in difficult cases) was provided 'in order to secure uniformity amongst all the various local tribunals'.[19] Language, later to become the watchwords of Franks, was again deployed to show how involving the courts would be detrimental to the scheme:

> Both this government and their predecessors attach great importance to having a system as cheap, inexpensive, rather informal and as speedy as possible under which these things can be dealt with.[20]

At report stage in the Lords the opposition proposed instead a right of appeal from the Commissioner on a point of law to the Court of Appeal. This brought into account a salient difference between Commissioner and High Court judge, namely the latter's security of tenure as opposed to the former's removeability. It reflected lingering perceptions of the Commissioner as a civil servant, and concerns that not even a Tribunal of Commissioner and two deputies would be sufficiently authoritative to resolve conflicting decisions on matters that had vexed the courts under workmen's compensation. The Lord Chancellor's riposte was to compare the Commissioner with a county court judge. He stressed again the need for speed, simplicity, and cheapness, but without sacrificing accuracy. This the Commissioner provided.

From past to present: some recurring themes

Consideration of the historical record shows the care with which was approached the matter of providing quality, accessible, expert adjudication of disputes, both at local tribunal and Commissioner level, a care the more surprising and laudable given that much of the planning took place in wartime. The examination of the

---

[18] *HL Debs*, Vol 142, col 668 (July 19, 1946).
[19] *Ibid*, at col 675.
[20] *Ibid*.

historical record, moreover, highlights issues and themes, which remain current concerns. Cheap, speedy and expert were watchwords of the Franks Report (1957).

Matters of delay, cost, expertise, the degree to which a system of adjudication dealing with complex law can remain informal, the reporting of and access to law-making decisions, are all central features of concern about the current role and work of the Social Security and Child Support Commissioners (see Chapter 1). Finally, matters of title do still matter. As we shall see (Chapter 7) the names of the new first- and second-tier tribunals and the titles of their judicial personnel in the reformed tribunal system are currently under review.

Changes in title and jurisdiction since 1948

Revising the Beveridge Plan: social security 1948-2003 [21]

The Beveridge vision – principal reliance on insurance-based benefits with means tested national assistance gradually withering away – never really came to fruition; the period instead has seen the balance reversed with the State encouraging heavy reliance on the means-tested sector in its various appellations. The perceived need for this encouragement – partly achieved through setting insurance-based benefit rates below those of assistance (which also embraced housing costs) and partly through restricting eligibility for insurance-based benefits, especially for the unemployed – came in response to demographic changes (an ageing population), the benefits of a national health service and the seemingly boundless achievements of medical science (increased life expectancy for all, including disabled people who would formerly have died at or soon after birth or in childhood) and economic pressures (unemployment, recession, the need to create a 'flexible' labour market, a need for restraint in public spending to aid a low-inflation economy).

For those without work through whatever cause, means-tested social assistance was provided successively by national assistance (1948-1975), supplementary benefits (1966-1988); income support (1988-date); and, from 1995, for the able-bodied unemployed required to seek work, income-based jobseeker's allowance rather than income support. In varying degrees, these schemes made payments in respect of housing costs, although since 1983 payments in respect of rent and local authority taxation (successively rates, community charge and council tax) have been the exclusive responsibility of local authorities. Initially, the centrally administered assistance schemes operated in terms of broad discretionary powers, albeit structured in terms of controlling 'officer' discretion by elaborate and often 'secret' administrative codes (Adler and Bradley, 1975; Bull, 1980).

> The use of discretion in social security provision in the United Kingdom has a very long history; it dates back to the Elizabethan Poor Law. In this field the same constellation of problems reoccurs: the establishment of a workable national administration aimed at

[21] See further Harris, (2000: 6-12, 61-63).

> the relief of poverty, the ever-present contradiction between providing relief and undermining work incentives, the influence of moral judgements concerning the status of the poor, and the balance to be struck between administrative efficiency and citizens' rights. (Buck, 2000: 2)

From 1980, the structure has been one of detailed legal rules, reducing or very closely 'structuring' discretion, with administrative guidance to decision-makers 'translating' the legal rules into civil-servant friendly language. The 'single payments' regulations, which made provision for one-off payments for supplementary benefit recipients, became the focus of a movement in Britain for the greater recognition of welfare 'rights'. The regulations contained detailed rules of 'entitlement' that were litigated strongly by an increasingly confident welfare rights lobby. Such deliberate efforts to produce test cases (see Prosser, 1983) inevitably meant the Commissioners were active in deliberating on such cases, as a perusal of Mesher's (1987: 272-344) annotations of the relevant legislation prior to its revocation will show. There were significant numbers of appeals to SBATs and then on to the Commissioners. The government, concerned about the spiralling numbers of claims for such payments, finally replaced this form of assistance with the discretionary social fund (see Buck, 2000) and produced alternative review mechanisms thus taking this form of social assistance outside of the regular social security appeal routes to tribunals and the Commissioners.

For family breadwinners in low-paid 'full-time' work, means-tested social assistance came through family income supplement (1970-1988) and family credit (1988-1999), replaced in October 1999 by working families' tax credit, and in 2003 by a wider regime of tax credits. The watchwords of the social security system have steadily become 'selectivity' or 'targeting' rather than 'universalism' (Ogus *et al*, 1995; CPAG, 1985).

An insurance-based scheme can only afford protection to those able to get into a position to be able, for some period at least, to contribute to the insurance scheme through payment of contributions during periods of work. Those disabled at birth or in childhood, or incapacitated very early in working life, could not do so, and would otherwise have had to rely solely on means-tested assistance. In response to a powerful political lobby on their behalf, a number of non-contributory benefits were introduced. Attendance allowance from 1971 and mobility allowance from 1976 aimed to provide for some of the extra costs that disability brings: care and mobility. A specific benefit – invalid care allowance – was also introduced in the mid-1970s to help carers, although initially excluding married and cohabiting women (a defect remedied from 1986 as a result of an adverse ruling in the European Court of Justice[22]). Since 1992, care and mobility needs have primarily been met through the care and mobility components of disability living allowance. In that same year, the needs of the disabled in low-paid work were sought to be met through the low-wage top-up afforded by disability working allowance (Disability Living Allowance and Disability Working Allowance Act 1991; Social Security

[22] See *Drake v Chief Adjudication Officer* 150/85 [1987] QB 166.

Contributions and Benefits Act 1992, s.129), modelled on family credit and replaced from October 1999 by the disabled person's tax credit, in turn replaced from 2003 with the disability component of tax credit. Various forms of non-contributory invalidity pension aimed to give those incapable of work long-term an element of income maintenance as of right, albeit at a rate lower than insurance-based benefits for incapacity. Embodying sex discrimination, these non-contributory pensions were replaced in 1984 by severe disablement allowance (SDA), covering those incapacitated before 20, and those incapacitated after that age who were also assessed as 80 per cent disabled through a process akin to that for assessing disablement for industrial injuries' purposes. SDA was abolished in respect of new claims from April 2001, but those incapacitated before 20 (or in some cases, 25) were afforded access to incapacity benefit without a contribution record. At the same time, the contribution conditions for access to incapacity benefit were tightened to require a more recent connection with the world of work, something done, though more strictly so, from 1988 with respect to unemployment benefit (and, from 1995, contribution-based jobseeker's allowance). Moreover, in the sphere both of unemployment and incapacity benefits, the line between means-tested (from 1988, income-related) and non-means tested benefits was blurred with unemployment benefit, jobseekers allowance and finally incapacity benefit being reduced for a variety of pension payments, and contribution-based jobseekers' allowance taking account of earnings from part-time employment to defeat, or reduce the rate of, entitlement.

Other changes were made in respect of insurance-based benefits underwriting incapacity for work and maternity. Responsibility for meeting the costs of short-term incapacity and of maternity pay were by stages transferred to employers in respect of most employees, leaving the state scheme to deal with self-employed and the unemployed persons sick or pregnant. Pressures on the social security budget, and the perception that invalidity benefit was underwriting both unemployment and early retirement, saw the abolition of sickness and invalidity benefits and their replacement in 1995 by incapacity benefit. Those benefits had operated on a broad-based test of incapacity – incapable of work by reason of some specific disease or bodily or mental disablement, work meaning work s/he could reasonably be expected to do – the bare bones of the statute being fleshed out by Commissioners' decisions, allowing a focus on the particular individual and extending beyond the medical matter (the claimant's state of health) also to embrace age, education, qualifications, experience and other personal factors, reflective of the interaction between medical and personal environmental factors which impede the access of disabled people to employment (Berthoud, 1995; Bonner, 1995). That was replaced by the central test of the new scheme, the medical/functional 'all work' test, since renamed the 'personal capability assessment'. Nonetheless, as with the test it replaced, decision-making at original and appellate level was essentially lay, albeit informed increasingly by medical evidence. In contrast, as with the industrial injuries scheme, medical matters within entitlement to attendance allowance, mobility allowance and the corresponding components of disability living allowance involved a much greater degree of medical involvement or control in decision-making at both original and appellate level.

Family protection was afforded through a range of dependants' additions to insurance-based benefits and through the concept of aggregation of 'requirements' and 'resources' in the 'balance sheet' forming a key component of means-tested social assistance or top-ups for low-wages. More direct financial assistance to those caring for a child was provided initially through family allowance (very rarely up-rated) and guardian's allowance. In addition, the tax scheme provided child tax allowances, of help, of course, only to those who paid tax. For part of the period, family allowances were in effect supplemented by the provision of free school meals and milk. From 1977, family allowance was replaced by child benefit and child tax allowances were phased out by 1980.

The range of industrial injuries benefits was steadily reduced – the earliest loss being that of injury benefit (a preferential incapacity benefit) initially allowing the industrially injured non-contributory access to sickness and invalidity benefits from 1982-1995 – to leave the scheme from 1990 concentrating on compensating through disablement benefit for the resultant disability of those disabled through work, and on affording the very severely disabled money for attendance needs through constant attendance allowance and exceptionally severe disablement allowance. But the central tests and issues (medical and otherwise) remained much the same as those established in 1948, and not significantly different to those in the workmen's compensation scheme with which this journey started.

Changes in the Commissioners' appellate jurisdiction 1948-2003

The legislation that was implemented in 1948, such of the Beveridge 'blueprint' as was accepted by the 1945 Labour Government – the National Insurance Act 1946, the National Insurance (Industrial Injuries) Act 1946 and the (thought to be residual) National Assistance Act 1948 – brought some, but not total, rationalisation of adjudication. The 'extended-three tier plus' (Micklethwait, 1976: 2) adjudication system, modelled basically on the system in 'unemployment insurance', extended to all national insurance benefits and to industrial injuries (other than Medical Appeal Tribunal) matters, but not to national assistance. Nor were family allowances within its purview. The Family Allowances Act 1945, introduced by the Coalition government, allowed appeal from the Minister to a court of referees but no further. The third-tier adjudication body was the Commissioners. Ostensibly (as a matter of law) there were two sets of Commissioners: the National Insurance Commissioners and the Industrial Injuries Commissioners. The reality from day one (5 July 1948) was that both jurisdictions were vested in the same persons, or, to put it another way, the same persons exercised each of the 'insurance based' jurisdictions (Micklethwait, 1976). Legal form was aligned with practical reality in 1966 when the two jurisdictions were merged as the National Insurance Commissioners.

Not all issues in respect of benefits covered fell within the Commissioners' jurisdiction. The exclusion of Medical Appeal Tribunal matters – the 'disablement and diagnosis questions – with respect to the industrials injuries scheme has already been noted. In addition, a number of questions (liability to pay contributions, whether the contribution conditions for access to an insurance-based benefit were met) were reserved to the Secretary of State and not appealable to the national insurance local tribunal (NILT), and so not appealable to the Commissioners. Family Allowances decisions were not appealable from the court of referees to the Commissioner. National Assistance was deliberately excluded from the Commissioner's remit. Appeals lay from the National Assistance Board to National Assistance Tribunals, designed to be even more informal than NILTs. No right to further appeal to the Commissioners was afforded. It was thought impossible and undesirable for a Commissioner to be asked to lay down general rules, binding as precedents, on the exercise of discretion. Since the right to assistance was not statutory in the same sense as insurance-based benefits, there was no need to have a system of case law binding throughout the country. That would create rigidity, whereas in this area flexible, broad discretion was needed. The Franks Report (1957) rejected such a right of appeal for similar reasons. When national assistance became supplementary benefits in 1966, the tribunals were renamed supplementary benefit appeals tribunals (SBATs). In 1970 they took on board appeals in Family Income Supplement cases. In 1978, the temporary step was taken to afford a right of appeal from an SBAT to the High Court on a point of law. In 1980, the National Insurance Commissioners (the merged body) became the Social Security Commissioners, when they acquired appellate jurisdiction, on a point of law only, over supplementary benefits, the successor benefit to national assistance, and over Family Income Supplement, a means-tested top-up for families with a breadwinner in low-paid work. In 1984 NILTs and SBATs were merged as Social Security Appeals Tribunals (SSATs).

In the intervening period, the Commissioners had gained jurisdiction over an expanding range of non-contributory benefits, including child benefit, attendance allowance and mobility allowance, these last two on points of law only. Certain disputes on employer-provided statutory sick pay and statutory maternity pay came their way in 1982 and 1986 respectively. In 1994, they took on appeals from disability appeals tribunals, thus embracing a range of benefits that now form a very significant part of their caseload (see Chapter 3, Table 3.7). In 1993, the Social Security Commissioners also became Child Support Commissioners.

As regards both national insurance and some industrial injuries matters, the Commissioners' appellate jurisdiction was full, covering both fact and law until 1987. As regards medical matters (e.g. the 'disablement questions' in industrial injuries disablement benefit, only added to their jurisdiction in 1959), however, their jurisdiction was confined to points of law, and Commissioners have proved appropriately deferential to decisions turning on medical expertise and judgment. When their competence was extended to the 'means tested' field, their appellate jurisdiction was founded on law only. In 1987, confinement to points of law was extended to the whole range of the Social Security Commissioner's appellate jurisdictions. Essentially a point of law will cover a breach of the rules of procedural fairness (natural justice), if the findings of fact are not supported by any evidence, a failure of the tribunal adequately to state the facts and reasons for its decision, or if the decision exhibits a false proposition of law (see Chapter 3).[23]

From 1 January 1993, the Commissioners took on appeals on a point of law from Child Support Appeals Tribunals. This system operates at the interface of public and private law. Instead of ordinary court processes, the child support system introduced public law procedures for assessing and enforcing child maintenance obligations, raising new problems for each Social Security Commissioner, each of whom simultaneously holds office as a Child Support Commissioner.

The Commissioners' jurisdiction in social security and in child support also covers procedural matters such as claims and payments (e.g. good cause for a late claim) and issues of overpaid benefit. In 1990, Commissioners acquired a new jurisdiction at the interface of social security and personal injury litigation, having in reality if not in precise legal form, insurance companies as one of the parties to the proceedings. The government introduced in that year a system whereby social security benefits, paid to persons who receive civil damages from compensators, could be recouped from the compensation payment.

Changes in the Decision Making and Appeals Structure in 1999

In 1999, the decision-making and appeals structure was radically overhauled by the Social Security Act 1998 (SSA 1998) and regulations made under it, and by the Social Security Contributions (Transfer of Functions, etc.) Act 1999. The Commissioners emerged relatively unscathed, these sea-changes largely affecting first-tier decision-making and the tribunals from which the Commissioners hear appeals. The impact on the Commissioners' procedures, workload and decision-making of the new DMA processes effected by SSA 1998, is examined in the next chapter. But one needs to note here that the Transfer of Functions Act 1999, by moving statutory sick pay and statutory maternity pay to the Board of Inland Revenue and its decision-making and appellate structure, removed these areas from the jurisdiction of the Commissioners. Perversely, when Family Credit and Disability Working Allowance were replaced by corresponding tax credits, which are the province of the Board of Inland Revenue, decisions made are nonetheless appealable to unified appeals tribunals under the jurisdiction of the Appeals Service (AS) and hence remain with the Commissioners. SSA 1998 replaced 'adjudication officers' (AO), who made the appealable first-tier decisions, with decision-makers (DMs) representing the Secretary of State. The old distinction between AO decisions (appealable to tribunals and Commissioners) and Secretary of State's decisions (not so appealable) had to be replaced with a boundary between those decisions subject to appeal to tribunals and those that were not. The boundary line

[23] *R(I) 14/75.*

is not the same, so that decisions on contributions conditions for access to insurance-based benefits, and those on contributions credits and home responsibilities, which help people meet those conditions, now fall within the purview of the Commissioners.

Acquisition of jurisdiction over council tax benefit and housing benefits

Since their creation in 1948, the Commissioners' jurisdiction has covered only decisions made by or on behalf of central government departments. Decisions on council tax benefit and housing benefit continue to be made by local authorities, rather than by officers of central government. From 2 July 2001, however, most of their decisions became appealable to unified appeals tribunals under the jurisdiction of AS, and consequently the Commissioners acquired jurisdiction over key aspects of these means-tested social assistance benefits.

Forfeiture: a first instance jurisdiction of the commissioners

Essentially, the Commissioners are a specialist *appellate* court. There is, however, one exception: the Commissioners have original jurisdiction with respect to deciding under the Forfeiture Act 1982 whether benefit should be forfeited as a result of an unlawful killing. This Act was passed after the Divisional Court in *R v National Insurance Commissioner, ex parte Connor*[24] had upheld a decision of the Chief National Insurance Commissioner[25] that a principle of public policy justified denying benefit to a woman whose widowhood came about as a direct result of her having killed her partner and committed the crime of manslaughter (see generally, Larkin, 2004).

Future jurisdictions

The Commissioners will in due course be taking on responsibility for deciding appeals from a much wider range of tribunals. These include: appeals from AS tribunals about the recovery of National Health Service costs from personal injury compensations, some decisions under the Child Trust Funds Act 2004, and appeals from Pensions Appeal Tribunals under the new armed forces pensions and compensation regime. Several other jurisdictions are likely to be added as part of the process of tribunal reform. As the Chief Commissioner put it in the Annual Report for 2003-04:

> The expansion has meant the respondents to claims have been extended beyond the central government department administering benefits, to the Inland Revenue and local authorities. In child support cases, in addition to the State, the mother and father of the

[24] [1981] 1 QB 158.
[25] *R(G) 2/79.*

relevant child are sometimes mutual protagonists. Further jurisdictions are shortly to be added. (Commissioners' Annual Report, 2004: 3)

Coming full circle? Challenging Commissioners' decisions[26]

Until 1980, from the point of view of the tribunals from which they heard appeals, the Commissioners were a superior tribunal. From the perspective of the High Court and its powers of judicial review, however, they ranked as an inferior tribunal, being amenable to *certiorari* (now called a 'quashing order'). While the courts were to have no appellate jurisdiction, the process of consideration by executive committees[27] and by Parliamentary counsel[28] shows that it was realised that the supervisory jurisdiction would not be excluded, despite statements about the finality of Commissioners' decisions. But that supervisory jurisdiction was only anticipated as regards lack or excess of jurisdiction. Those examining the matter could not foresee the revival of review for error on the face of the record in and since *R. v Northumberland Compensation Appeal Tribunal, ex parte Shaw.*[29] While attempts to oust the jurisdiction of the courts ultimately proved futile, the status of Commissioners and respect for their experience and expertise produced a degree of judicial deference to their decisions: see further Chapter 6. That deference in judicial review in turn arguably made it easier to effect a right of appeal on a point of law to the Court of Appeal, so that by 1980 the adjudicatory structure became one argued for by Conservative peers and two Law Lords in 1946 (an appeal on a point of law to the Court of Appeal). A degree of deference to the expertise of the Commissioners continues to be expressed by the Court of Appeal and by the House of Lords in handling social security and child support cases (see Chapter 6), And, from 1987, the Commissioners were restricted to matters of law only, so that, ironically, particularly when sitting as a Tribunal of Commissioners (see further Chapter 3), the model proves not so very different from Morrison's CAT, rejected in 1944.

We consider that this restriction to law only was a watershed, changing the nature of the Commissioners' role and relationship with users from the system described by Micklethwait (1976).

A changing workload

The Commissioners and their staff deal with a significant caseload. As we have seen, in Chapter 1 (Table 1.1), OSSCSC is a smaller operation in terms of the number of cases than the immigration, tax and mental health areas, but it handles

---

[26] This matter is more fully addressed in Chapter 6.

[27] National Archives catalogue ref CAB 87/12 and 87/13.

[28] Office of Parliamentary Counsel, *Family Allowances 1945*, Vol. II: Correspondence, p.238.

[29] [1952] 1 KB 338.

more cases than some other important tribunals. Tables 2.1 and 2.2 below give the figures for applications for leave and appeals 'received' and 'disposed of' by OSSCSC respectively.

As we shall see in Chapter 3, an appeal to the Commissioner is preceded by an application for leave to the AS tribunal chair, and if s/he refuses, an application for leave arrives directly at the Commissioners' office. Therefore, the 'appeals' received in Table 2.1 will have already been given leave by the AS tribunal chair. However, the 'applications' in Table 2.1 have come in directly to the Commissioner because these have been refused leave by the AS tribunal chair. One can see that the general balance between applications and appeals has changed when we come to consider applications and appeals 'disposed of'; there are generally more appeals in Table 2.2 than in Table 2.1. This is because the 'appeals' in Table 2.2 now include a proportion of applications for leave that the Commissioners have previously granted themselves. These applications are then treated as 'appeals'. The appeals and applications in both the DCA's annual reports of judicial statistics and the Council on Tribunals' annual reports are presented as aggregate figures. For example, this would give respectively a total of 6,695 cases received and 6,721 cases disposed of in 2003.

Table 2.1 The Social Security Commissioners: applications and appeals *received* in England and Wales, 1998-2003

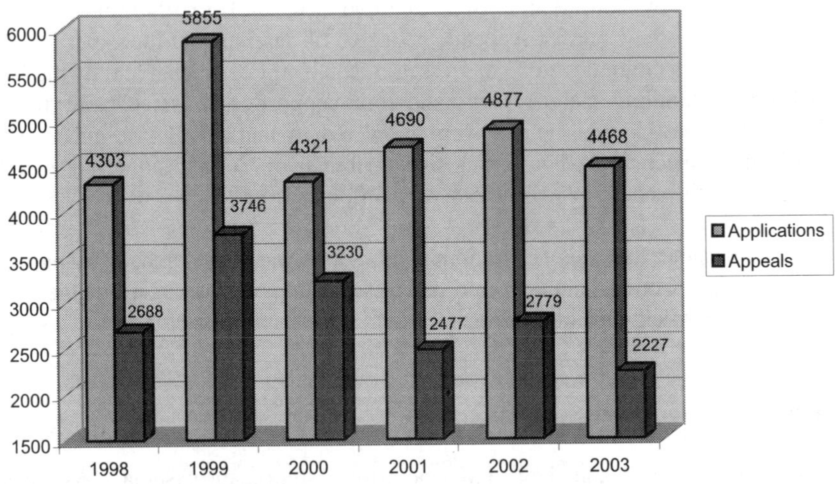

Source: LCD/DCA, Judicial Statistics annual reports: 1998-2003.

However, as we shall argue in Chapter 6, there is an element of 'double counting' in presenting the figures in this way. Figures for 'applications' and 'appeals' *received* are also given in Chapter 3 (Tables 3.2 and 3.3). The attentive reader will notice that the figures given in those Tables differ to the ones here. This is mainly because the figures in Tables 2.1 and 2.2 appear to be collected in relation to a *calendar* year while the ones in Chapter 3, derived from the Commissioners' annual reports, relate to *financial* years.

Table 2.2 The Social Security Commissioners: applications and appeals *disposed of* in England and Wales, 1998-2003

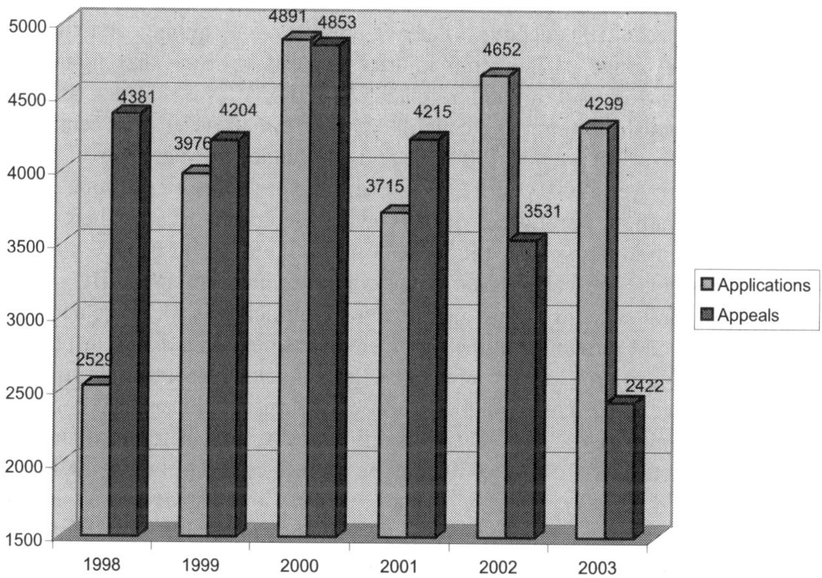

Source: LCD/DCA, Judicial Statistics annual reports: 1998-2003.

Nevertheless, from Table 1.1 we can see a diminution of appeals received (leave having been given by the tribunal chair) from 1999 onwards. This provides some evidence that the DMA changes introduced by SSA 1998 have had some influence in restricting appeals. On the other hand, applications received have lessened to a degree having reached a peak of 5,855 in 1999, though the numbers in subsequent years do not suggest that claimants' desire to appeal has been significantly abated.

Turning to Table 2.2, there are two points to note. Firstly, appeals disposed of appear to have fallen consistently since 2000. They have nearly halved in numbers from 2000 (4,853) to 2003 (2,422). Again, this provides some evidence that the DMA changes have had their effect. Secondly, the *proportion* of 'applications' and 'appeals' disposed of by the Commissioners over the period has changed dramatically. In 1998 there were 2,529 (37 per cent) applications and 4,381 (63 per cent) appeals. In 2003 the proportions had practically reversed. There were 4,299 (64 per cent) applications and 2,422 (36 per cent) appeals. There are a number of explanations for why this switch in the proportion of applications and appeals has occurred and these are examined further in Chapters 3 and 7.

Commissioners operate in a demand-led environment with little effective control over the number of cases that come to them. The variation in workload depends on a number of factors, such as the changes in jurisdiction charted above and the stacking of 'lookalike' cases. It clearly responds to changes in the benefit system. For example, in 1948, the importance of industrial injuries benefits warranted a separate system of adjudication. However, improved industrial safety in the last 50 years, the decline of heavy industry and mining and the drastic reduction in the range of industrial injuries benefits to three, has lightened the Commissioners' workload in relation to such benefits. As we shall see (Chapter 3, Table 3.7) industrial injuries benefits was some seven per cent of the Commissioners' workload for 2004-05, and just under ten per cent of all cases disposed of from April 2001-April 2004. There are pressures on the appeal process when a new benefit is introduced. It may be litigated more because there has been little time and/or administrative preparation in producing good quality information about the benefit. Jobseeker's allowance was introduced in 1996. By 1999, one could see the first signs of a growing number of applications for leave and appeals from unemployed claimants, but the figure since has been less than four per cent of cases disposed of. Ambiguities and other flaws in the legislative drafting invite challenge by welfare rights groups. New disability and incapacity benefits are intensely scrutinised by a resourceful disability lobby, and there are other reasons why losers in terms of those benefits may be more inclined to pursue their 'rights' (see Chapters 4 and 7). The workload of the Commissioners in relation to incapacity benefit after its introduction in 1995 increased significantly, and there was a less dramatic growth in disability living allowance (DLA) cases in the period 1996-1999. From April 2001-April 2004, incapacity benefits have formed some 15 per cent of all cases disposed of, while disability benefits (DLA and AA) cases account for almost half. Finally, income support cases used to account for a much higher proportion of the Commissioners' caseload. However, when income-based Jobseekers Allowance was introduced a key client group was removed from income support. Currently, income support appeals and applications amount to about nine per cent of the Commissioners' workload and jobseeker's allowance to about two per cent (see Chapter 3, Table 3.7).

The role of the Commissioners and the perceived relevance of the background of those holding office

In the Commissioners' Annual Report for 2003-04, Chief Commissioner Hickinbottom encapsulated the formal role of the Commissioners

> The Commissioners hear appeals on points of law. These mainly concern welfare benefits and tax credits, involving complex domestic statutory provisions, and often human rights and European Union law. It is the Commissioners' role not only to do

justice between the parties in an individual case – important as that is – but also where appropriate to give guidance on matters of legal principle to the relevant government authorities and other benefit claimants. In Great Britain, nearly 5 million people of working age claim a key welfare benefit. In terms of tax credits, the numbers are even higher, 6.2 million households (involving 10.4 million children) receiving such credits. And, of course, all children are entitled to child benefit. In giving guidance on the proper construction of benefit provisions, the decisions of the Commissioners therefore directly affect the lives of very many people.

Whilst not ignoring the importance of dealing with cases efficiently, the Commissioners have at the forefront of their minds their dual judicial functions of correctly deciding individual appeals, and giving guidance on the law more generally when appropriate. These will continue to be their priorities, whatever their future might be within the tribunal system. (Commissioners' Annual Report, 2004: 2).

He also made the important point that in evaluating their role and their success (or lack of it) in fulfilling it:

...statistics cannot give a complete picture. The antithesis of 'Justice delayed is justice denied' is not that decisions delivered promptly and cost-efficiently are necessarily just. Statistics alone give no indication as to the quality of Commissioners' individual decisions, or the extent to which their decisions have contributed to the development of a coherent body of welfare law. Yet, to the Commissioners, these aspects of their work are vital. (Commissioners' Annual Report, 2004:2).

Our interviews indicate that, generally, the Commissioners would endorse that encapsulation of their work. Some would also add a role of identifying for the lawmakers areas of difficulty and injustice in the existing rules. Others saw their roles as very much of setting quality standards for tribunals in respect of which they had a supervisory role. Most thought they were writing judgments for tribunal chairs, the Secretary of State and claimant's representatives, rather than directly for the claimant who was more concerned with the result than the reasoning.

At the beginning of our research, there were 19 full-time Commissioners in Great Britain, including the Chief Commissioner. There were also two Commissioners in Northern Ireland. Of the 21, four were women. The number increased to five with the appointment of Mrs Jupp, but dropped back to four with the retirement of Commissioner Heggs in August 2002 (see Appendix 3). Nevertheless, this is a slightly better gender ratio than in the higher echelons of the judiciary. There are currently only nine per cent of High Court judges who are female and around ten per cent of circuit judges.[30] There are, at the time of writing, 20 full-time Commissioners in the United Kingdom, including the Chief Commissioner for Great Britain, currently HH Judge Hickinbottom, appointed in September 2003 (Bonner and Buck, 2004), and a Chief Commissioner for Northern Ireland, currently HH Judge Martin, appointed in 1997. There are two

[30] DCA, *Judicial Appointments Annual Report* 2003-04. There were, in post at March 2004, 60 women circuit judges (out of 611), eight women High Court judges (out of 106), two Lady Justices of Appeal (out of 37) and one Law Lord (out of 12).

Commissioners sitting permanently in Scotland under the Great Britain jurisdiction.[31] Each Commissioner constitutes in law a separate tribunal (Micklethwait, 1976). A full list of the current Commissioners and past Commissioners retiring from 1997 is given in Appendix 3.

The Commissioners were envisaged to be members of the senior judiciary, the Lord Chancellor undertaking to recommend appointment of the type of person he would consider for the High Court bench (see above), but in many respects – remuneration, qualification for office, tenure and removeability – they more closely emulate county court or circuit judges. It is suggested here, however, that this is a body of judges which has apparently developed from an inferior tribunal subject to the supervisory jurisdiction of the High Court to be instead in many ways, though not in strict legal form, the equivalent of a specialised branch of the High Court.

In formal terms, Commissioners are appointed by the Monarch on the advice of the Lord Chancellor from among those holding a 10 year general qualification (barrister or solicitor) or those who are advocates or solicitors in Scotland of at least 10 years standing, the same as those for a county court or circuit judge. Making it a Crown appointment was, as was seen earlier, one of the ways of winning support for the exclusion of the courts in favour of this specialist, equivalent level jurisdiction. They are independent in the exercise of their judicial functions, hold office generally only until aged 70, and may be removed from office by the Lord Chancellor on the ground of incapacity or misbehaviour (SSA 1998, s.14, Sched. 4). There are (currently) 17 deputy Commissioners (a reduction from 27 in the light of decreased Commissioner workload), appointed by the Lord Chancellor from those with the same formal qualifications as Commissioners. All Commissioners in Great Britain fall under the jurisdiction of the Lord Chancellor. Nine legal officers (in the London office) exercising significant quasi-judicial functions aid the work of the Commissioners and deputies (Social Security Act 1998, s. 14, Sched. 4, para. 6). There are currently 21 administrative support staff[32] at the London office of the Commissioners (Procession House) and seven support staff at the Edinburgh office who further assist them.

The office of Chief Commissioner was established by the National Insurance Act 1966. There had been no need for one earlier since the adjudication scheme operative from 5 July 1948 had seen its two jurisdictions (National Insurance Commissioner and Industrial Injuries Commissioner) vested in one person, assisted by deputies in an obviously hierarchical structure. The first incumbent was Sir David Davies QC, a former county court judge. Appointment from that jurisdiction was very apt because of the link between the new industrial injuries' work and that executed until 1948 by the county courts under the Workmen's Compensation

---

[31] Commissioners May (the 'Senior Commissioner for Scotland') and Parker. Scottish Commissioners also hear appeals from tribunals north of North Yorkshire and from Workington in the North-West: see Select Committee, 2000: 'Memorandum from OSSCSC in Scotland' (APP 18), *Minutes of Evidence II*.

[32] Personal communication to the authors from OSSCSC, 27 April and 3 May 2005 respectively.

legislation. Criticism of the judiciary in a litigious scheme had been directed at the higher courts, particularly the Court of Appeal (Cornish and Clark, 1989: 533-36). 1966 saw a formal fusing of the two jurisdictions, the elevation of the then Commissioner, Sir Robert Micklethwait, to Chief Commissioner, with his deputies becoming full Commissioners.

Then, as now, the statutory criteria for appointment require a relevant legal qualification (barrister, advocate or – since 1979 – solicitor) of at least 10 years standing. The Lord Chancellor told Parliament in 1946 that he would choose as Commissioner a person he would otherwise consider appropriate for the High Court bench. Little is known otherwise on the criteria for selection. Only one public record office file on appointment of National Insurance/Industrial Injuries Commissioners and deputies is as yet available for scrutiny. It makes interesting if dated reading in terms of attitudes and language, with a later leading Commissioner found not ready for elevation to Deputy Commissioner at that much earlier career stage.[33] All Chief Commissioners prior to Judge Hickinbottom (Davies, Micklethwait, Temple, Griffiths, Bromley, Machin and Harris) have come from the Bar, either being a former Commissioner or, mostly, a circuit/county court judge. Judge Hickinbottom is a circuit judge, the first Chief Commissioner appointed from the solicitor's branch of the profession. Judge Martin, the Chief Commissioner in Northern Ireland was a county court judge on appointment, but came from the Bar.

The statutory role of the Chief Commissioner is very limited; he is empowered to have cases involving a question of law of special difficulty heard by a Tribunal of Commissioners, appointed by him, one of which may be himself, although it is more common for him not so to sit. He has no power to reverse other Commissioners' decisions. Nor can he give directions on how an appeal should be decided; each Commissioner is in this sense an independent judicial tribunal. He has no statutory presidential powers, although administratively an analogy might be drawn with the President of the Appeal Tribunals. As a sort of *primus inter pares* or, perhaps, actor-manager, his administrative role in relation to other Commissioners and the practical operation of this second appellate tier of adjudication, albeit established by what the first incumbent, Micklethwait called 'accepted custom', is much more important, the centrality of his work. As he put it:

> The Chief Commissioner decides which decisions shall be reported, though he consults the other Commissioners on this and many other administrative matters both from day to day and at the periodical conferences of all the Commissioners. In the last resort he decides all internal administrative matters relating to the three offices in London, Edinburgh and Cardiff and also speaks for the whole body of Commissioners in external matters. (Micklethwait, 1976:43)

Our interviews with three Chief Commissioners (Judges Machin, Harris and Hickinbottom) and the other Commissioners indicate that increasingly the incumbents of the Chief Commissioner's office have seen it as essentially an

---

[33] National Archives catalogue ref LCO 2/7110.

administrative one. The Chief Commissioner liaises with the Department for Constitutional Affairs (DCA), the Department for Work and Pensions (DWP) and other government departments and is normally the chair of the users' group committee (see further Chapter 6). The Chief Commissioner has input into the current tribunal reform process through membership of the Tribunal Presidents' Group (see Chapter 7). He also has a personnel role in interviewing candidates for appointment as deputy or Commissioner. His judicial management role involves some control of the workload and setting up procedures that get the work through at an appropriate speed.

He exercised his power of choosing which decisions to report by convening and chairing a small group of Commissioners including one from Scotland and one from Northern Ireland. This body was known under Judge Machin's regime as the 'Star Chamber' and reporting is now decided by an editorial board of Commissioners and a legal officer, chaired by the Chief Commissioner (see further, Chapter 5). The Chief Commissioner's work on procedure is also now aided by a committee, which also makes recommendations on procedural rules to the DCA. There is also now a development and training committee organising training sessions for Commissioners and deputies. Like Leggatt (2001), a significant number of Commissioners would like the Chief Commissioner to take a stronger and more pro-active 'judicial leadership' role in terms of development of the law and setting good judicial standards. The current Chief Commissioner seems very much to see giving a lead in this area of law as one of his roles.

From our interviews with the Commissioners, we found that, behind the formal appointment qualifications, they had professional backgrounds, broadly, as legal practitioners, tribunal chairs and academics. There were a number of Commissioners who had overlapping professional backgrounds in more than one of these categories, six in all three if one took account of part-time academics. Not all the tribunal chairs had sat in the social security field at all; several were from industrial/employment tribunals, VAT and Duties tribunals or Pensions appeal tribunals. All three Chief Commissioners were circuit judges, and one, Judge Harris, served coterminously as President of the Appeals Service, from whose tribunals come most of the appeals dealt with by the Commissioners. About half had served first as deputy Commissioners, one for a very brief four-week period. Several also held other judicial appointments while serving as a Commissioner (member of the Employment Appeal Tribunal, chair of War Pensions Tribunal). Our research has certainly dispelled the notion of the dominance of Chancery barristers; only four had that background. Experience as a practitioner was quite varied: criminal and civil law, some international work. Indeed, one had prior to appointment a mainly paper practice dealing with appeals from colonies and Commonwealth countries to the Judicial Committee of the Privy Council.

This work does not analyse particular decisions or subscribe to any crude theories of 'judicial behaviouralism'. The authors postulate, however, a relevance of background experience to the approach to one's professional work. While there seemed no clearly discernible pattern of allocating particular types of work to Commissioners with a particular background, there was evidence that, in terms of their own perceptions, their professional backgrounds had important impacts on their role as Commissioners.

Only four Commissioners had come to the job as practitioners or academics expert in social security law (the academics, however, saw their other background as tribunal chairs rather than academia as being the basis for their appointment). Ten, however, had gained experience in the area by sitting as chairs of a range of appeal tribunals now under the AS umbrella. But a range of legal backgrounds could impact in less direct ways. For example, the Commissioners deal with often-complex legislation in their benefits, tax credits and child support jurisdictions, and the legal issues encountered can raise quite complex aspects of property law and accounts. One Commissioner with all three professional backgrounds, including a practice advising international agencies and governments on tax, thought they had, in different ways, been good preparation for the job of a Commissioner:

> I've been running with the administrative side of the job and the social security side of the job for all my professional career. The other aspect and the common ground between tax, social security and my European experience is that it is very much a statute-based subject dealing with extremely complex legislation and my whole training, in a sense, has been handling in everyway you could think of extremely complex legislation.

Familiarity with the tax and revenue side had assisted this Commissioner very much in dealing with tax credits and pensions' work. Familiarity with accounts had been valuable both in respect of child support and the resources of the self-employed as regards a range of benefits, especially income–related ones. Several Commissioners, with a property and trusts background, thought that helped in child support and more complex aspects of the financial balance sheet at the heart of the income-based benefits where there are complicated structures as to how people own different assets. It also aided the drafting side of a Commissioner's work. A chancery and pensions practice, involving practising in quite a wide area of very technical subjects, meant that another Commissioner was used to being given sets of papers to advise on matters s/he knew almost nothing about. Being used to getting to grips quickly and accurately with topics s/he had not dealt with before helped with learning a completely new field. Pensions work had involved construing complex legal documents and statutes. General legal training, another thought, prepared one for getting to the heart of a matter and sorting out what was actually relevant. One Commissioner thought practice in the higher courts advantageous as enabling the rapid identification of whether there was in an appeal an arguable point of law. Another thought lack of experience in social security law and tribunal work a great advantage:

> ...one of the problems about getting involved exclusively or to a great extent in the Commissioners' work is that you come with a certain degree of baggage and perceived views that the Appeals Service has about the way in which cases ought to be decided or certain aspects of the law and one of the advantages of coming to it fresh is that one had a totally fresh view on it. It's complicated work, there is a different way of thinking, but what it has, like all legal jobs, is the fundamental ability to analyse a legal problem and

> come to a conclusion thereon and I did find that with my previous experience in relation to the way in which appellate jurisdictions worked, once I began to master the law then it worked okay. … I have actually had the ideal background for doing the work of a Commissioner.

Life and the caring profession of one's spouse might give useful insight into disability benefits. Several whose practice had mainly been paper-based found quite easy the transition to an adjudicative role in which oral hearings are largely absent. For those whose experience was court-based or tribunal based, the lack of well-qualified legal representation and oral hearings took some getting used to. Those who had been full-time or part time chairs of social security tribunals thought that experience particularly valuable for their work as a Commissioner.

> …my formative experience is the grass roots involvement in tribunal decision-making and appeal processes, I do think that was very important. I do think that from my perspective to realise when I'm writing decisions as a Commissioner I'm not just looking at how they are received by the parties, or by the profession I don't think we could say the wider public, as it is very rare that the wider public is even interested but I do think it helps me to focus on what I think is important, the tribunal which is receiving and applying that decision.

Another – with a background extending beyond social security tribunals – thought:

> …professional background obviously helped as a full time tribunal chairman in knowing what goes on in a tribunal in knowing the sort of pressure they're under. Not that it necessarily affects my judgment in any appeal, but knowing what happens at the level below I think is useful, otherwise it's a bit like being parachuted in as a General to Whitehall not having been in the field as it were. I've seen both sides of it. But I think the other jurisdictions I've sat in help me to know the different styles of representation the different sort of issues and the different styles of the tribunal that you can come across.

A Commissioner with an employment tribunal background found that very helpful in dealing with European Community laws aspects. That practical experience – in social security and/or other tribunal fields – helped tie what might otherwise be a remote jurisdiction to reality on the ground. A third thought tribunal experience was as important as his/her academic expertise in social security law:

> …the background in having sat on tribunals is useful because it gives you a feel for the way that things go on in tribunals. It gives you a feel for the sort of guidance and directions that tribunals like, if cases are being sent back to them. Obviously as time goes on that perhaps fades out a bit. It is useful at the beginning but obviously Commissioners who come in without that background develop a feel for it as well and your experience becomes more remote, less relevant. I think the academic background is also useful as you know you spend most of, a lot of our time telling students where the Court of Appeal went wrong or where the House of Lords went wrong and they didn't

> consider this, or that. Sort of teach students to answer exam questions as if they are in the Court of Appeal and it's a challenge to actually then do it but I think it gives you a useful perspective on the approach. Maybe it leads to some of us with that background to go off into long frolics on explaining principles that don't actually bite but I think my view is that it is still helpful in decisions not simply to announce the result, but to explain where the result fits in to an overall framework of principles. It is actually one of the strengths of what the Commissioners have done. I think the academic background is helpful from that point of view.

In contrast, another former practitioner/academic turned chairman, with a background in welfare rights advice work, considered that all his/her experiences were important, but thought that the welfare rights background gave:

> ...appreciation of the law and how it works in practice... and, I suppose the way it will seem to lay-people, the way it seems to claimants, the kind of language they have to use to enable people to understand what's going on.

Another stated that since s/he

> ...came from the tribunal with a knowledge of social security law and child support law, I have experience of how the tribunal operates in practise I often understand what the procedures have been and where things may have gone wrong and hopefully understand the practicalities of hearing cases and writing decisions.

But that intertwined with and reinforced her/his practical bent from time at the Bar:

> ...that has always influenced me. I've always been very practical, a sense of not seeing things in terms of theory but how does this right actually work in a court, how do you prove it, what evidence are you going to have to prove this, what factors in real life are going to influence it, rather than what appears on the page to be perhaps something rather different from the way it will work in practise.

His/her more remote academic background – both in time and subject area (commercial/company) was rather played down, but s/he brought from that a skill in 'handling legislation, legislation that is continuously changing and is very technical in the company field'. The broader base of appointments achieved over the last decade had resulted in a stronger collective pool of expertise, but arguably at the expense of 'collegiality', an attribute or non-attribute on which there were very mixed views – some regarding it as wholly non-existent, others as there but not efficient in promoting a common view (see further, Chapter 6). Increased size has exacerbated difficulties in achieving consistency in decision-making.

Table 2.3 Commissioners' and Chief Commissioner's salary rate: 1974-2005

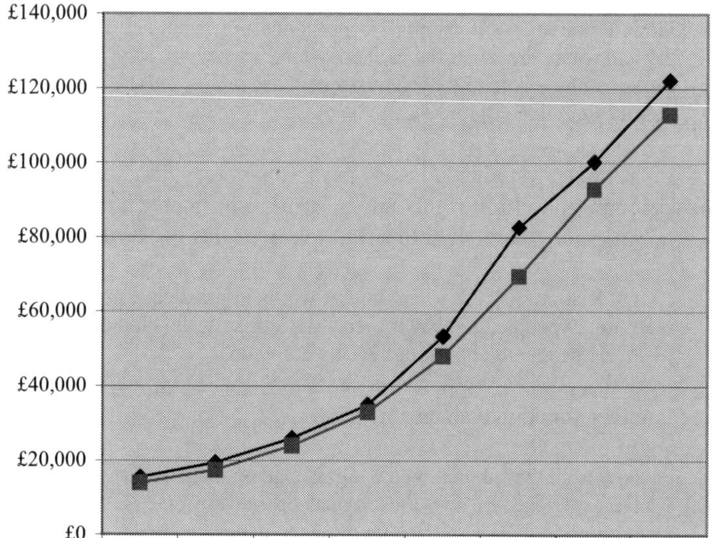

	1974	1978	1980	1985	1990	1995	2000	2005
Chief Commissioner	£15,500	£19,500	£26,000	£35,000	£53,400	£82,641	£100,209	£122,139
Commissioner	£14,000	£17,500	£24,000	£33,000	£48,100	£69,457	£92,810	£113,121

Source: Reports of the Review Body on Senior Salaries; 1974 – 2005.

The Commissioners' remuneration

No account of the development and nature of the Commissioners is complete without some reference to their remuneration. To an extent, their remuneration locates them within a wider judicial hierarchy. Despite early comparisons in the history of the Commissioners with High Court judges, their tenure is more comparable to that of circuit judges and indeed they have received the same salary level as circuit judges since 1974. Commissioners are in category 'group 5' along with, for example, circuit judges, the Deputy Chief Immigration Adjudicator and the senior district judge of the principal registry of the Family Division. The Chief Commissioner is placed in the same senior salary scale ('group 6.1') as, for example, senior circuit judges, the Chief Immigration Adjudicator, the President of the Appeals Service and circuit judges at the Central Criminal Court in London ('Old Bailey' judges). The increases in their salary rates from 1974 to present are charted in the Table above.

The prospect of tribunal reform reflected in the Leggatt review of tribunals prompted the Scottish Commissioners to remark that 'there would be a considerable dent to the morale of office holders were the fixing of salaries to be removed from the Senior Salaries Review Board' (Walker, 2001: para 12).

The importance of this historical perspective

This chapter has shown the *ad hoc* way in which pre-World War II adjudication structures developed and how the Commissioners are very much based on the model of adjudication developed for unemployment insurance: 'Umpire' transmuted into 'Commissioner'. It reveals in surprising contrast some very thoughtful planning amidst the dark days of that war for a post-war structure, very deliberately using Commissioners – independent Crown-appointed specialist judges of the calibre of those in the High Court – rather than the courts. The aim was to create an 'enabling' system to help the unrepresented claimant seeking to assert his or her rights. Watchwords like cheap, expert, speedy and informal are shown to predate the Franks report (1957), but to link, through that report and consequent reforms to the report of the Leggatt review, with its concerns with tribunal independence, user-friendliness, minimisation of delay, regulation of precedent-setting decisions and stress on an enabling function envisaging do-it-yourself rather than publicly funded representation. The chapter shows graphically how the Commissioners' jurisdictions and roles examined by Micklethwait (1976) have changed and broadened beyond the national insurance and industrial injuries sectors into a world of means-tested benefits and an array of disability benefits.

We consider that a watershed change was that in 1987, confining to a point of law only appeal to the Commissioners across the whole range of their appellate jurisdiction, which, we consider, alters radically the Commissioners' role and their relationship with lay users (see Chapter 7). The next chapter examines the role played by the Commissioners in the modern decision-making and appellate processes. Readers should bear in mind that, in the vast majority of cases, appeal to the Commissioners proves the final stage in the appellate process of challenging or defending a decision on social security benefits, tax credits, housing and council tax benefits, and child support matters.

Chapter 3

The Decision-Making and Appellate Process

Introduction

Our project looked at the appellate work of the Commissioners against a backdrop of a falling workload and the implementation of the decision-making and appeal (DMA) changes introduced by the Social Security Act 1998 (SSA 1998). The essence of the decision-making structure is unaffected: initial decision by an official in the Department for Work and Pensions (DWP), the Department for Social Development in Northern Ireland, the Inland Revenue, the Child Support Agency (CSA) or a local authority; a full right of appeal (fact and law) to an Appeals Service (AS) tribunal; a right of appeal from that tribunal to a Commissioner, with leave, on a point of law; and a right of appeal, again with leave on a point of law, to the Court of Appeal from the Commissioner. Most appeals come from DWP areas. Relatively few proceed beyond Commissioner-level.

There are millions of benefit decisions made by officials of the DWP every year. About 1 per cent of these (around 250,000) will go to the AS tribunals (National Audit Office, 2003: 1). The Commissioner's workload is only some 2.5 per cent (around 6,250) of that of the AS tribunals. However, as will be seen, there are relatively few categories of benefit that make up the bulk of appeal work. In recent years, by far the largest source of appeals to both the tribunals and Commissioners has been Disability Living Allowance (DLA). There are some 2.5 million claimants in receipt of the benefit. There are annually some 40,000 appeals to AS tribunals about that benefit, and about 3,000 cases each year to the Commissioners. Incapacity Benefit, Income Support and Industrial Injuries benefits also constitute significant proportions of the workload of both the tribunals (Table 3.6) and the Commissioners (Table 3.7). There is also a long 'tail' of several dozen other benefits that in aggregate constitute significant workloads and, because of their relative infrequency at the appeal stages, may be more demanding of judicial and other resources to resolve them.

It will be seen that appeal rights in social security are subject to a number of limitations and restrictions. They come not as of right but must be clearly located within constantly changing statutory material (see Chapter 2). Whole areas of decision-making are excluded from appeal. There are at each stage provisions which can delay or obviate (by correcting an error) appeals, whether to tribunal or

Commissioner-level, and the DMA changes have attempted to apply some limits on the appeal tribunal's inquisitorial jurisdiction and the point of time on which they must focus, although, in both instances, the Commissioners, in the face of poorly drafted legislation, have made strenuous efforts to maintain the interests of justice.

Figure 3.1 below sets out the basic structure of the appeal route: from the initial decision of a departmental official to the AS tribunal, the Commissioners and then on to the courts. This chapter briefly examines aspects of departmental decision-making and AS tribunal-level determinations. The chapter then focuses in greater detail on the various procedural stages at Commissioner-level and includes an account from our research of the Commissioners' own views about their work.

Departmental decision making

As explained in Chapters 1 and 2, the jurisdiction of the Commissioners is in the process of expanding. The initial decision-making that might eventually produce an appeal from the AS tribunal to the Commissioners now includes not only the officials of the DWP, but also officials within the Inland Revenue making decisions about tax credits, officials of the CSA making decisions about child maintenance and officials within the local authorities making decisions about housing benefit and council tax benefit. The departmental administration of these benefits and credits by the various government authorities involves millions of decisions each year.

The DWP's operation administering welfare benefits is huge. There are over 11 million recipients of both contribution-based retirement pensions and winter fuel payments. There are over 14 million recipients of benefits for the disabled (including DLA) and working age benefits and over two million recipients of Income Support. The CSA currently deals with around two million parents with care and non-resident parents. The Inland Revenue recorded 5.9 million families, containing 10 million children as tax credit recipients in December 2004. The local authorities are handling the work generated by around 3.8 million housing benefit and 4.6 million council tax benefit recipients.

Most appeal processes have the dual function of being both a means whereby the claimant can assert his or her rights where the administration of the benefit is in error or the relevant legal rule is in need of challenge, and a repressive function whereby complaints can be filtered out. This repressive function is usually controversial. To what extent does the 'filter' of the appeal process result in the evaporation of otherwise meritorious complaints? It is certainly the case, as will be seen, that there is little relationship between the scale of benefit and the profile of appeal work handled by both AS tribunals and the Commissioners. Retirement pensions and child support, for example, though requiring a huge administrative effort at the departmental level of initial decision-making infrequently find their way into the appeal system.

Figure 3.1 The Appeal Process: statutory rights of appeal

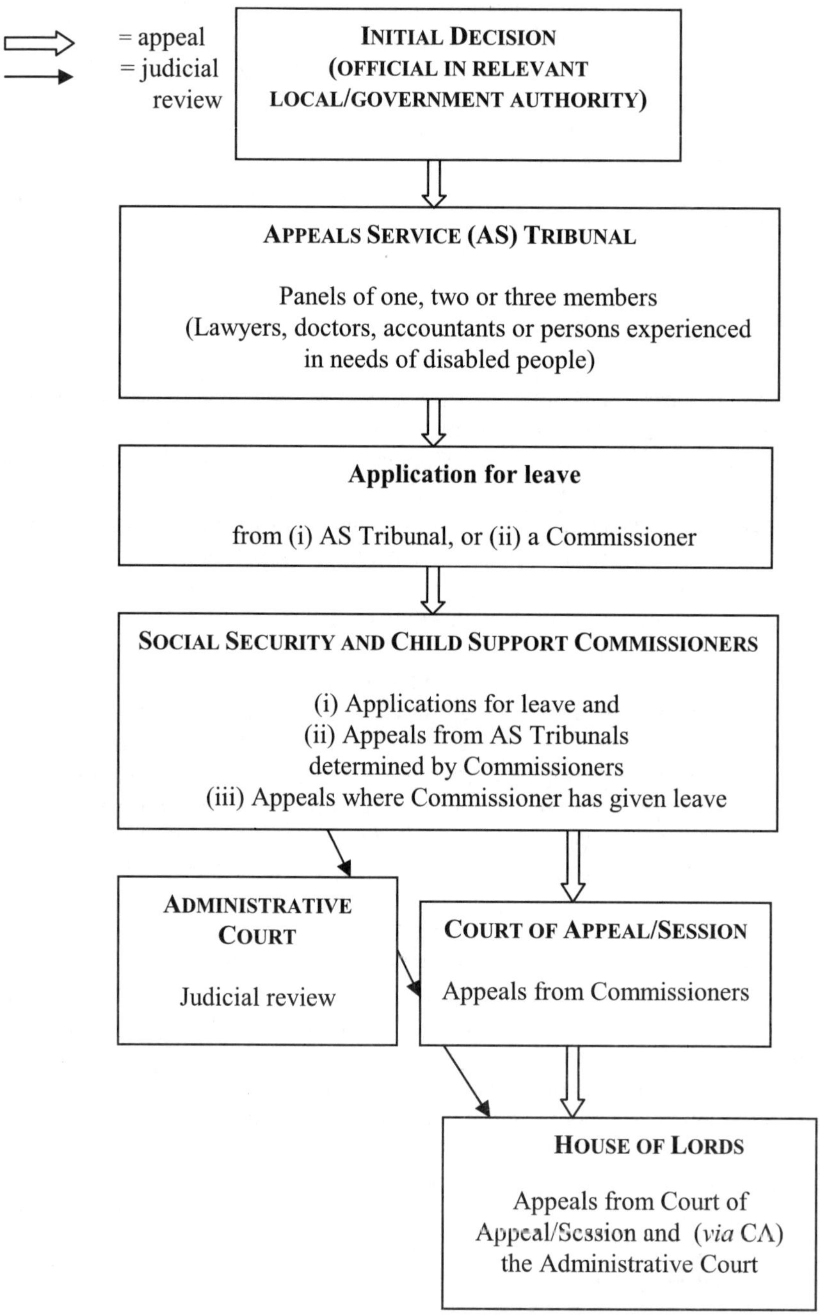

A departmental decision on a benefit, credit or child support matter will classically require a written notification of the decision to be given to the claimant. For example, in respect of benefits and child support, the notification must contain information setting out whether there is entitlement and where appropriate the amount payable and the date when it is payable from in addition to information about any available appeal rights. Where an appealable decision has been notified but without a statement of the reasons for the decision, the claimant can request a written statement within a month from the notification and the decision maker must supply such a statement within 14 days.[1]

The following paragraphs of this section, for the sake of clarity, focus on this particular form of 'departmental' decision making in the DWP, but the reader should not lose sight of the increasing number of initial decision-makers in other government and local government authorities as explained above. As regards DWP decision-making, it is the 'Secretary of State' who has the legal responsibility for making decisions. Once a decision on benefit has been made there are in essence three ways in which it can be disputed and changed: by revision, supersession or on appeal.

The initiative underlying SSA 1998 to improve DMA is assisted by a number of statutory 'filtering' tools intended to make the appeal process more efficient. These include powers at the departmental level to revise and supersede and stay earlier decisions. It also includes, at the AS tribunal and Commissioner levels, powers to supersede, set aside and to stay appeals. These procedures are explained in outline in the following sections. Figure 3.2 below also provides an overview of the location of these devices alongside the appeal route.

The decision-maker or the claimant can initiate a *revision* of the original decision (SSA 1998, s.9). There is however, no appeal against a decision to refuse to revise. The right to appeal survives only as applied to the original decision. However, the time period for appealing is brought forward to commence from the date of the revised decision (or a decision not to revise). Consequently, asking for a revision before making an appeal will not prejudice a claimant. Any outstanding appeal however, will generally lapse if a revised decision is made prior to the determination of the appeal. This provision has therefore been of great utility for the Secretary of State to head off appeals in circumstances where it is appropriate to concede the case or to correct an 'official error'.

The decision-maker or the claimant can also initiate a decision to *supersede* an earlier decision (SSA 1998, s.10). This power may be applied not only to an original decision, but also to a revised decision or a decision of an AS tribunal or a Commissioner. The supersession will also take effect from the date it is made, in contrast to a revision, which generally takes effect from the date of the original decision.

---

1 Social Security and Child Support (Decisions and Appeals) Regulations 1999, SI 1999/991, reg. 28. (Hereafter 'SI 1999/991').

Figure 3.2 The Appeal Process: 'filtering' tools

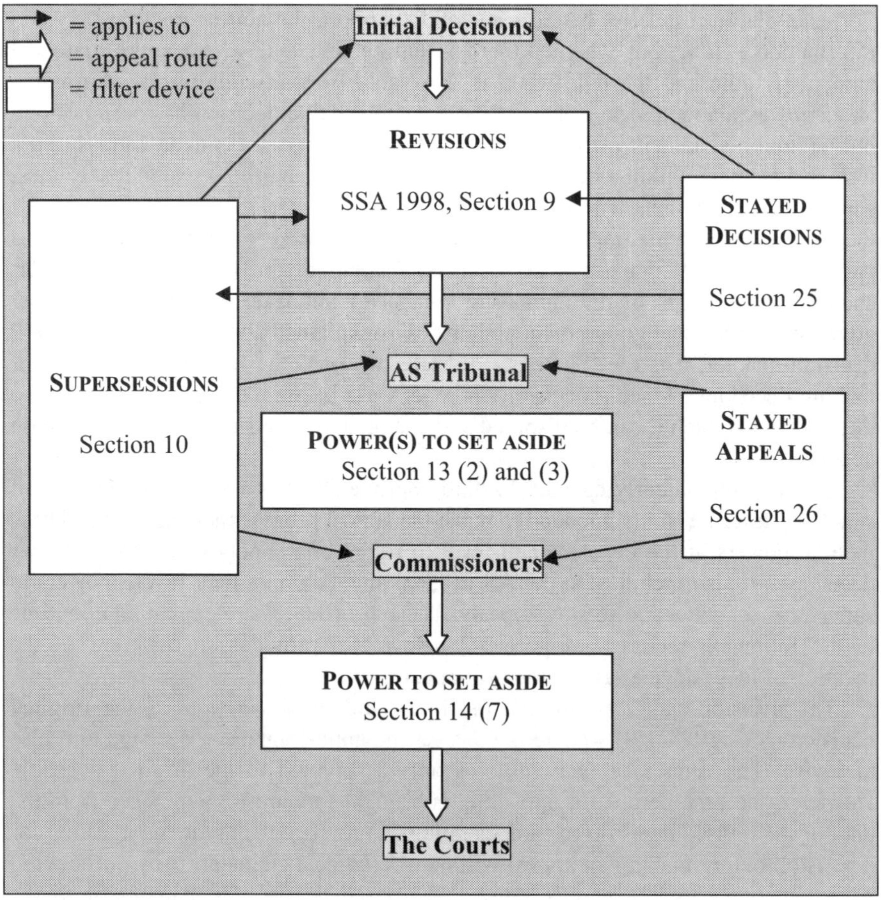

One or more of three constraining criteria must be met if the decision-maker is to supersede a tribunal or Commissioner's decision.[2]

Where an original, revised or superseded decision falls to be made, the Secretary of State has a broad discretion to *stay such decisions*. The circumstances that trigger this power will be that there is an appeal pending in a 'lead' case, either to the Commissioners or the courts, which could possibly affect the 'lookalike' case to be stayed (SSA 1998, s.25).[3]

---

[2] SI 1999/991, reg 6(2). See also *Wood v Secretary of State for Work and Pensions* [2003] EWCA Civ 53, reported as *R(DLA) 1/03* overruling a Tribunal of Commissioners decision in *R(DLA) 6/02*.

[3] '[The Secretary of State] has a broad discretion and much will depend on such circumstances as the number of cases, the amount of money at stake, hardship to the claimants and the degree of probability that the court's decision will provide significant

Appeals Service (AS) tribunal-level decision-making

The numbers of appeals received by AS over the past six years is set out in the Table 3.1. This illustrates to an extent the impact of the DMA changes on the overall number of appeal cases. After a significant fall from the figure in 1997-98 the total number of appeals received has hovered a little below 250,000 cases per annum since 1998-99.

Table 3.1 Appeals received by the Appeals Service 1997-98 to 2003-04[4]

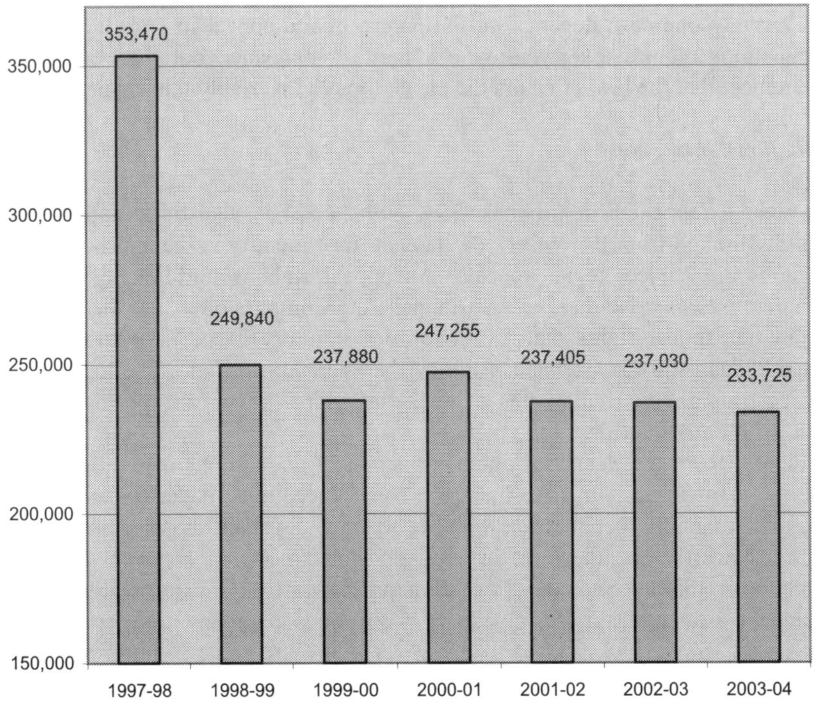

Source: Derived from DWP, Quarterly Appeal Tribunal Statistics: June 2004, Table 1.

The 'Appeals Service' replaced the Independent Tribunal Service in April 1999. Under the DMA changes, responsibility for the *administration* of appeals passed from the President of the Independent Tribunals Service to the Secretary of State. AS is made up of two distinct bodies within a single organisation. The

assistance with the determination of the cases before him.' (Rowland and White, 2004: para 1.427).

4 Each 'year' is calculated from monthly figures given from October to the following September. Figures for the last three months in 2003-04 were noted as 'provisional'.

administrative side of the AS was launched as an executive agency within the Department of Social Security (DSS) (now the DWP) in April 2000. The Chief Executive, with delegated powers from the Secretary of State, is the head of the agency and has responsibility for the administration of appeals. The *judicial* functioning of tribunals operates as a non-department public body headed by the President of Appeal Tribunals. Appeals are heard in tribunals in over 140 venues throughout England, Scotland and Wales and are processed at eight major operational sites throughout Great Britain.

An appeal tribunal is made up of panels of one, two or three members (SSA 1998, s.7). Panel members must be lawyers, doctors, accountants or persons experienced in dealing with the needs of disabled people.[5] The composition of the panel in any one case depends on the nature of the appeal in question. All the permutations require a lawyer to be a part of the panel, but there is no legal requirement that the lawyer chairs the panel, though invariably this happens.

Limitations on appeals

The right to appeal to a tribunal (SSA 1998, s.12) is, like other appeal rights, carefully limited from the outset. Parliament must identify in the legislation which decisions are subject to an appeal. An appeal right is traditionally entirely a creature of *statute*. Neither the AS tribunals, the Commissioners nor the courts can conjure up appeal rights that lack a proper statutory basis. An appeal is not available against *every* decision made by the Secretary of State. The legislation in essence provides two categories of decision against which an appeal lies (SSA 1998, s.12(1)(a) and (b)).

Firstly, there are decisions about the statutory 'conditions of entitlement' for benefits. However, even here there are some exceptions made; for example, no appeal lies against the question whether to treat a person as 'present' in Great Britain. Nevertheless, this category of appealable decision is given some legal protection in that the Secretary of State is precluded from making regulations that would take away appeal rights in respect of questions that relate to the conditions of entitlement (SSA 1998, s.12(3)). However, there are areas in both the primary legislation and in the regulations where it is stated that no appeal will be available; for example, the time and manner of certain payments and making certain deductions from benefit.[6] There are a number of Commissioners' decisions that have questioned the legal validity of these limitations on the appeal right, on the basis that the prescribed decisions may well 'relate' to the conditions of entitlement and thus fall foul of SSA 1998, s.12(3).[7]

Secondly, an appeal lies against a number of miscellaneous types of decision not falling within the 'conditions of entitlement' formula; for example, decisions about whether to make payments to a third party, disqualifications, recovery of

---

[5] SI 1999/991, reg 35 and Schedule 3.
[6] *Ibid*, Schedule 2.
[7] See *CIS/540/02*.

benefit and certain contribution decisions. A Commissioner's decision has identified a connecting thread between 'appealable' decisions.

> Standing back from the details of the Social Security Act 1998 and the regulations made under it, there is a clear theme uniting most of the decisions that are appealable. This is that they are, to use the new jargon, 'outcome decisions'. This is not a term of art. It is merely a useful expression to refer to decisions that have, in crude terms, an impact on a claimant's pocket. In other words, an outcome decision is one that directly affects the money that the claimant receives or might receive in the future.
>
> The determinations that are the building blocks of outcome decisions also, of course, affect the money that the claimant receives or might receive in the future. But they do not have this effect directly. They have this effect only when incorporated in an outcome decision. The claimant is able to appeal against the outcome decision and is able to challenge, as an issue arising on that appeal, the underlying determination.[8]

The legislation also sets out three categories of people who have rights of appeal: the claimant; any other 'prescribed' person (e.g. an appointee for a claimant unable to act or deceased); and, any person from whom the Secretary of State has decided benefit is recoverable (SSA 1998, s.12(2) and (4)). It also sets out the time within which, and the manner in which, appeals are to be brought (SSA 1998, s.12(7)).[9] Generally, an appeal must be brought within one month of the date of notification of the decision. There is provision for a late appeal on the basis of two alternative conditions: (a) the legally qualified panel member is satisfied that there are reasonable prospects of success, or (b) the panel member is satisfied that it is 'in the interests of justice' that the application is granted. In any event no appeal is possible after one year following the end of the (one month) period allowed for appealing. The manner in which an appeal is made is that it shall be in writing either on an approved pro-forma or in another format acceptable to the Secretary of State.

One of the new DMA changes introduced in SSA 1998 in order to reduce the numbers of appeal cases was a provision instructing that a tribunal 'need not consider any issue that is not raised by the appeal' (section 12(8)(a)).[10] Obviously, the wording 'need not' does not appear to provide a total bar to considering issues not raised. Indeed, as Rowland and White (2004: para 1.379) comment, this subsection 'implies a power to consider new issues but makes it clear that there are limits to the extent to which the inquisitorial role of a tribunal imposes a duty to consider such issues.' In a Tribunal of Commissioners decision it was stated that:

> Everything will depend on the circumstances in any given instance. We would be slow to convict a tribunal of failure to identify an uncanvassed factual point in favour of the claimant in the absence of the most obvious and clear cut circumstances.[11]

---

8 *CIB/2338/00*, paras 23-4.

9 See also SI 1999/991, regs 31-3.

10 See also the comparable provisions relating to revisions (SSA 1998, s.9(2), and supersessions (SSA 1998, s.10(2)).

11 *R(SB) 2/83(T)*.

Another limiting provision specifies that a tribunal *shall not* take account of any changes in circumstances absent at the time when the decision appealed against was made (SSA 1998, s.12 (8)(b)). The starkness of this provision in the field of social security, where claimants' circumstances can change quite rapidly has, to an extent, been mitigated by the Commissioners who have held in a number of decisions[12] that this provision will not prevent the consideration of post-decision evidence for the purposes of drawing inferences from it as to the circumstances present prior to or at the time of the decision. This is especially relevant in relation to cases where entitlement depends upon a medical prognosis. Nevertheless, as Rowland and White indicate, this provision could benefit from an element of discretion, but as it is, it 'introduces an unwelcome element of technicality into appeals to tribunals that were once supposed to be user-friendly.' (2004: para 1.379).

Notification of decision and right of appeal

A claimant who is dissatisfied with the tribunal's decision has the right of appeal to a Commissioner, subject to obtaining either the tribunal chair's permission, or if that is not granted, a direct application to the Commissioner for leave. An application for leave to a tribunal chair is examined in the following section. A direct application to a Commissioner for permission to appeal is dealt with later in this Chapter.

Application for leave/permission to the tribunal chair

A claimant's application for leave/permission[13] from a part-time tribunal chair will in fact be heard by one of his or her full-time colleagues.[14] The legislation was amended in May 2002 to formalise this existing practice in the Appeals Service whereby the full-time legally qualified panel members determine *all* these applications for leave.

The Regulations provide that an application for leave is sent to the clerk of the tribunal within a period of one month from the date the applicant has been sent a written statement of the reasons for the decision.[15] A copy of that statement should be annexed to the application. The tribunal chair determining an application for leave must record his or her decision in writing and send a copy to every other party. Late applications can be accepted (up to a limit of 13 months from the date of the notification of reasons) for 'special reasons' as a matter of discretion. The

---

[12] For example, *R(DLA) 2/01, R(DLA) 3/01.*

[13] 'Permission' is the modern usage, but 'leave' is retained as it still appears ubiquitously in legal literature.

[14] SI 1999/991, reg 58(6). Rowland and White (2004: para 1.383) question whether this was how section 13 was intended to operate.

[15] SI 1999/991, reg 58.

discretion is a broad one. It is not only the reasons for the delay itself that may be considered.[16]

Setting aside and redeterminations

Another of the DMA changes introduced by SSA 1998 (s.13(2)) was a new facility for tribunal chairs, at their discretion, to set aside appeal decisions and direct that the case be heard again by the same or a differently constituted tribunal on the basis that the decision was 'erroneous in point of law' (see Figure 3.2 above). A precondition for the availability of this power is the existence of an application for leave to appeal to the Commissioners made to the tribunal chair.

The provision was obviously intended to stem the flow of unnecessary appeal cases to the Commissioners, and the Commissioners' Annual Report (2004: 4) appears to confirm that this specific power has contributed towards a drop in their own caseload. From a 'users' perspective of the system it may well be that claimants would generally prefer to have an adverse decision set aside and be given a further chance at the tribunal level. However, it should be remembered that in perhaps a small but significant class of case, it may also be important to bring the error of law in question to the attention of the Commissioners. A key point of statutory interpretation and/or other matters of wider public interest may be at stake. Rowland and White advise that '[i]f there is active opposition to a setting aside and there is a serious point of law to be determined, it is suggested that the panel member should grant leave to appeal rather than set aside the decision' (2004: para 1.384).

However, no doubt to limit the workload, the Secretary of State has generally waived any right to be consulted in relation to claimants' applications for leave under this power. On the other hand, it has been held that it is a breach of the rules of natural justice to set aside a decision that was favourable to the claimant without any consultation with the claimant.[17]

The legislation also obliges the tribunal chair to set aside and refer the case for redetermination 'if each of the principal parties to the case expresses the view that the decision was erroneous in point of law' (SSA 1998, s.13(3)). This provision is controversial in that it places a *judicial* decision – the determination of whether there is an error of law – into the hands of the parties. If they agree, the chair must set aside the decision. In addition, to be operational, the Secretary of State must of necessity break his/her own waiver in relation to being consulted. Finally, it should be noted that this provision would also allow a setting aside in circumstances where both parties identified *different* errors of law.

---

[16] Other factors might be; the strength of the grounds of appeal, the amount of money at stake, whether the decision affected current entitlement, whether there was an adequate alternative remedy, the difficulties that delay would have on making further findings of fact and the parties' conduct of the case, including their contribution to the delay. See the annotation in Rowland and White (2004: para 2.484) and the cases cited therein.

[17] *CIS/4533/01*.

There is no right of appeal against the tribunal chair's decision to set aside (or not to set aside) [18] though a judicial review challenge is a possibility. The right to appeal will still be attached to the redetermined decision of the tribunal. However, a Commissioner's decision has suggested that the creation of a right of appeal against the exercise of the set aside power might in exceptional cases be appropriate. The case is incidentally a classic example of the Commissioners using their decision writing to prompt the legislature into action.[19]

Stayed appeals procedure

The power to stay *appeals* is comparable to the 'stayed decision' procedure at the departmental decision-making level (SSA 1998, s.25). In this context, it is available at the tribunal or Commissioner level (SSA 1998, s.26): see Figure 3.2 above. Where a Commissioner or a court is considering a lead case, any 'lookalike' appeal that is to be heard by a tribunal or a Commissioner can be stayed, pending the result of such a case. In essence, the Secretary of State has powers to issue a notice requiring the tribunal or Commissioner to refer lookalike cases to him/her. The Secretary of State will then hold back the lookalike cases from the appeals process and has powers, following the resolution of the lead case, to revise or supersede the original decision without the need of the tribunal's involvement.

Alternatively, the Secretary of State's notice will specify that the tribunal (or Commissioner) will stay the lookalike cases until the lead case is resolved. Finally, another alternative available is for the tribunal (or Commissioner) to decide the lookalike case on the basis of a notional determination of the lead case which would be least favourable to the claimant, if the tribunal considers it to be 'in the interests of the appellant' to do so. This provision is largely intended to enable claimants to have some benefit paid while the lead case is still pending even though this might fall short of their entitlement if the lead case turns out to be in their favour.

It does however seem curious that the decision whether lookalike cases are held back by the Secretary of State or referred to the judicial authorities is a decision in the hands of the Secretary of State who will be a party in both the lookalike and lead cases. The Secretary of State's choice of procedure on this matter is not itself appealable though it is challengeable by way of judicial review. Rowland and White offer the following explanation:

> The perception that this provision was desirable appears to have arisen out of an occasion when the then President of social security appeal tribunals directed tribunals to

[18] *CIS/4533/2001*.

[19] 'Those responsible for proposing legislation in this field may wish to consider whether it would be desirable for there to be a right of appeal to a Commissioner from decisions of a legally qualified panel member. Given the nature of such decisions, appeals would be rare but this case may illustrate the desirability of having some proportionate way of dealing with the exceptional case in which a significant error is made' (*CIS/4533/2001*, para 15).

> determine a vast number of appeals notwithstanding the fact that an appeal against a Commissioner's decision was pending in the courts. This resulted in some thousands of extra appeals being brought before the Commissioners. It may be thought that this is unlikely to be repeated. In practice the Secretary of State is very content to allow tribunals and Commissioners to manage blocks of 'lookalike' cases without resorting to serving a notice under this section and where a notice is served it is usually after consultation with the President of appeal tribunals and the Chief Commissioner (2004: para 1,432).

In the London office of the Commissioners,[20] 50 cases were stayed under this procedure pending the outcome of *Gillies*[21] in the Court of Session. There were 104 cases stayed pending the outcome of *Hinchy*[22] in the Court of Appeal (since heard in the House of Lords), 39 cases pending the outcome of *Hooper*[23] in the Court of Appeal and 20 cases stayed pending the case of *Carson and Reynolds*[24] pending an outcome in the House of Lords.

Notice of appeal to the Commissioners

If the tribunal's decision is not set aside and the tribunal chair grants leave, then certain information and documentation will need to be included in the notice of appeal.[25] It must include, for example, the grounds on which the appellant intends to rely, the notice informing the appellant that leave to appeal has been granted, the decision against which leave to appeal has been granted, and the written statement of the reasons for the tribunal decision. The notice of appeal will not be valid unless it is sent to a Commissioner within one month of the date on which the appellant was sent written notice that leave had been granted.[26] If the tribunal chair refuses to give leave, the appellant can apply for leave directly to the Commissioners.

Commissioner-level decision making

The Office of the Social Security and Child Support Commissioners (OSSCSC) records 'applications' (i.e. applications for leave to appeal) separately from

---

[20] Figures supplied by OSSCSC to the authors 16 March 2005.
[21] *Secretary of State for Work and Pensions v Gillies* (28 November 2003) 2004 SLT 14.
[22] *Hinchy v Secretary of State for Work and Pensions* Court of Appeal (20 February 2003) [2003] 2 All E.R. 289; House of Lords (3 March 2005) [2005] 2 All ER 129.
[23] *R (on the application of Hooper) v Secretary of State for Work and Pensions*, Court of Appeal, (18 June 2003) [2003] EWCA Civ 875.
[24] *R (on the application of Carson) v Secretary of State for Work and Pensions, R (on the application of Reynolds) v Secretary of State for Work and Pensions*, Court of Appeal (17 June 2003) [2003] 3 All ER 577.
[25] Social Security Commissioners (Procedure) Regulations 1999, SI 1999/1495, reg 12. (Hereafter ' SI 1999/1495').
[26] *Ibid*, reg 13.

'appeals' arriving in the office after a tribunal chair has granted leave. In fact, applications currently constitute about 66 per cent and appeals around 34 per cent of the Commissioners' caseload. As can be seen from Tables 3.2 and 3.3 below, applications and appeals received have both fallen over the past four years. The reasons for this trend are analysed further at the end of this chapter.

Applications for leave to a Commissioner

As the statutory ground for an appeal to the Commissioners is that the decision of the tribunal was 'erroneous in point of law' (SSA 1998, s.14), it is clear that the Commissioner must focus on whether such an error of law appears when considering an application for leave. A Commissioner's decision[27] has provided a useful synthesis of the meaning of error of law in this context. It put forward eight categories of errors. These are further explained in the section below in this chapter concerning appeals to the Commissioners. However, it should be apparent to the reader that the potential breadth of these formulations, especially in the hands of a good advocate, will mean that many tribunal decisions are likely to contain an arguable 'error of law'.

An application for leave to a Commissioner must usually be made within one month of the notification of a refusal or rejection by the tribunal. A Commissioner also has a discretionary power to accept a late leave application for 'special reasons'.[28]

Given that it has been repeatedly accepted that the Commissioners have an 'inquisitorial' jurisdiction, the question arises as to how far a Commissioner is bound to inquire into the reasons given for the application for leave. It has not been disputed that a Commissioner may give leave on the basis of grounds not raised in the application. Indeed, as will be seen later in this chapter, the formulation of 'error of law' referred to above includes a failure or neglect to 'ask material questions in pursuance of their duty to act inquisitorially'.[29] So an obvious failure on the part of the tribunal or Commissioner to properly inquire and raise appropriate issues in a case could itself be an error of law.

However, the High Court has indicated that there are some limits to the Commissioners' ability to raise new points.

> Commissioners are well versed in Social Security law and if it is apparent on the face of the papers that there is a strong arguable point not taken by the appellant, they should, nevertheless, give leave unless there is a compelling reason to the contrary. But they are not required to hunt through the papers for points of law like a legal bloodhound. (*R (Begum) v Social Security Commissioners*[30])

---

[27] *R(IS) 11/99.*
[28] SI 1999/1495, reg 9(3).
[29] See *R(IS) 11/99*, para 4, quoted later in this chapter.
[30] [2002] EWHC 401, para 36.

Table 3.2 Applications *received* by the Commissioners (2001/02– 2004/05)

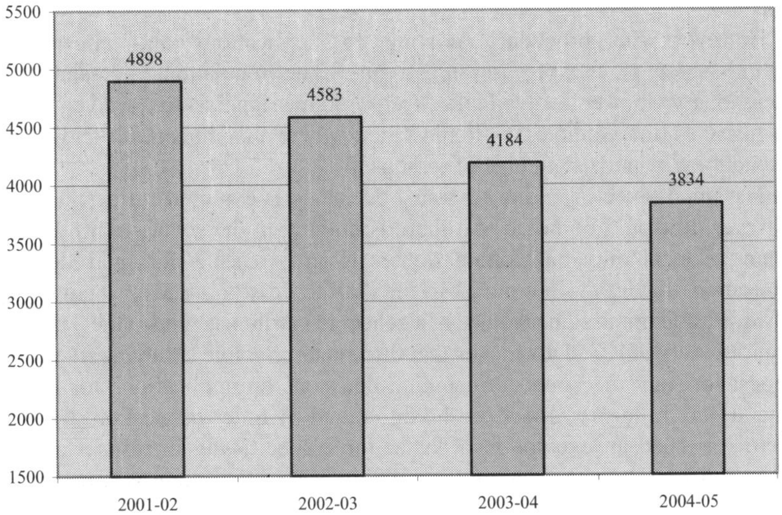

Source: Commissioners' Annual Reports, 2003, 2004 and 2005[31]

It was pointed out in *Begum* that 'arguability' was not sufficient but a higher threshold was required. 'The point must be obvious; that is one which would have a strong prospect of success were leave to be granted.'[32]

Prior to SSA 1998, the legislation was unclear what to do about applications for leave where no reasons had been given by the tribunal. In fact, the long delays in extracting reasons for the decision from the tribunal chair was a common cause of complaint cited in the evidence to the Select Committee (2000) inquiry into the Commissioners (see Chapter 1). The 1998 legislation makes the position clearer; a tribunal cannot grant leave in such circumstances but a Commissioner can. An application can be made to a Commissioner where one has been 'refused' by the tribunal chair, or where it has been 'rejected'.[33]

The regulations[34] detail the documentation required for making an application for leave to a Commissioner. It includes a similar list to that required for a notice of appeal after a tribunal chair's leave has been granted and includes, for example,

---

[31] The statistical data for inclusion in the Commissioners' annual report 2005 was supplied to the authors by OSSCSC ahead of its publication date.

[32] 'An obvious point, it seems to me, is one that stands out and not one that can only be gleaned by a paper chase through various documents which may underlie the decision maker's decision. Accordingly, it will, in my judgment, ordinarily be difficult to bring a reasons challenge within such a category, unless the reasons are obviously deficient on their face' [2002] EWHC 401, para 20.

[33] SI 1999/1495, reg 9(1). See also *CSDLA/536/99.*

[34] SI 1999/991, reg 58.

the grounds on which the applicant intends to rely; the decision against which leave to appeal is sought and the written statement of the reasons for the tribunal decision.

However, the procedure relating to applications and appeals to the Commissioner is flexible to an extent. The regulations contain a general discretionary power[35] available for Commissioners to waive procedural irregularities, for example, in circumstances where an applicant for leave has failed to send the tribunal's statement of reasons.

The importance of giving reasoned decisions is explored further in Chapter 6. However, it should be noted that there is nothing in the social security legislation placing a legal duty on Commissioners to give reasons for their decisions on applications for leave, in contrast to the duty to do so on the substantive appeal.[36] However, a Commissioner ranks as a scheduled 'tribunal' under the Tribunals and Inquiries Act 1992.[37] This means that there is in principle a duty to give reasons on request for 'any' decisions,[38] including decisions on applications for leave. The general duty in the 1992 Act can be disapplied by order of the Lord Chancellor.[39] There was such an exemption order in force specifically in respect of decisions given by Commissioners on applications for leave[40] but there was no general use made of it.[41] In our interview work, some of the Commissioners mentioned that they had given reasons in suitable cases during the period when the exemption order was in force. One of the Chief Commissioners interviewed referred to his discussions with the Lord Chancellor in which he recommended that this exemption order be lifted. No doubt the impending Human Rights Act legislation was a prompt for this action.

Once an application for leave is determined by a Commissioner, notice of it must be sent to the applicant and respondent.[42] Where leave is granted, then, subject to any contrary direction by a Commissioner, this notification is deemed to be a 'notice of appeal' (see above) and to have been sent on the same day as the notification of the application for leave decision.[43] This regulation is invariably applied where the Commissioner grants leave. The Commissioner may also 'treat and determine the application as an appeal'.[44] This provides a useful discretion for Commissioners to clear cases without further ado. A determination to refuse leave to appeal, which must be communicated in writing to the applicant, cannot be

---

[35] SI 1999/1495, reg 27.

[36] *Ibid*, reg 28(1) and (2).

[37] Tribunals and Inquiries Act 1992, Schedule 1, para 41(d).

[38] Tribunals and Inquiries Act 1992, s.1.

[39] *Ibid*, s.10(7).

[40] See the Tribunals and Inquiries (Social Security Commissioners) Order 1980, SI 1980/1637, reg 2, which exempted social security commissioners from the requirement to give reasons for their decisions on applications for leave. See also *R v Secretary of State for Social Services, ex parte Connolly* [1986] 1 WLR 421.

[41] Wade and Forsyth (2000: 917).

[42] SI 1999/1495, reg 11(1).

[43] *Ibid*, reg 11(2).

[44] *Ibid*, reg 11(3).

appealed. The only remaining remedy will be to take judicial review proceedings in the Administrative Court (see Chapter 6).

The Commissioners' views on applications for leave

The Commissioners views on applications, currently a sizeable proportion of their total caseload, focussed on four issues. Firstly, their approach to the crucial question of what constitutes a decision that is 'erroneous in point of law'. Secondly, their views on the way in which OSSCSC personnel could best organise themselves to handle this work. Thirdly, their views on the role of tribunal chairs and appellants in this context. Finally, their explanations for the variability in their practice were considered.

Approaches to identifying errors of law The Commissioners generally agreed that most of the applications fell into the category of what they referred to as 'facts and reasons' applications. In other words, an error of law could be identified in one of two overlapping categories. Firstly, where the tribunal had made a totally inadequate finding of fact usually unsupported by the evidence. Secondly, where it had failed to adequately explain the reasons for its decision. The Commissioners also referred to a number of *ad hominem* issues, such as 'the chairman was not listening', or had already made up his mind, indeed a whole range of natural justice issues were referred to.

They gave examples of cases in which they would invariably *grant* leave; for example, where the tribunal had not seen the claimant when it was quite obvious there was a clash of evidence that needed resolving in an oral hearing. Another 'classic one' was where the tribunal was split, but the minority's opinion had not been recorded. Sometimes decisions could be perverse and/or run against the weight of the evidence or the legislation had been simply misapplied or a significant point made by the claimant had not been dealt with at all. An example of the latter was the tribunal's failure to deal with a General Practitioner's report favourable to the claimant that conflicted with the Department's examining medical practitioner's report.

The Commissioners also gave examples of the types of case where they would invariably *refuse* leave, for example, cases where there was already copious and consistent authority. A small point of law, probably covered already with an authoritative Commissioner's decision was unlikely to be given leave. However, where Commissioners' decisions were either absent or inconsistent on the point, leave was more likely to be given. For example, one Commissioner referred to a case concerning the status of prelingually deaf persons and the help needed with reading and writing in respect of DLA entitlement. The Commissioner took the view that the inconsistent Commissioners' decisions on this matter had been a nuisance for tribunal chairs and needed tidying up.

There was some concern amongst Commissioners that applications based on inadequate reasons or insufficient findings of fact were sometimes too generalised. Too often applications did not clearly demonstrate why findings of facts or reasons were inadequate. There was a tendency for claimants and their representatives to produce mere assertions rather than properly constructed contentions supported by evidence. It also appeared that the Commissioners were more psychologically prepared to give leave in the minority of applications where the Secretary of State was the applicant. This was because it was much rarer for the Secretary of State to apply for leave against tribunal chairs and, all other things being equal, it was therefore more likely that proper legal advice had been used and that there was a point of substance in such applications. A few of the Commissioners said they used a rule of thumb – if they had to think about the applications for more than five minutes there must be some substantial error of law point there to justify granting leave. Most Commissioners were also able to identify, albeit a minority of cases, where the tribunal had given a perfectly good explanation of its decision but the point of law itself remained contentious and might be in need of investigating and developing further, in which case leave would be granted to provide the closer focus available at the Commissioner level. Another (minority) category of case identified was where the error of law point was a borderline one but there remained issues in need of attention. In such cases, some of the Commissioners referred to their attempts to give a hint that they had not granted leave because they thought it would necessarily succeed but because further exploration of these issues was desirable. One Commissioner's practice was to deliberately leave such 'borderline' applications for a day or two in order to return to it with a fresh mind.

Our interviews with the Commissioners also brought out 'other considerations' apart from errors of law that might persuade them to grant leave. Some of the Commissioners appeared to mediate the strict criterion of error of law with quite practical considerations. One Commissioner referred to cases where there may have been a technical error of law but if the point was not ultimately going to make any difference to benefit it was less likely to be given leave. The Commissioners generally had a keen awareness of the potential impact of their decisions on the parties. Many of them indicated their wish to avoid falsely raising the hopes of claimants and they were also concerned lest they should (unnecessarily) demoralise tribunal chairs.

> There are some [tribunal decisions] where you may take the view that the tribunal haven't dotted every 'i' or crossed every 't', but in the final analysis it's not going to make much difference to the eventual outcome of the case. And in that view it is probably actually fairer to the claimant just to refuse it, on the basis that if the claimant gets leave, then it raises a false sense of hope which just results in more bitter disappointment later on.

One element that appeared to affect the Commissioners' approach to applications was the extent to which they viewed their function as 'inquisitorial', or 'enabling' to use the Leggatt Review terminology. There was recognition that in this jurisdiction it was relatively easy to construct a 'point of law' argument from practically any tribunal decision, however well written. The Commissioners generally thought it appropriate to fill the 'representation deficit' experienced by many unrepresented claimants, and to conduct enquiries that might reasonably have been pursued by a good representative. However, there were limits perceived to the inquisitorial function, as reflected in *Begum*,[45] (a case heard around the time of our interviews). One Commissioner felt strongly that it was not his job 'to fine tooth-comb the case and effectively act as a second advisor to the claimant' but if there was a blatant error of law the parties had missed then that would be a reason for granting leave. However, despite this constraint, some of the Commissioners evidently had a certain amount of professional pride in their ability to independently spot a point no one else had.

> ...that is part of the fun of the job because it gives rise to a certain amount of smugness, if you spot a point which nobody else has spotted, it's rather like being the brightest boy in the class!

From a wider perspective, one of the (three) Chief Commissioners interviewed thought that the full implications of the provision in SSA 1998, whereby an appeal tribunal need not consider any issue not raised in the appeal,[46] had not really yet been taken on board throughout the system. He thought this and another provision[47] – preventing a tribunal from taking into account any circumstances not obtaining at the time when the decision appealed against was made – had the potential to convert the tribunal jurisdiction from a merits review to an appellate function. He thought that the Commissioners also ought to be looking in a much more confined way at what constituted an error of law. However, these provisions, which are replicated for revisions and supersessions and form significant elements of the DMA changes, do *not* appear in the legislation applying at Commissioner-level. It might therefore be equally plausible to conclude that it was intended the Commissioners' jurisdiction retains its inquisitorial flexibility to address the failures of a curtailed jurisdiction in the level below.

Applications and the organisation of work During our interview work with the Commissioners a case management initiative was underway to address some of the concerns, in particular delay, raised by the Select Committee inquiry (see Chapter 1). One early decision was to better deploy the efforts of legal officers (see below). The legal officers had been looking at every application for leave arriving at OSSCSC and then passing it on to a Commissioner, often with a note of recommendation. It was thought this arrangement had resulted in some duplication of effort and legal officers were taken off looking at DLA applications, mainly on the basis that most of the Commissioners were very experienced and knowledgeable about DLA and would not need further assistance, at least in routine cases. A new policy was established to try and ensure that, normally, the same Commissioner who decided to grant leave would also be responsible for the

45 [2002] EWHC 401. See the quote from *Begum* given in the main text above.
46 SSA 1998, s.12(8)(a).
47 *Ibid*, s.12(8)(b).

substantive appeal. Some of the Commissioners discussed the principle whether legal officers, who have a number of delegated quasi-judicial and administrative functions,[48] might be suitable persons to determine applications, perhaps in categories of routine cases. There were differing views about this question and, indeed, at the time of our interview work, there was much concern about the future role of the legal officers, an issue taken up in further detail later in this chapter. One Commissioner expressed strong views against devolving the leave function in any way to the legal officers, a function that was 'too much at the heart of judicial responsibility to be delegated.' Another Commissioner thought that legal officers tasked with this decision might be inclined to err on the side of caution and so increase the overall number of appeals.

In addition to addressing the issue of a more efficient use of legal officers, OSSCSC also turned its attention to the role of Deputy Commissioners in handling applications. Deputies themselves do not generally hear applications for leave. The policy of judicial continuity will generally mean that the logistics of having (part-time) Deputies determining an application and then determining the appeal is too difficult. There is now a system whereby a Commissioner granting leave who is not going to hear the appeal has to indicate whether the appeal is fit to be heard by a Deputy. Deputies will usually hear the more routine cases, though there are currently a number of very experienced Deputies who are likely to be allocated cases of greater difficulty and, in particular, cases involving their own specialisms. Deputy Commissioners have been, and can be, used to clear applications for leave where there has been a sudden increase in the caseload and/or a number of 'lookalike' cases need dealing with.

Views on tribunals and applicants Some of the Commissioners commented regretfully on the ability of tribunal chairs to make proper findings of fact. One common flaw perceived by the Commissioners was where the tribunal chair simply listed pieces of evidence without making coherent conclusions about the facts of the case. Most of the Commissioners were acutely aware that their role on applications was *not* one of primary fact finding. One Commissioner expressly stated that s/he would not grant leave simply because s/he would have probably taken a different view had s/he sat on the original tribunal. Another Commissioner raised concerns arising from chairmen sitting on their own, writing up their decisions long after the event:

> ... one has to have the faint suspicion that the decisions are not always necessarily a reflection of actually what was thought about on the day, but justification for a decision later.

Another Commissioner was concerned that tribunal chairs simply did not have enough time to write up decisions properly. The Commissioners only had the written evidence to assess leave. There were cases that could have been avoided if

[48] See SI 1999/1495, reg 7.

a better quality decision was produced by the tribunal, an issue perhaps to be addressed by better training of tribunal members. In the view of this Commissioner, the system had become top-heavy. Policy makers, he said, were looking at 'quantity' at the tribunal level and 'quality' at the Commissioner level, but emphasis on 'quality' at the decision-making level would mean fewer appeals in the system.

Variability of practice A dominant and persistent theme in our interview work with Commissioners on questions about applications was their confirmation and concern that their practice was very variable. One Commissioner stated 'there is no doubt that some Commissioners grant leave more easily than others'. There was also some evidence of unacceptable variability in the approach to identifying 'special reasons' for late applications.

> I mean we get bizarre ones, up to three or four years old. But there is a very wide variance between [them] – whilst I think most people say the longer the delay, the more coherent the reasons would have to be – but I mean there are people, and probably most people wouldn't baulk at a couple of days, but some people are very much stricter than others. Some people I think are very, very lax.

To some extent, this was unsurprising. The approaches to exercising a discretionary power are likely to be variable as the range of types of case and benefit type will require a range of different responses. Another Commissioner pointed to OSSCSC figures that showed one Commissioner allowing 90 per cent of applications for leave while another only allowed 30 per cent. Two Commissioners reported that in the past a (now retired) Commissioner used to allow applications in *every* case. One Commissioner thought that *new* Commissioners tended to be more generous and then later realised that an overgenerous use of leave was a waste of time and resources. One (experienced) Commissioner, who had been a tribunal chair, and viewed himself as relatively generous on the question of granting leave, thought that one needed to defer in particular to the findings of fact of the first instance tribunal. For example, the 'cooking test' (in DLA), in his view, should really be regarded as 'a conglomerate factual issue' in which tribunals of fact should be allowed a 'margin of appreciation' in deciding what is relevant. Some Commissioners were less willing to grant leave unless there was a really substantial point with prospects of success.

The Commissioners' various positions along a spectrum of generosity in approach to applications appeared to rely on underlying views about the overall purpose of the appeal system and claimants' motivations. One Commissioner, for example, said 'there is an "appeal culture" these days and people just don't want to take "no" for an answer'. Another influence detected was the important, though difficult to define, element of 'collegiality' amongst the Commissioners (see Chapter 6). One Commissioner thought that his own rather stricter approach to applications had in fact been picked up by a few other Commissioners and, almost by a process of osmosis, had spread further amongst the Commissioners to produce a more robust approach to refusing applications in which a greater proportion were likely to be refused on the basis that they had very poor prospects of ultimately succeeding.

It was surprising that, given the variability in approach to granting or refusing applications for leave, there had been little formal discussion within OSSCSC, at least at the time of our interviews. One of the Commissioners said s/he would have welcomed a structured training day on this issue so long as this did not involve any prescriptive direction as the determination on applications was seen pre-eminently as a judicial function. Some of the Commissioners pointed out that if a proper job was done at the application stage, either by stopping it there or by better identifying issues, this would save time later on.

Appeals to the Commissioners[49]

Table 3.3 below shows that appeals received from 2001/2 – 2004/5, like applications (see Table 3.2 above) have also declined. The reasons for this are examined in the evaluation section at the end of this chapter. However, it can be noted here, that on the basis of these figures appeals currently constitute around 34 per cent of the Commissioners' workload and there has been a slight decline in the overall proportion of appeals over applications during this period.[50]

An appeal lies to a Commissioner from a decision of an appeal tribunal on the ground that the decision was 'erroneous in point of law' (SSA 1998, s.14). There is no appeal available against a tribunal chair's decision to set aside. There is also no appeal available against a tribunal chair's decision to refuse to adjourn a case.[51] An appeal lies at the instance of a claimant and other prescribed persons, the Secretary of State, a trade union in certain cases and a person from whom it is determined any amount is recoverable, for example, where an overpayment has been made. The legislation prescribes cases where unions can appeal to a Commissioner, for example, where the case relates to industrial injuries benefit and the claimant was a union member.

[49] There are *separate* rights of appeal in respect of the recovery of benefits from those making compensation payments in relation to personal injury (Social Security (Recovery of Benefits) Act 1997, s.13) and in relation to housing benefit and council tax benefit under (Child Support, Pensions and Social Security Act 2000, Sched 7) not detailed in this book.

[50] The ratio of appeals to applications on the basis of the figures given in Tables 3.2 and 3.3 was 37:63 in 2001-02, 35:65 in 2002-03 and 34:66 in both 2003-04 and 2004-05. However, these figures may contain a certain amount of 'double counting': see further Chapter 6.

[51] *Carpenter v Secretary of State for Work and Pensions* [2003] EWCA Civ 33, reported as *R(IB) 6/03*.

Table 3.3 Appeals *received* by the Commissioners (2001/02– 2004/05)

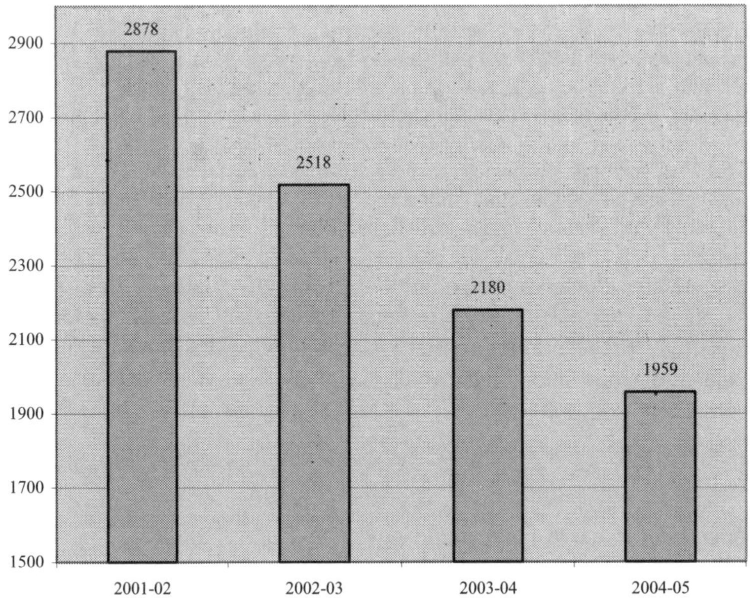

Source: Commissioners' Annual Reports, 2003, 2004 and 2005

Where a Commissioner holds that the decision was erroneous in law it must be set aside. A Commissioner will then have three alternative courses of action. Firstly, a Commissioner may substitute his or her own decision 'if he can do so without making fresh or further findings of fact'. Secondly, a Commissioner may make findings of fact if s/he considers it expedient and then go on to substitute his or her own decision. Thirdly, a Commissioner may refer the case back to a tribunal 'with directions for its determination' (SSA 1998, s.14(8)). This referral will be to a differently constituted tribunal (subject to any contrary direction of a Commissioner).

The ground for appeal: error of law

Appeals to a Commissioner may only be made on the ground of an error on a 'point of law'. Appellants frequently misunderstand the limitations of this legal concept and frame their appeals in terms of a dispute on the *facts* rather than the law. The Commissioner's decision already referred to in relation to applications (above) sets out the categories of case that might contain an error of law for these purposes.

> Any attempt to list the circumstances in which an error of law may be revealed is bound to be incomplete and at the same time to identify overlapping categories … An error of

> law may be revealed if a tribunal (a) have recorded a false proposition of law in their reasons for decision, (b) have reached a decision that is supported by no evidence, (c) have found facts such that no person acting judicially and properly instructed as to the relevant law could have come to the determination under appeal, (d) have taken into account matters which they ought not to have taken into account, (e) have refused to take into account or neglected to take into account matters which they ought to have taken into account, or (f) have failed or neglected to ask material questions in pursuance of their duty to act inquisitorially … . A decision will also be erroneous in point of law if (g) there has been a breach of the rules of natural justice or (h) there has been a *material* breach of the other procedural rules, statutory and implied, that must be followed by tribunals, chairmen and clerks. (*R(IS) 11/99*, para 4)

In short, the grounds are very similar to those available to the Administrative Court on an application for judicial review.[52] These include 'illegality', 'irrationality', 'procedural impropriety' and, following the Human Rights Act 1998, a breach of a Convention right which, in many cases will involve a question of 'proportionality'.

Setting aside and redetermination

A Commissioner has a comparable power to the AS tribunal (see above) to set aside the decision where each of the principal parties to the appeal expresses the view that the decision appealed was erroneous in point of law (SSA 1998, s.14(7)). This power arises *after* leave has been granted. The Commissioner will then refer the case to a tribunal with directions for its redetermination and the legislative assumption is that this will be to a differently constituted tribunal (subject to a contrary direction from a Commissioner).

> A setting aside under this subsection does not necessarily imply that the Commissioner is satisfied that the decision under appeal was erroneous in point of law. The point of this provision is to enable a decision to be set aside without the Commissioner having to go into the case in the depth necessary to make that judgment. (Rowland and White, 2004: para 1.393)

Precisely because a Commissioner need not necessarily be satisfied that there is an error of law, it is thought that Commissioners' decisions to set aside do not establish any propositions of law. In one Commissioner's decision[53] it was stated that '[i]n my view, no determination under section 14(7) should be regarded as providing an authoritative statement of the law. The Secretary of State should not cite such decisions'. There is some logic in this approach. The usual requirement for a Commissioner to provide reasons for a decision is disapplied in the case of section 14(7) decisions.[54] However, the practice had arisen for the parties to cite

---

[52] See Lord Diplock's formula in the 'GCHQ' case: *Council of Civil Service Unions v Minister for the Civil Service* [1985] AC 374, at 408.
[53] *CI/3596/2001.*
[54] SI 1999/1495, reg 28(2).

such material. This practice was robustly disapproved of in a Commissioner's decision.

> It is not in my view appropriate for the Secretary of State to rely on a direction made in a decision without reasons as authority for a proposition. This is because the decision has been given without reasons and it is not possible to deduce from it the basis upon which the Commissioner has reached the proposition he is making as a direction. ... I have noted a tendency by both representatives and the Secretary of State to use directions in decisions without reasons in this way and it is a practice which ... is disapproved and must stop. (*CSDLA/101/00*, para 4)

There are also a number of Commissioners' decisions criticising the Secretary of State's over-willingness to accept error of law arguments based upon inadequate reasons.[55] One decision states that the power to set aside is inappropriate where there is a serious dispute of law between the parties upon which the tribunal ought to be given full guidance.[56]

Representation before the Commissioners

The legislation provides that the Commissioners' procedure regulations can include 'a power to make provision as to the representation of one person, at any hearing of a case, by another person whether having professional qualifications or not' (SSA 1998, s.16 (3)(a)). The regulations provide that a 'party may conduct his case himself (with assistance from any person if he wishes) or be represented by any person whom he may appoint for the purpose.'[57] In a predominantly paper-based jurisdiction it is no surprise that the regulations also provide for the exchange of 'written observations' on the appeal. A respondent may submit 'written observations' within one month of receiving written notice of the appeal. Where the Secretary of State is (usually) the respondent those written observations must include not only the grounds on which the respondent intends to rely but also a statement indicating whether or not the Secretary of State will oppose the appeal. Copies must then be sent to every other party. At this point the Commissioners are specifically authorised to make a section 14(7) order setting aside the decision where the principal parties are agreed that the decision at issue was indeed erroneous in point of law. Otherwise, the paper exchanges may continue. Within one month of being sent written observations any party may submit written observations in reply and these in turn must be copied to every other party.[58]

In March 2001, the then Chief Commissioner, Judge Machin QC, issued a *Practice Memorandum*[59] noting the introduction of new case management

---

[55] For example, *CSIB/596/99*, *CSIB/611/99* and *CSDLA/505/99*.
[56] *CDLA/4102/99*.
[57] SI 1999/1495, reg 17.
[58] *Ibid*, regs 18 and 19.
[59] 'Written Observations on Appeals in Social Security and Tax Credit Cases in England and Wales', 9 March 2001, reproduced in Rowland and White (2004: para 2.304).

procedures to encourage improvements in the quality of written submissions and to remove unnecessary delays. The memorandum confirmed two changes in practice. Firstly, that the Commissioners would be giving reasons for granting leave (see above). Secondly, that they would usually issue 'directions' setting out the procedure appropriate for the type of case at issue. The memorandum notes one category of case where the parties would be asked if they had any objection to the Commissioner setting the decision aside on grounds identified by the Commissioner.

The Commissioners have faced particular challenges to do justice in a context where public funding for legal representation is practically absent. The Lord Chancellor could only fund legal representation for an appellant through the legal aid scheme in England and Wales where s/he considered it appropriate to do so in 'exceptional circumstances'.[60] This provision was used very sparingly. At the time of our interview work there had been an indication from the Scottish Executive that more public funding might be forthcoming in the social security jurisdiction.

A majority of applications and appeals arrive at OSSCSC where the claimant is representing him or herself. If the claimant is represented this may be a friend, relative or a layperson from a voluntary organisation, the Citizens Advice Bureau (CAB), for example, or a local authority welfare rights officer. It is unusual to find a claimant formally represented by a private solicitor. Surprisingly, given the importance of representation in this jurisdiction noted by a number of researchers in the past (e.g. Genn and Genn, 1989; Baldwin *et al*, 1992), OSSCSC do not appear to collect any statistics on the representation profile in respect of either oral or paper hearings before the Commissioners.[61]

If a case goes to an oral hearing it is more likely that a representative will appear on behalf of the claimant. There are no 'rights of audience' however in front of the Commissioners. In principle, anyone can represent the appellant. Sometimes the claimant will represent him or herself at oral hearings. Otherwise, it is likely to be a CAB adviser or local authority welfare rights officer. In particularly difficult or complex cases where the appellant and/or appellant's representative have been in touch with, for example, the Child Poverty Action Group or the Free Representation Unit in London, counsel may appear on behalf of the appellant. A specialist solicitor will represent the DWP. Where there is a case of special difficulty or complexity and there are wider matters of public interest and resources at stake, the Secretary of State will engage counsel. Although our research did not extend to representation given at AS tribunals one of the Commissioners interviewed was keen to point out that the Department's policy not to send solicitors or indeed any representative to the AS tribunals was affecting the quality of decisions arriving at OSSCSC. Good representation at that level, in

---

[60] Legal Aid Act 1988, s.4(2) and (4). These powers have been carried over into the Access to Justice Act 1999, section 6(8), now exerciseable by the Secretary of State for Constitutional Affairs.

[61] Personal communication to the authors from OSSCSC, 16 March 2005.

his/her view, could preclude the need to appeal to the Commissioners. See further, Chapter 4, for details of the Commissioners' views on representation.

Hearings: paper and oral hearings

A feature of the jurisdiction of the unemployment benefit Umpires, the Commissioner's appellate ancestors, was the high proportion of cases determined on the papers (Chapter 2). This is also a distinctive feature of the modern Commissioners. It is estimated that around 96 per cent of cases are dealt with in this way, leaving only 4 per cent of cases listed to be heard orally.[62] It would appear that this proportion has remained steady over the past five years despite some speculation by the Commissioners at the time of our interview work that the Human Rights legislation would compel greater use of oral hearings. These figures are further examined in the evaluation section at the end of this chapter. However, oral hearings often contain interesting and usually complex legal issues. They are also perceived by many of the Commissioners as significant 'events' in their work and provide much material for Commissioners' discussions with each other and useful benchmarks for defining their overall function.

Our limited observation of three oral hearings, one by a Tribunal of Commissioners and in all cases with representation for all parties, indicated that, while not as formal as a court, they were nonetheless rather more formal than AS tribunal hearings. This, in the two single Commissioner's hearings, one of which seemed more formal than the other, was partly a product of individual style as well as the layout of the Harp House oral hearing room which places the Commissioner in a slightly elevated position facing the parties and representatives. The Tribunal hearing was on compensation recovery and, given nine counsel and accompanying solicitors for four of the parties (in reality insurance companies), for logistical reasons had to be held in a formal courtroom at the Royal Courts of Justice in the Strand, thus adding extra formality to the proceedings, which, apart from mode of dress, did not appear very different to the observer's impressions of hearings before the Court of Appeal.

The regulations assume that, where a request for an oral hearing has been made by either party, the Commissioner will grant the request, unless the Commissioner 'is satisfied that the proceedings can properly be determined without a hearing'. Indeed, our interview work with the Commissioners (see below) revealed some surprise that so few claimants actually requested an oral hearing. A Commissioner refusing such a request must send his or her reasons to the appellant before or at the same time as the appeal determination.[63] A Commissioner also has discretionary power to direct an oral hearing 'without an application and at any stage'.[64] In order to support a policy of judicial continuity, oral hearings in London are normally determined 'by the Commissioner currently seized of the case'. Exceptionally, a

---

[62] Figures supplied to the authors by OSSCSC in March 2005.
[63] SI 1999/1495, reg 23(2) and (3).
[64] *Ibid*, reg 23(4).

London-based Commissioner at a venue in Scotland may hear an English or Welsh case.[65] Any party has the right to request an oral hearing in a Welsh case be held in Wales and where practicable before a Welsh-speaking Commissioner.[66]

In a Court of Session case[67] it was held that even where a claimant's appeal has been 'supported' by the Secretary of State, there was no compulsion on the Commissioner to direct an oral hearing. Parties should be given at least 14 days notice of the hearing. The Commissioner can go ahead with a hearing if any party fails to turn up. There is a mandatory requirement for the hearing to be in public unless the Commissioner makes a direction that there are 'special reasons' for holding it in private.[68] The claimant, the claimant's representative and the Secretary of State's representative, and other persons entitled to be heard, can address the Commissioner at the hearing and, with leave, can 'give evidence, call witnesses and put questions directly to any other person called as a witness'.[69] A Commissioner also has a power (used rarely) to summon witnesses to the hearing and produce relevant documents and may require a witness to give evidence on oath.[70] The power is analogous to the power of a tribunal chair to summon witnesses.[71] In both cases, however, there is no legal sanction for non-compliance. There is a power vested in the High Court to issue a summons in aid of a tribunal,[72] but this is dependent on the tribunal having no power itself. As the tribunal (and Commissioner) do have, albeit *unenforceable*, powers to summons witnesses, it is thought the High Court power cannot be applied.

Practice has varied over the years, but at present, oral hearings are held regularly in London, Edinburgh, Cardiff, Bury, Doncaster, Plymouth and (exceptionally) in other court centres if people are unable to travel.[73] More recently, video-conferencing facilities for hearings have been employed. This involves the use of a three-way video link between the Commissioner in London and the claimant/representative and the Secretary of State's representative. The facilities for video-conferences were available at the time of writing in the following locations: Birmingham, Cardiff, London, Leeds, Manchester, Plymouth, Winchester and Preston.

---

[65] *Practice Statement: Oral Hearings of English and Welsh Cases*, 26 June 2001. However, it should be noted that under the terms of *Practice Memorandum No 1*, issued by the Chief Commissioner on 31 December 2004, all previous Practice Memoranda and Directions were revoked.

[66] See *Practice Memroandum No 3*, 31 December 2004.

[67] *Miller v Secretary of State for Work and Pensions*, Court of Session (Inner House), 12 July 2002, unreported.

[68] SI 1999/1495, reg 24(5).

[69] *Ibid*, reg 24(6) and (7)

[70] *Ibid*, reg 25.

[71] *Ibid*, reg 43.

[72] Civil Procedure Rules, r 34.4.

[73] OSSCSC Explanatory Leaflet (2004).

Oral hearings: the Commissioners' views

At the time of the Select Committee (2000) inquiry there had been a downward turn in the number of oral hearings. However, by the time of the interview work it appeared that more oral hearings were being held. There were four principal, interlinked issues that emerged from the interviews with Commissioners on this topic: the extent to which the oral legal tradition should be supported; the criteria used to call an oral hearing; the conduct of the hearing; and the implications for case management.

Oral tradition Most Commissioners were strongly supportive of the value of oral hearings, an attitude that in many cases was firmly based on their respective professional backgrounds and experience; for example, in the county court or as tribunal chairs. They generally cited two main benefits. Firstly, an oral hearing had a number of advantages over paper hearings in getting to the heart of the matter on a point of law. In their view, there was little substitute, in appropriate cases, for the face-to-face contact of a hearing with the parties present. One Commissioner thought it was 'the most effective way of reaching out to the educationally disadvantaged litigant.' Many of the Commissioners related accounts of the different slant on an argument that could occur, sometimes unexpectedly, in an oral hearing. One Commissioner characterised the oral legal tradition as the 'white hot crucible of debate'. Secondly, there was a clear view that, in appropriate cases, the claimant could 'have their day in court' and 'let off steam' to obtain a 'sense of release'. There was obviously some professional pride in the hearings where the Commissioner had felt that the case had been properly explained to the claimant and, even if the appellant did not win the appeal, he or she would go home with a lessened sense of grievance. One Commissioner made an interesting comparison with the Immigration Appeal Tribunal where the work was nearly all in oral hearings. S/he thought that in the long term it would be preferable to adopt a clearer oral hearing framework in social security, though this would involve the 'regionalisation' of Commissioners' work. This Commissioner was also distinctly unimpressed with his/her experience of a German tribunal system that had adopted a largely paper-based system of review but where, 'the productivity is absolutely appalling, the delays are monstrous'. Another compared the oral tradition favourably with paper reviews:

> One of the defects of the written procedure is that everything operates in sequence and simply carrying on a complicated legal argument through written submissions. It is very time consuming because each new submission produces a new point and a new stage. Whereas an oral hearing can collapse all of that, providing you have got reasonable Reps. So, there is a lot to be said for oral hearings, even if you could actually deal with the issues on paper it would take a lot longer. And I think there is a lot to be said for getting oral hearings in quickly in cases which you think it's worth it, which cuts down delay.

Another Commissioner noted that however brilliant a written judgment might be it did not carry the same flavour as the feeling claimants had coming away from an oral hearing. One Commissioner however, unlike most of his colleagues, viewed oral hearings as largely wasteful of time. His (minority) view was that the claimant had already had an opportunity to have an oral hearing with the AS tribunal and it was not the function of the Commissioners to provide a symbolic 'day in court'.

Criteria for calling oral hearings The criteria used by Commissioners to decide whether to order an oral hearing were quite variable though most were generally positive about holding oral hearings if only 'to relieve the tedium of looking at sterile papers'. Some Commissioners would always grant an oral hearing where one had been requested unless it was clearly going to be decided in favour of the person requesting it. Two Commissioners admitted that they would almost invariably be predisposed to grant an oral hearing in overpayment cases. Many of the Commissioners found it difficult to precisely identify any particular criteria for ordering an oral hearing, either on request or directing it on their own initiative. One Commissioner thought that oral hearings would be more useful in respect of applications for leave rather than appeals. Most put it in terms of a 'gut instinct' born of experience. Some referred to situations where the AS tribunal's reasons were not coherent, an inadequate record of the hearing and other poor quality decision indicators, which would put the Commissioner on notice that something was sufficiently wrong in the papers to justify an oral hearing. Some referred to the impression, when reading the papers, that there was a significant 'gap' in the evidence that remained unexplained.

There was some disagreement on the approach to be taken, in particular in relation to where a hearing had been requested. Some Commissioners took a rights-based view that such requests should almost always be accepted as the claimant should in principle be able to have a hearing, particularly, for example, where a lot of the claimant's money was at stake in an overpayment case. Some Commissioners thought it important to provide an oral hearing where there was a real sense of grievance underlying the case even in circumstances where the arguments were already quite clear on the papers. One Commissioner explained that oral hearings tended to be used more frequently when a new benefit had been introduced (e.g. housing benefit) but then levelled off as areas of legal uncertainty were settled.

It was evident that Commissioners would only use sparingly their discretion to direct an oral hearing on their own motion; for example, where there was a clear point of law of some difficulty that had not been properly addressed. At the time of our interviews the Human Rights Act 1998 had only just been implemented but the status of social security appeal hearings under article 6 of the European Convention on Human Rights was not clear and many of the Commissioners perceived, at least, informal pressure for them to agree to oral hearings where these were requested. Some cited the Human Rights Act 1998 as an explanation for the perceived rise in oral hearings. However, Commissioners with longer service took the view that the long-term trend had been a *decrease* in the numbers of oral hearings. A few Commissioners said that they would exceptionally direct an oral hearing where there had been no request but the paperwork revealed a point that had not been properly addressed and it needed full argument.

There were only a few who articulated a clear and structured approach to selecting an oral hearing. One Commissioner, for example, distinguished three areas where it was appropriate: where there was an important and substantive point of law, where the case was hopelessly confused on the papers or where there was an important point not being addressed, and finally, where the party has requested it but the Commissioner was minded to reject it and a hearing was necessary to give that party the chance of oral argument. This Commissioner rejected the suggestion however, that a set of 'guidelines' might be useful to provide some consistent structure to selecting cases for oral hearing on the basis that this would inevitably lead to a fettering of judicial discretion.

Running the hearing Some of the Commissioners thought of themselves as 'very activist in oral hearings'. The Commissioners' backgrounds, particularly those who had been tribunal chairs, often informed the way in which they ran oral hearings. In particular, former tribunal chairs had greater confidence that they could spot arguments in favour of unrepresented litigants. One Commissioner felt that oral hearings were a good opportunity to 'teach representatives what their job should be at this level'. Most of the Commissioners thoroughly enjoyed engaging intellectually in a good argument with the Secretary of State's representative or counsel when they appeared, but the variability of quality, particularly in the representation of the Secretary of State, affected their satisfaction. 'I would have liked a nice sort of ding dong of an argument, and sometimes you get it but other times you think … it's like wringing out a wet sponge'. Most Commissioners consciously tried to run oral hearings without too much formality and one or two deliberately paid attention to not using legalistic language with non-lawyers. However, a minority of oral hearings involve counsel on either side and these hearings are run much like any case in the High Court. There were also complaints that on occasion appellants and/or representatives did not turn up to hearings. Attendance by the appellant was appreciated.

> I mean I know from sitting for instance as a Chancery Master that your attitude to a matter is totally different if somebody turns up even if they actually don't say anything. But if they are there it changes your thinking.

One Commissioner, who had at the time administrative responsibility for training, pointed out a useful spin-off benefit of his experience of oral hearings in Liverpool, Leeds and Newcastle had been the attendance of observers from local welfare rights organisations and local departmental staff. The Commissioners generally acknowledged that their general conduct of oral hearings could have a particularly significant effect on their public image.

Implications for case management There was some awareness that oral hearings might be costly but equally there was a view that early intervention with an oral hearing in suitable cases could prevent lengthy proceedings. One Commissioner thought that an appropriate use of oral hearings in child support cases could be used to 'short-circuit' such cases and bring them to a conclusion.

Some of the Commissioners indicated problems with the accessibility of hearings. One Commissioner remarked that s/he had read too many times 'I would have come to an oral hearing but it is too far to travel'. Several Commissioners mentioned the possible regionalisation of their work. Most thought it worthy of further consideration in order to increase user accessibility. However, two possible difficulties were identified. Firstly, there was a danger of becoming isolated from developments, and the consequent inconsistent decisions. Secondly, there was a concern about Commissioners becoming over familiar with the tribunals in their region. However, some Commissioners were very positive about the possibilities of having more oral hearings using more centres around the country. One Commissioner commented that the Court Service had not been very co-operative in finding convenient, regular venues around the country, though they were hearing more regularly cases in the North of England.

Another Commissioner pointed out the particular need, given the high proportion of DLA and incapacity benefit appeals (see Table 3.7 below), to provide venues that were accessible for disabled people. New court centres were accessible but the older buildings tended not to be. By contrast, the smaller geography of Northern Ireland enabled most people to get to Belfast relatively easily. In addition, courthouses outside Belfast, in Londonderry for example, were used on an *ad hoc* basis. It would appear that a much greater proportion of cases are heard orally in Northern Ireland.

One Commissioner discussed the potential of video link conferencing, pointing out that it would be particularly suitable where the hearing was in essence on arguments relating to a point of law. S/he foresaw problems where evidence was being taken on questions of fact in which case it was important to observe witnesses directly, but could not see any reason why the strictly legal forensic process could not be delivered using video conferencing facilities. One of the Chief Commissioners interviewed was particularly interested in the possibilities of using such facilities and was organising consultations with welfare rights groups at the time of our interviews about the use of such facilities and the use of physical venues too. He thought there was more room for *ad hoc* arrangements to accommodate claimants' needs to use an accessible venue.

Determination by a Tribunal of Commissioners

One of the functions of the Chief Commissioner (or a nominated Commissioner if the Chief is unable to act) is to direct that an application for leave or appeal, that 'involves a question of law of special difficulty', is heard by a Tribunal of Commissioners, that is, three or more Commissioners, which may or may not include the Chief Commissioner. The presiding Commissioner has a casting vote where the votes are equally divided (SSA 1998, s.16 (7)). The provenance of the Tribunal of Commissioners is discussed further in Chapter 2. Traditionally, such Tribunals are appointed where there has been disagreement amongst Commissioners on a particular point of law. Decisions of Tribunals of Commissioners ought usually to be followed by single Commissioners[74] but do not have to be followed by subsequent Tribunals of Commissioners.[75] See further Chapter 5 on how a Tribunal of Commissioner's decisions fits into the system of precedent.

Determination by a Tribunal of Commissioners: the Commissioners' views The three Chief Commissioners interviewed over the course of our research project had rather different views about how to use Tribunals of Commissioners (hereafter 'Tribunals'). One thought there was a sense in which the use of a Tribunal was redundant, as when they were first established there was no right of further appeal to the Court of Appeal. He commented that his predecessor had made more use of them but he would use them in cases of complexity or difficulty. Another Chief Commissioner refrained from sitting himself, no doubt because of the possible conflict of interest that this would highlight given that he also carried the appointment of President of the Appeals Service (Bonner and Buck, 2004). One Chief Commissioner said he would 'like to give them a bit of a whirl' but pointed out there had been some criticisms that Tribunals had tended 'to produce a bit of a wish-wash' and if that were to happen then he would not use them. The third Chief Commissioner interviewed had already set up five Tribunals at the time of our interview. He thought there would be around twelve Tribunals each year. This Chief Commissioner, though aware of the need to decide an individual case, was acutely aware of the special role of the Tribunal to elucidate legal principle and its possible impact on the public.

> The statutory criterion is a point of law of 'special difficulty', but it seems to me in considering the criteria for selection one has to look at the importance generally in this area of law. 'Supersession' and 'revision', they are decisions taken thousands of times every day by appeal tribunals and decision makers and the fact that the law was not clear – as to when one…decision should be taken and when the other, and the ability of a tribunal to correct defects in the decision by a DM [decision-maker] so that area was not clear – seems to have warranted clarification by a Tribunal of Commissioners.

He agreed that the case for directing a Tribunal hearing on a point of special difficulty relating, for example, to transitional regulations[76] was less compelling. Another Commissioner agreed that the confusion there had been about supersessions and revisions was exactly the kind of case where a Tribunal could

---

[74] *R(I) 12/75(T)*, para 21.
[75] *R(U) 4/88*.
[76] Transitional regulations are regularly required in social security law to govern the rules relevant to a period of transition between the law prior to and after legislative amendments and reforms.

have flushed out the issues. He pointed out 'there clearly is an argument for them where different lines of authority are building up within Commissioners.'

One long-serving Commissioner remarked that until around 1992 a Commissioner's decision was followed unless it was blatantly wrong whereas the modern tendency had moved towards greater disagreement. 'You know, you have got a basic decision which gives guidelines, and after all you should give guidelines, and they sort of go and add tramlines to it all.' It appeared that the allocation of individual Commissioners to a Tribunal was undertaken on the basis of two considerations: ensuring that at least one of the Commissioners had a specialist knowledge in relation to the question at issue; and making sure that Commissioners generally got a fair turn to sit. One Commissioner also had a word of caution.

> The problem with the Tribunal of Commissioners is of course, if it does not get things right. Unless it gets overruled by another Tribunal fairly soon afterwards, it can cause the law to go off the wrong angle for quite a long period. And I also think there's an acknowledgement that one or two Tribunals over the last decade have not really contributed positively to the development of the law. So one's got to be careful.

Determinations of Commissioners on leave to appeal to an appellate court

Whereas the right of appeal to a Commissioner can only be applied to decisions of a tribunal found in sections 12 or 13 of SSA 1998, an appeal *from* a Commissioner to an appropriate court will lie from 'any decision' of the Commissioner (SSA 1998, s.15). This appeal right is not limited to appeals arriving from the tribunals under section 14. It also applies to Commissioners' decisions under the Social Security (Recovery of Benefits) Act 1997 and under section 4 of the Forfeiture Act 1982.

An appeal to the appellate court is subject to leave being given by a Commissioner, or, if refused, by the appropriate court (SSA 1998, s.15). The 'appropriate court' is specified by the Commissioner dealing with the leave application from one of the following: the Court of Appeal, Court of Session or the Court of Appeal in Northern Ireland, if it appears that the relevant place is in England & Wales, Scotland or Northern Ireland respectively. Even if the relevant place is Scotland, for example, a Commissioner has a discretion nevertheless to specify either the English or Scottish courts 'having regard to the circumstances of the case and in particular to the convenience of the persons who may be parties to the proposed appeal'.

A decision of a Commissioner to *refuse* leave to appeal to Commissioner level is not however a 'decision' against which an appeal could be launched under section 15 of SSA 1998. Such refusals can only be challenged by judicial review proceedings. This was the conclusion in *Bland v Chief Supplementary Benefit*

Officer,[77] which was mainly based upon the reasoning that to recognise such an appeal right would defeat the whole purpose of applications for leave to filter out 'needless and frivolous appeals'.

Applications to the Commissioner for leave to the appellate court must be in writing, stating the grounds, and made within three months from the date of the written notice of the Commissioner's decision.[78] The time limit may be extended under the Commissioners' general procedural powers[79] but if he or she refuses to do so the court cannot.[80]

An application to the appropriate court to appeal, or for permission to appeal, must be brought within six weeks of the refusal or grant of leave to appeal being sent to the parties.[81] If permission is refused the Court of Appeal will give 'short reasons' to inform the applicant why the application was refused. The general test for permission to appeal to the Court of Appeal is laid down in a *Practice Direction*.

> The general rule applied by the Court of Appeal, and thus the relevant basis for first instance courts deciding whether to grant permission, is that permission will be given unless an appeal would have no real prospect of success. A fanciful prospect is insufficient. Permission may also be given in exceptional circumstances even though the case has no real prospect of success if there is an issue which, in the public interest, should be examined by the Court of Appeal. Examples are where a case raises questions of great public interest or questions of general policy, or where authority binding on the Court of Appeal may call for reconsideration.[82]

There is a somewhat different statutory test however where the Court of Appeal is considering an application for permission from a county court or the High Court where those courts in turn are considering appeals from the court below, a position at least analogous to the second-tier appellate status of the Commissioners. The issue whether this modified test should apply to the Commissioners was addressed in *Cooke v Secretary of State for Social Security*.[83] Hale LJ (as she then was) ruled that 'a robust attitude to the prospect of success criterion ought to be adopted'. In other words, the Court of Appeal 'should take an appropriately modest view ... of how likely it is that the commissioner will have got it wrong'.[84] The deference

---

77 [1983] 1 W.L.R. 262, also reported as *R(SB) 12/83*.

78 SI 1999/1495, reg 33(1).

79 *Ibid*, reg 5.

80 See *White v Chief Adjudication Officer* [1986] 2 All ER 905, also reported as *R(S) 8/85*.

81 See Civil Proceedings Rules Part 52 and *Practice Direction 52*, para 21.5 for the procedure in the Court of Appeal. See R.C.290 and 293B for procedure in the Court of Session.

82 *Practice Direction* [1999] 1 WLR 1027, 1033.

83 [2002] 3 AER 279, reported as *R(DLA) 6/01*.

84 '[T]he practical effect may be that, unless there is an important point of principle or practice, it will be necessary to persuade a Judge hearing an application for permission to appeal that the Commissioner was *probably* wrong, rather than *possibly* wrong' (Rowland and White, 2004: para 1.398).

shown in Hale LJ's judgment is important, and is considered further in Chapter 6, as it indicates a number of points about the perceived relationship between the Commissioners and the appellate courts, and the extent to which the Court of Appeal is likely to interfere with the Commissioners' specialist knowledge in the social security field.

Leave to an appellate court: the Commissioners' views

The cumulative number of applications for leave to appeal to the Court of Appeal received in the London office for the calendar years 2001 to 2004 inclusive was 244,[85] an average of around 60 each year (or around three applications per annum per Commissioner). The number of cases actually reaching the appellate courts is even smaller: only 21 cases in 2003, see Chapter 6, Table 6.1. Each individual Commissioner will therefore have a relatively limited experience in making this type of determination. One Commissioner said s/he had to deal with about six applications each year.

There were three main themes that emerged from our interview work. Firstly, a variety of views about the perceived correct approach to determining leave. Secondly, views on the competence of appellate courts to handle social security cases and the general relationship of the courts with the Commissioners. Thirdly, views about the impact of the decisions of the appellate courts on the Commissioners and their professional esteem.

The *Cooke*[86] decision in the Court of Appeal (see above) had been decided shortly before our interview work and had clearly been considered carefully by most of the Commissioners. One Commissioner claimed the case endorsed what his/her practice had always been. Unsurprisingly, the Commissioners generally approved the 'deference' this case showed to their own specialist knowledge (see further Chapter 6). One Commissioner thought the decision had in effect designated the Commissioners as the final court of appeal in social security matters on points of law 'in all but a tiny minority of the most extremely important cases.' Another Commissioner pointed out that most of the Court of Appeal judges would simply not know much about the social security area: 'there are about four or five who know their onions in this field, but the rest, I think, just run.'

Indeed, there was a perception by several Commissioners that when a case went up to the House of Lords – around one case annually, see Chapter 6, Table 6.3 – the Commissioner's decision was usually upheld. Some Commissioners took the view that if they felt their decision was right they would simply refuse leave. The appellant could always take the application to the Court of Appeal and try there for permission.

> … we should not foist appeals on the Court of Appeal when they may not want them, and they may think that specialist judges in this area, a sort of *Cooke* point, should really

[85] Figure received by the authors from OSSCSC, 16 March 2005.
[86] [2002] 3 AER 279, reported as *R(DLA) 6/01*.

> be given their head on some of these issues. I don't have any problem in refusing leave to appeal. The Court of Appeal will decide, in a sensible way, whether they want to hear a particular point.

Others took the view, even where they were sure their decision had been right, that if there was room for two legitimate points of view they would grant leave. Some of the Commissioners stressed the element of the potential impact of the case in how they approached the determination of leave. One Commissioner stated he would give leave 'if it's a general point of importance that spreads across more than one case, I refuse leave if it's just an individual argument.' Some of the Commissioners were less anxious about refusing leave to an appellate court than refusing leave from an AS tribunal to Commissioner level. In the former case, the appellant could always try the Court of Appeal for leave. In the latter case, a refusal was likely to be the end of the road. In the past, one (now retired) Commissioner *always* refused leave to the appellate court and simply regarded the task of deciding whether a case should go further as belonging to that court. Another Commissioner thought that, in an appropriate case, it might be worth hinting that although s/he would follow an established line of Commissioners' authority, in fact s/he may well have decided the issue differently without such precedents. This strategy could be deployed to encourage an appeal to the Court of Appeal to explore the alternative viewpoint.

As regards the impact of the Court of Appeal's intervention, it did appear to be something of a 'rite of passage' in the Commissioners' professional development. One relatively new Commissioner said that it was received wisdom amongst colleagues that a Commissioner only genuinely matures 'when your decision is overturned by the Court of Appeal'. Quite a few of the Commissioners appeared to keep a private 'score' of their own decisions that had been scrutinised by the Court of Appeal, but one Commissioner claimed strenuously that keeping a personal count or tally would not be a proper approach, though s/he was quick to point out a case in which his/her decision had been preferred by the House of Lords to the opposing view of another Commissioner. There was sometimes disappointment in cases where the parties had settled and obtained a consent order from the appellate court when it was thought the issues could have done with a full airing. One Commissioner bemoaned what s/he perceived as a quite arbitrary process by which some cases arrived in the Court of Appeal whereas other (more suitable) cases evaporated.

Most of the Commissioners were naturally extremely interested in how the appellate court dealt with their own decisions. Once the decision was available it was clear that Commissioners were eager to consider what lessons could be taken from it. Sometimes, the appellate court's decisions were criticised. For example, one Commissioner remarked that the 'lack of intellectual rigour in the *Mallinson*[87]

[87] *Mallinson v Secretary of State for Social Security* [1994] 2 AER 295. The lead case on 'attention *in connection with* bodily functions'. Lord Woolf held that '[t]he attention is in

decision has resulted in huge numbers of extra appeals coming to us…'. One of the Scottish Commissioners identified an interesting difference between the impact of a decision from the Court of Session compared to the Court of Appeal.

> We don't regard the decisions of the Court of Appeal as 'the holy grail'! They are signposts on a way, but they are signposts on a way where we can all see where they came from and how it's going. Therefore, we should be able ourselves to map out what should happen next or in the future because the whole idea of a Scots legal mind is to apply the statutory provision precisely to a set of facts …. Whereas, I think in England there's much more what's called *stare decisis* – you try to relate how the law has been developed through the cases. So there is a cultural difference.

Original jurisdiction: the forfeiture rule[88]

This exceptional *original*, rather than *appellate*, jurisdiction of the Commissioners was referred to briefly in Chapter 2. The Forfeiture Act 1982 placed responsibility at first instance with the Commissioners for making decisions whether widows' benefit (now 'bereavement benefit') could be paid in whole or in part in circumstances where the survivor had been responsible for the death of the deceased. Section 4 of the 1982 Act sets out the rule of public policy that a person should not benefit from his or her own wrongdoing in such circumstances. Under an amendment in 1986, the Commissioners were given the power to modify the effects of the rule of forfeiture to achieve greater equity in individual cases (Larkin, 2004: 70). Unsurprisingly, given the nature of these cases, they are relatively 'rare birds' in the words of one of the Commissioners. In 2001-02 there were only two forfeiture cases disposed of; in 2002-03 there were six, in 2003-04 there were 17 and in 2004-05 there were ten.[89]

Commissioners' views on forfeiture cases

Regarding forfeiture cases, we were told that 'traditionally the more experienced Commissioners have been allocated them'. One of the senior Commissioners said that s/he might see one or two such cases a year at the most. One of the Commissioners noted that these cases, though involving the application of reasonably well-settled principles of law, had 'an almost total element of discretion which is not usual for other decisions which we have.' The Commissioner recognised, that in these circumstances it was important that the Commissioners, as a body, developed consistent decision-making.

---

connection with the bodily function if it provides a substitute method of providing what the bodily function would provide if it were not totally or partially impaired'(p 306).

[88] See generally, on the forfeiture rule in social security, the excellent article by Larkin (2004).

[89] Figures supplied by OSSCSC to the authors 16 March and 26 April 2005. The two prefix codes for forfeiture cases are CFG and CFP: see Appendix 4.

> ...once you have decided that rule applies so that that person whose benefit is forfeited, then your discretion to lift the forfeiture is pretty unrestricted. And we've developed, I've been trying to develop, some kind of guidelines in decisions that I've made on this, to give people an indication of when one asks for submissions on forfeiture cases. You very often find that the representative for the claimant, and often also the representative for the Secretary of State, doesn't address the potentially relevant factors in the case that might cause you to be more disposed to lift the forfeiture rule 100 per cent or whatever. So I've adopted the practice of issuing a direction, and giving a few earlier decisions of particularly [Commissioner's name] and my own who – we both happen to have some forfeiture cases at the same time – simply to give them the idea of the kind of factors that currently Commissioners ... are taking into account on forfeiture cases.

The approach of the Commissioners appeared to be to start with a consideration of the trial judge's view of the severity of the crime.

> ... the starting point is, you get the judge's remarks on summing up to the jury and the basis on which the jury have convicted the claimant of manslaughter. And if for example the charge against her has been murder, and if it was only a manslaughter conviction, that means that the jury accepts that there has been very severe provocation and that's a factor that is reflected in the judge's sentence, and you take account in general, unless there is some particular reason against it, of the judge's remarks on sentencing and the sentence he imposes. If he only imposes a sentence of two years' probation, which is unusual for a manslaughter conviction, then you can take it that neither he nor the jury viewed the killing as anything more than something near an accident. And you therefore are much more ready to accept that the forfeiture should be lifted.

Another factor mentioned to take into account when considering this discretion was whether the person (usually the widow) still had any responsibility for children. One Commissioner had lifted the forfeiture rule in such circumstances leaving it to operate much later in order to prevent the children from being indirectly penalised.

The legal officers

Legal officers were formerly known as 'nominated officers' but this was changed in 1999 because the title was widely misunderstood.[90] The Lord Chancellor's Department (LCD) consulted the Commissioners on the change of nomenclature. One suggestion had been 'registrar' but according to one Commissioner, 'the LCD threw a wobbly at that, they weren't going to have them called "registrar"'. One of the Commissioners pointed out that the title 'registrar' had a variable content ranging from a purely administrative role, for example the registrar of a tax tribunal, to a purely judicial one. In between, there was a 'legal administrative' role, for example, the registrar to the Lands Tribunal, a role requiring a qualified

90 Social Security Commissioners Procedure Regulations 1987, SI 1987/214. These Regulations were revoked by SI 1999/1495, reg 2(b), as from 1 June 1999.

lawyer to perform it. At the time of the passage of SSA 1998 it had been envisaged that the role of legal officers might be widened. One interviewee informed us that 'the LCD nearly gave [the legal officers] the power to do 14(7) decisions[91] and they got cold feet at the last minute.'

The legislation provides for the delegation of certain judicial and administrative functions to the legal officers; for example, giving directions, determining requests for oral hearings, summoning witnesses and extending or abridging time limits.[92] Any party can make a written request within 14 days for a Commissioner to reconsider a legal officer's direction. However, such a request will not stop the proceedings under the direction or order unless a Commissioner authorises it.[93] The legal officers are qualified solicitors or barristers. There were 12 legal officers in post at the London office at the time of our interviews. There were nine (including the senior legal officer and two part-time) in post in March 2005. There were also two legal officers in the Edinburgh office and one in the Belfast office in March 2005.

One of the long serving legal officers aptly described the mindset required for their specialist tasks.

> You need to be a person who doesn't mind spending a lot of time on your own. I mean I always say to people, there's no point in coming here if you want a lot of external stimulation. You haven't got clients, you've got to be prepared to be self motivated, you've got to be a self-starter, you've got to have these files constantly coming in front of you, you've got to maintain interest. You've got to like the sort of crossword puzzle of the law really; you've got to want to unpick things. But also, on the other hand, you have got to be able to take a balanced view and not get stuck on something for a month because that won't go down at all well. So you've got to be able to process work but also to do what's necessary, you've got to be able to see the wood from the trees and that is something that people find quite hard in the beginning. They either tend to be the kind of people who get stuck in the wood or they don't see the wood. I haven't, fortunately, had anybody like that; I think I've been quite good at choosing people.

The legal officers: the Commissioners' views

Our interviews took place at a time when the position of the legal officers was in a state of flux. There had been an increase in the numbers of legal officers due mainly to the surge in work caused by *Bate*.[94] There had been an immediate need for experienced people to tackle the increasing workloads. Consequently, some of the legal officers had been recruited through a special competition from welfare rights organisations. However, the case management committee established at OSSCSC following the Select Committee intervention had opened up the whole

---

91 SSA 1998, s.14(7). The Commissioner's power to 'set aside' where the parties agree there was an error of law.

92 See SSA 1998, Schedule 4, para 6 and SI 1999/1495, reg 7.

93 *Ibid*, reg 7.

94 *Bate v Chief Adjudication Officer and another* [1996] 2 AER 790 (HL) (16 May 1996), a case concerning contentious points about the Income Support severe disability premium.

question of how best to use legal officers within the organisation. The increasing management control exercised by the Commissioners in this way had lowered the morale of the legal officers at the time of our interviews. There was a perception that the interlocutory work was being taken away from them; 'we have effectively had all our delegated powers taken away from us, the Commissioners are doing everything'. One reason for this exertion of control had been that some of the legal officers in the past had, in the view of some of the Commissioners, gone off 'on a frolic of their own' in pursuing lines of inquiry in respect of the casework.

There was a general concern that the notes of recommendation on cases that the legal officers used to write to individual Commissioners had changed to a system whereby the legal officer was expected to write a note to an *unnamed* Commissioner. However, different Commissioners had required different types of help. Some preferred a more thorough research effort; others preferred a shorter note on a particular point. One legal officer interviewed said, 'we have found this very difficult because there is a desire for a standardised product but it is a standardised product that doesn't suit many people.'

Our interview work revealed three themes. Firstly, the Commissioners' general recognition of the legal officers as an extremely valuable resource within the organisation. Secondly, doubts about how to best use this resource depending on how Commissioners viewed legal officers' dual judicial/administrative function. Finally, their views about the legal officers' possible future role. This is followed by some brief comments about the role of legal officers in the Belfast and Edinburgh offices.

A valuable resource The Commissioners mostly agreed that the legal officers represented an important and useful resource that was not being used to its full potential in a number of ways. We were told that the legal officers' knowledge stretched back over years (some had given several decades of service to the Commissioners) and was regarded as quite invaluable in this jurisdiction notorious for its technical complexity. One of the Chief Commissioners pointed out that OSSCSC was very privileged to have their legal officers[95] and that they were essential for two reasons. Firstly, because there was a greater burden on the Commissioners to investigate points of law in the claimant's favour as most appellants were unrepresented. The legal officers were in a good position to undertake that type of research. Secondly, the law was extensive, complex and fast moving, but legal officers were able to keep on top of new developments and helped to keep the Commissioners up to date.

One Commissioner thought the nearest analogy to a legal officer's post was a Master of the Supreme Court; another said that the European Court of Justice *judge-rapporteur* exactly described their role. However, legal officers, who were qualified barristers or solicitors, were not judicial appointments. They were civil servants and it appeared there had been an uncomfortable relationship between

[95] 12 legal officers at the time of our interviews. There were nine legal officers (including the senior legal officer and two part-time) in post in March 2005.

them and the clerical/administrative staff of OSSCSC supplied by the Court Service. One Commissioner said that the senior legal officer was not subject to instruction by the senior administrator. It should be the administrators taking directions from the senior legal officer, not the other way round. Another Commissioner remarked that their long serving senior legal officer 'could do the Commissioner's job with both hands tied behind her back'.

However, the Commissioners' general regard for the legal officers was not quite universal. One Commissioner said 'if we did not have the legal officers I would not reinvent them.' He noted their variable ability and that the office had stopped using them for interlocutory control as 'some of them were not able to really exercise judgment on what issues were relevant and what issues should be raised before us as opposed to the tribunal.' He thought a research assistant role was all that was required to help the Commissioners. He gave an example of the sort of research point that might need pursuing. It concerned a case relating to assistance with a funeral payment where a relative lived in the Channel Islands. The legal officer had done some research on the system of welfare support in the Channel Islands. Some legal officers were known to be interested in and expert in various areas of law, for example, European Law or Human Rights and such points were readily referred to such individuals.

Deploying legal officers and their dual function Most Commissioners recognised that legal officers had a dual function. They were part judge's clerk/research assistant and part quasi-judicial officers with an interlocutory jurisdiction. Some Commissioners felt they ought to focus exclusively on the research role in difficult and complex cases and should not be drawn into the case management and administrative roles. At the time of our interviews the system whereby legal officers would look initially at *all* applications was reviewed. Legal officers had been relieved of doing the initial filter on most of the DLA cases on the basis that most of the Commissioners were not going to miss points on DLA cases, a benefit with which they were well acquainted. Legal officers were often expected to write a 'note' commenting on the application or appeal for the Commissioner. It appeared they were commenting on around half the cases arriving in OSSCSC. In addition to obtaining the legal officer's note of recommendations in a case, some Commissioners also referred their draft decisions to them for checking. New Commissioners and those who were dealing with an unfamiliar point of law might do this to discover whether it contained some 'elementary howler'.

Many of the Commissioners perceived that the legal officers were not entirely happy in their jobs, not least because of the lack of clarity in their role and function. For example, they had been increasingly used to sort out files on routine cases. One Commissioner attributed this to the inadequacy of the general administrative support staff. Some of the Commissioners thought that their use in an administrative support role was undertaken at the expense of developing a more expert role in OSSCSC. Some of the Commissioners were aware that the legal officers were generally unhappy about writing notes of recommendation 'into the void', that is, not knowing to which Commissioner the note was sent. The legal officers were aware that different Commissioners liked different kinds of notes, some wanted very brief notes, and others wanted fuller research efforts.

Several Commissioners referred to instances where the legal officers had been instrumental in encouraging the claimant to secure a good representative in difficult cases. One Commissioner gave an example of this occurring in a difficult 'additional pensions' case where a particularly interesting point of law arose for an oral hearing. The Commissioners generally reported that some of the legal officers would be capable of doing very detailed and well-argued notes to assist their decision-making. It appeared that a few of the Commissioners felt that the legal officers' detailed knowledge might prompt them to recommend the claimant should have a 'second bite at the cherry'. This was an approach that one Commissioner described as 'the vice of this jurisdiction'. The facility to obtain a legal officer's view of a case was also mentioned as useful by Commissioners who, for a variety of reasons, wanted to 'stand back' from a case and re-establish their own objectivity.

The legal officers appeared to be quite actively involved in the training sessions organised by one of the Commissioners. The Commissioner had encouraged them to produce briefing documents on a number of issues; for example, the impact of the Human Rights legislation on social security law. The legal officers were also active in other parts of the OSSCSC; for example, a legal officer regularly attended the meetings of the 'Star Chamber' (see Chapter 5) and provided representation on the 'user group' (see Chapter 6).

The future role of legal officers and team working One of the Chief Commissioners interviewed thought that legal officers might be specifically assigned to one or two Commissioners, working with a clerk and perhaps one or two Deputies attached in a team formation. The team would decide how best to distribute the work. However, he believed that the file should initially come directly to the Commissioners. The team, supervised by the Commissioner(s) would be responsible for the file from beginning to end. This would also have the advantage of integrating the administrative support staff into the case management process. 'They're totally isolated from the end product of what they're doing, that makes it difficult for them to make sense of what they're doing, and it makes it difficult for us to work efficiently.' Where there was some legal or procedural complexity it could be referred to the legal officer and then returned for further consideration. Interestingly, the team-working idea reflected what a long-serving Commissioner told us had been the position many years ago; one legal officer attached to two Commissioners. This Commissioner, and others, regretted the fact that legal officers had become less integrated into the organisation and were not linked to particular Commissioners. There were a number of Commissioners who supported the principle of maintaining judicial continuity over case progression, a principle recognised in other areas of civil justice reform.[96]

Most Commissioners agreed the need for greater clarity about the legal officers' two primary functions and that more consideration was needed to address what their future role could be. One Commissioner noted that in the past the legal officers' role was more obvious as Commissioners tended to have little or no knowledge of social security law on appointment. However, with the arrival of new Commissioners, sometimes with considerable experience in the area, the original justification for legal officers was disappearing. Some Commissioners very much supported the idea that legal officers should play a more centre-stage role in case management and giving directions. To an extent, this process had started; for example, where a batch of 'lookalike' cases was detected one legal officer was given the task to coordinate their progress. One Commissioner mentioned this had happened in 'vibration white finger' cases,[97] a task that could not have been delegated to administrative support staff lacking the necessary legal expertise.

There was not of course universal approval for the team working idea. One Commissioner pointed to past failures at OSSCSC where too many people had been involved in reading case papers leading to duplication of effort and delay. S/he also thought it would be problematic working out how to allocate cases to teams. There was also some concern that if the legal officers were not looking at every case but only getting involved in more difficult cases, this would isolate them from a more comprehensive understanding of what was happening in the organisation. One of the Chief Commissioners thought that further judicial functions could be delegated to legal officers in the future. For example, it was possible that section 14(7) determinations (see 'setting aside and redeterminations' above) could be undertaken by legal officers, comparable to the role of registrars in the Court of Appeal.

Legal officers in Northern Ireland and Scotland In Northern Ireland there was one legal officer looking at practically every case arriving at the office, though if he became overloaded cases went directly to the (two) Commissioners. He would generally allocate cases alternately to each Commissioner. This was thought appropriate in the Northern Ireland context 'so there is nobody going to accuse us of packing the court'.

In Scotland the legal officers used to look at all the applications for leave and appeals as they arrived and write notes on them for the Commissioners. However, that was not considered a good use of their time. One of the Scottish Commissioners said, 'I don't see that I'm particularly advantaged by the legal

[96] For example, in care proceedings; see the *Protocol for Judicial Case Management in Public Law Children Act Cases*, (2003), Family Policy Division, Lord Chancellor's Department, June 2003, London: LCD.

[97] 'Episodic blanching, occurring throughout the year, affecting the middle or proximal phalanges' of at least three fingers on a person's hand. See Social Security (Prescribed Diseases) Regulations 1985, SI 1985/967, Sched 1, para A11.

officer either telling me that there are sufficient facts or reasons or insufficient facts or reasons when I can see that perfectly plainly for myself.' S/he thought that legal officers could be best utilised in relation to difficult cases, in particular, to identify points both parties had missed. The legal officers in the Edinburgh office like the London office appeared to have a key role in coordinating efforts on batches of 'lookalike' cases when these occurred. There were also a number of other administrative tasks thought difficult to be performed by non-legally qualified administrative support staff. Indeed, one of the Scottish Commissioners thought there was a 'third dimension' to the role of the legal officer in the Edinburgh office, in particular the senior legal officer who had to act as a bridge between the administrative staff (supplied by the Scottish Executive) and the Commissioners. The formulation of standard letters would be his/her responsibility because ordinary administrative staff would not have the legal knowledge to gauge whether such letters fitted within the terms of the regulations.

Evaluation: the appellate process in transition

Commissioners' caseloads

The cases dealt with by the Commissioners in the form of both applications for leave (Table 3.2 above) and appeals (Table 3.3 above) amounts to only around 2.5 per cent of all AS appeals. This small proportion is unsurprising given the fact that appeals to the Commissioners are on a point of law. The Commissioners' workload has fallen in the last few years in absolute terms although, as their annual report for 2003-04 makes clear, 'the decrease is not as great as sometimes portrayed'. In 1998 the Commissioners disposed of 6,846 cases in the London office. In 2004-05 this figure was 5,793 made up of 3,834 applications for leave (66 per cent) and 1,959 appeals (34 per cent). In the intervening years the total figure had reached a peak of 8,000 cases 'disposed of' in a year though this reflected a reduction of cases 'pending' before the Commissioners rather than an increase in the numbers of cases arriving at OSSCSC. Figures for applications and appeals to the Edinburgh and Belfast offices are given in Tables 3.4 and 3.5 below.

Nevertheless, there has been some reduction in the number of cases in the last few years. The Commissioners' Annual Report (2004) identifies three possible causes. Firstly, the general state of the economy has meant fewer benefits claimed overall and this has been reflected in the reduction of appeals going to both the AS tribunals and onwards to the Commissioners. Secondly, a number of procedural reforms in SSA 1998 have reduced the Commissioners' workload; for example, the ability of AS tribunals to review their own decisions. Thirdly, improved training for tribunal members. The President of the Appeal Tribunals has a statutory duty to arrange appropriate training for tribunal members (SSA 1998, Sched 1, para 8). It was reported that in 2003-04 the Appeals Service held 47 training events and 2,900 panel members received training over 3,200 days delegated for training. (Appeals

Service, 2004: 15). However, there has been a change in the balance of applications for leave and appeals dealt with by the Commissioners. In 1998, 4,317 cases of the 6,846 London cases (63 per cent) went to full appeal. In 2004-05, as stated above, only 34 per cent went to full appeal. The Commissioners' Annual Report claims that these changes not only reflect the tribunals' power under SSA 1998 to review their own decisions but also 'a more robust approach of Commissioners to the refusing of leave to appeal in cases of little merit' (2004: 4). The report concludes that this has not affected the quality of decisions but has improved the time within which cases before the Commissioner are handled.

Table 3.4 Scotland: applications and appeals, 2002-03, 2003-04

Applications for leave		
	Received	Disposed of
2002-03	807	609
2003-04	674	487
Appeals		
	Received	Disposed of
2002-03	465	516
2003-04	447	421

Table 3.5 Northern Ireland: applications and appeals, 1999-2003

Application for leave			Cleared			
	Outstanding	Lodged	After hearing	Without hearing	Total	Outstanding
1999	146	298	40	308	348	96
2000	96	190	23	201	224	62
2001	62	185	4	137	141	106
2002	106	272	8	244	252	126
2003	126	194	13	233	246	74
Appeals			Cleared			
	Outstanding	Lodged	After hearing	Without hearing	Total	Outstanding
1999	166	142	91	100	191	117
2000	117	93	54	85	139	71
2001	71	65	29	79	108	28
2002	28	122	26	59	85	65
2003	65	107	34	89	123	49

Source: NI Judicial Statistics (2003: 106).

Caseloads by benefit

It is useful to know the caseload of the appeal process broken down by *type* of benefit. A breakdown by benefit is given below for both AS tribunal appeals (Table 3.6) and applications and appeals to the Commissioners (Table 3.7). The reader should note these are only broad indicators of the profiles of work at both levels, as the statistical basis for each table is slightly different. Nevertheless, the tables do provide a clear picture of DLA emerging as the most heavily litigated benefit of all, occupying 38 per cent of tribunal and as much as 46 per cent of Commissioner caseload. DLA is followed at both appeal levels by incapacity benefit, income support and industrial injuries disablement benefit cases in significant proportions. Further along the spectrum the same benefits appear, though in smaller and different proportions, child support, for example, at 1 per cent of the total at the tribunal level, but 5 per cent at the Commissioner level.

Table 3.6 Proportion of AS tribunal appeals in benefit categories (2004)

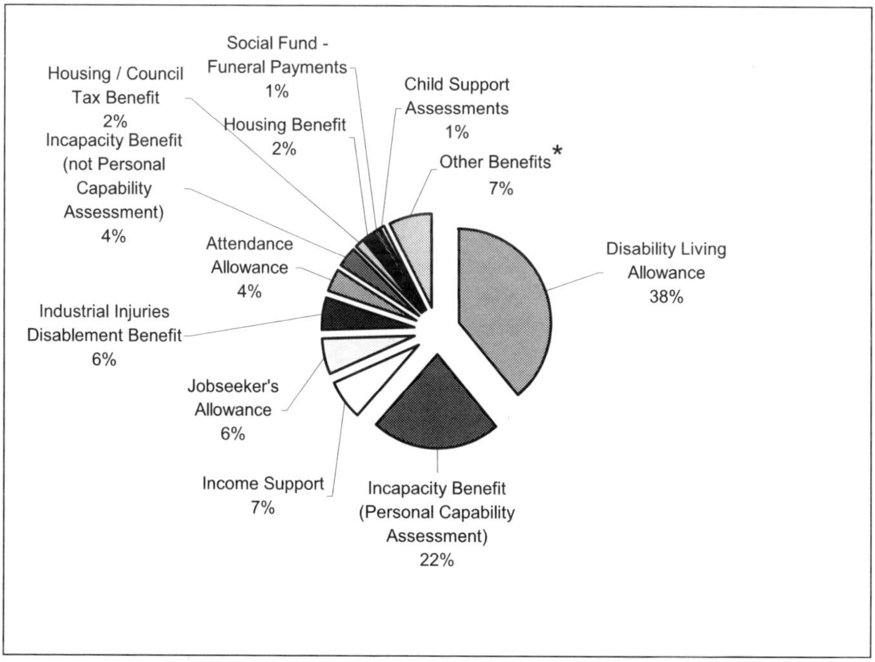

Source: *Derived from DWP, Quarterly Appeal Tribunal Statistics: June 2004, Table 2. The percentages were derived from figures from the quarter ending 30 June 2004.*
*Note: The 'other benefits' category includes around 27 benefits/credits, including, for example, pension credits, carer's allowance, child benefit, social fund maternity payments. Each of these 'other' benefits accounted for less than 0.9 per cent of the total.

These figures are also volatile over time. New benefits in the system – for example, housing and council tax benefit – may be more litigated upon introduction for a year or two until the problems giving rise to appeals are 'settled down', sometimes by providing better information to the public, sometimes by providing clearer interpretation from the Commissioners, which then may preclude many appeals from occurring, or a combination of such factors. One can also note the long 'tail' of 'other benefits' at both levels. Statistically, these may reflect small numbers of cases; however, they have certain implications for the deployment of judicial resources.

Table 3.7 Proportion of applications and appeals to the Commissioners in benefit categories (2004-05)[98]

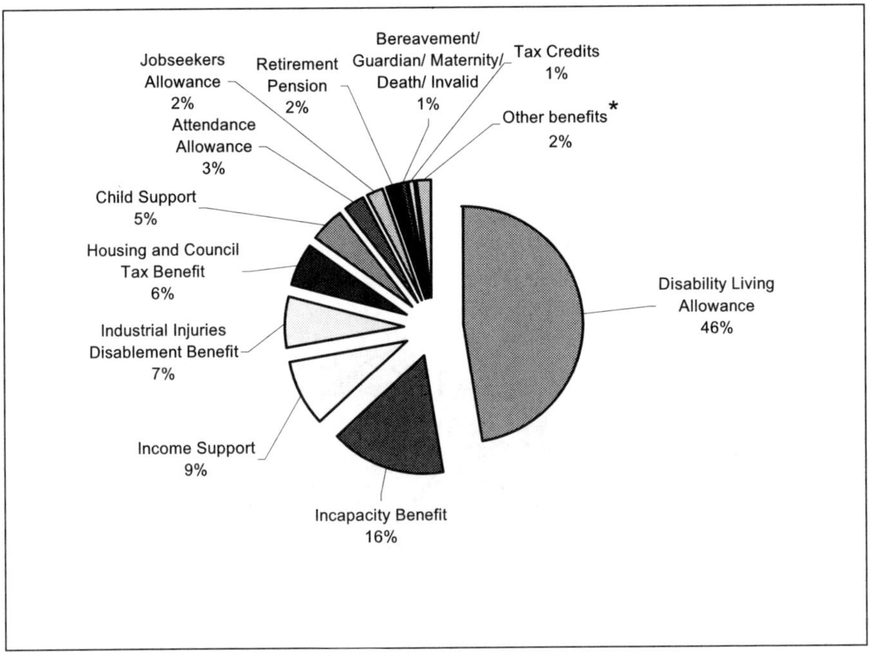

Source: Figures supplied by OSSCSC to the authors 26 April 2005.

*Note: The 'other benefits' category included 15 benefit categories; CPC (0.7%), CF (0.4%), CS (0.3%), CFP (0.1%), CCR (0.1%), CFG (0.1%) and a 'tail' of eight other categories with hardly any or no cases at all. See Appendix 4 for prefix definitions.

98 The figures relate to the financial year 2004-05. They are based on 'new cases' received, that is the sum of all applications for leave arriving at OSSCSC and the appeals arriving directly from the Appeals Service (leave having already been given by the AS tribunal chair).

A benefit rarely encountered may consume proportionately more judicial time, precisely because the tribunal chair or Commissioner is unfamiliar with the particular benefit, and could be grappling with its complexities perhaps for the first time. When one considers, in particular, the benefit breakdown of work at Commissioner-level in Table 3.7, it is evident that the Commissioners are in fact handling an overwhelming number of cases concerning disability and incapacity-related benefits and allowances, a total of 72 per cent (DLA, incapacity benefit, industrial injuries and attendance allowance) in 2004-05. No doubt the contentious nature of disability-related benefits, in terms of the political priority they receive and the legislative formulas used, both contribute to the creation of legal regimes that are more likely to be challenged. One must not forget also the growing influence of the disability lobby in Great Britain that has made efforts to provide good quality information and representation on all disability-related issues. Moreover, adverse decisions in these areas might be thought to reflect badly on the claimant's integrity, in some instances seeming to stigmatise the individual as an unworthy malingerer.

It will be seen that the breakdown by benefit of the Commissioners' workload in Table 3.7 above includes a total of both 'applications' and 'appeals'. When these figures are separated out however, there is very little difference between them in terms of the benefit breakdowns.

Case Management

Due to a number of case management techniques that were initiated around the time of our interview work with the Commissioner, there have been some steady improvements in the efficiency of managing the workloads of both applications and appeals.

Following the Select Committee inquiry into the Commissioners (see Chapters 1 and 6) OSSCSC initiated a case management initiative to expedite the backlog of cases and address the problem of delay in the system. This involved some reorganisation of the way in which the Commissioners, legal officers and administrative staff were working; for example, a Commissioner who gives leave on an application will now normally make the decision on the substantive appeal, thus providing greater judicial continuity in dealing with cases. There has also developed, as stated above, a more 'robust approach' to applications for leave in routine cases, and there are more developed systems for dealing with batches of 'lookalike' cases where these occur. There is also a clearer Committee structure at OSSCSC to assist in undertaking the administrative functions of the Chief Commissioner. This has included the development of an 'Editorial Board' to deal with the process of reporting Commissioners' decision (see Chapter 5). There is also a Procedure Committee that considers procedural rule changes and makes recommendations to the DCA and DWP, considers *Practice Memoranda* and other explanatory guidance to be made available to the parties.

There have also been developments in the technology used by OSSCSC and a review of the administrative staff structure and organisation. A more efficient electronic case management database was introduced in April 2002 to replace the ERIC ('Every Record is Casetracked') system. The new system allows case data to be imported into documents at a keystroke and management information can be more easily extracted in order to monitor office standards and targets. OSSCSC also uses email communication more frequently and now receives 'written submissions' from the Department via email as a permanent arrangement. (Commissioners Annual Report, 2003: 14; 2004: 22). The office standards include targets to register applications and appeals within five working days of receipt; to reply to correspondence within ten working days and to issue Commissioners' decisions within five working days. (Annual Report, 2003: 5; 2004: 24).

The DMA changes and waiting times

The DMA changes referred to throughout this chapter – for example, the 'set aside' powers of both the tribunals and the Commissioners (see Figure 3.2 above) – have undoubtedly made a contribution in preventing the numbers of appeals from increasing. It does make sense to have flexible powers available to 'short-circuit' the full extent of the appeal route in appropriate cases and there is little evidence from welfare rights' organisations that these devices are a cause of injustice. Such devices have also assisted in speeding up the appeal process where it must be used. The progression in 'waiting times' at the level both of the Appeals Service and the Commissioners provides some evidence that the changes have had a beneficial effect.

Before the Select Committee (2000) scrutinized the Commissioners (see Chapters 1 and 6), it had already undertaken an inquiry into the modernization of social security appeals and published its report in November 1999 (Select Committee, 1999). The government's reply to that report (Select Committee, 2000a) had noted the efforts of the Department to heighten efficiency by means of the twin strategy of trying to clear the backlog of older cases and improving the waiting times for new cases. A backlog of over 70,000 cases in February 1999 had reduced to around 9,500[99] in November 1999. The President and the Chief Executive of the Appeals Service later reported to the Select Committee that by April 2000 the backlog figure had fallen to 728 (Select Committee, 2001: para 2.2). Furthermore, by the end of March 2001 the average waiting time was reported as haven fallen to 13.6 weeks.

Finally, in 2001-02, a new target was set for cases returned by the Commissioners to the AS tribunals. The average waiting time for a re-hearing should be no more than eight weeks from the date of return to the Appeals Service (Select Committee 2001). Currently, this target co-exists with two more set by the Secretary of State: the average waiting time for an appeal is to be not more than 11 weeks from the time of receipt by AS; and the number of cases over 20 weeks old

[99] 5,000 of these 'lookalike' cases were awaiting a lead decision from the courts.

as at 1 April 2004 is to be reduced by at least 15 per cent by 31 March 2005 (Appeals Service Agency, 2005: 11). The Appeals Service reported in their 2003-04 annual report (Appeals Service, 2004: 4) that on average, cases returned from the Commissioner were re-heard in 8.4 weeks. The average waiting time for an appeal to be heard by an AS tribunal from the time of receipt was 11.2 weeks, and the number of cases over 24 weeks old was reduced by 29 per cent. There had also been progress in reducing the amount of waiting time discrepancies between local offices.

At the level of the Commissioners, waiting times had clearly stretched to embarrassing lengths, an average of 64 weeks in 1998.[100] The picture now could not be more different. In the latest Commissioners' Annual Report (2004: 18) the target for the average waiting time from 'application' to ruling was 10 weeks. The target for 'appeals' was 20 weeks. In 2003-04 both of these targets appear to have been achieved. The OSSCSC headline figures for waiting times over the past four years are given in Table 3.8 below.

Table 3.8 Waiting times for applications and appeals to the Commissioners

Average waiting times shown in weeks

	2000-01	**2001-02**	**2002-03**	**2003-04**
Applications*	19.0	15.7	9.9	8.1
Appeals**	40.8	34.1	21.2	19.7

* from receipt of application to disposal of application, either being refused or granted
** from when an application is granted or upon direct receipt of an appeal

Source: Commissioners' Annual Report (2004: 22).

However, it should be noted that in the case of applications that are *granted*, the waiting time, from the appellant's point of view is the aggregate time for applications and appeals, for example, 27.8 weeks in 2003-04. However, even that ungenerous notional figure is much better than the average of 488 days we observed in our own survey of appellants' experiences of the appeal process in 2000-01: see Chapter 4.

The future role of legal officers and tribunal reform

The Leggatt (2001: 186) report, as mentioned in Chapter 1, had made favourable comments about the legal officers' role at OSSCSC consistent with their views on

[100] This figure was given in answer to a Parliamentary Question put by Mr Dismore MP and apparently inspired the Select Committee inquiry into the Commissioners the following year. See Chapter 6 and Hansard, House of Commons, *Written Answers*, 9 November 1999, cols 503w-504w.

the use of 'registrars' in a reformed tribunal system. In particular, the suggestion that section 14(7) powers (set aside where parties agree) be given to the legal officers was accepted in principle as a task suitable for their notion of a registrar under their recommended 'Divisional' tribunal structure (see Chapter 1). The Leggatt notion of a registrar (2001: 101) was based on the model of the Registrar of the Lands Tribunal. Interestingly, during our interview work, one of the legal officers had been deputising in the Lands Tribunal. We were told that this legal officer 'said it's so different because you're dealing with inter-party disputes where … you have summons for directions and much more formal things.' However, the registrar, according to Leggatt, would carry out some similar tasks to the legal officers at OSSCSC. They would perform an initial scrutiny of cases, they would have a range of interlocutory powers; 'registrars would undertake preparatory pre-hearing work and make interlocutory decisions for the tribunal under direction.' Finally, Leggatt suggested it might be useful to set out their powers and duties in legislation.

However, there does appear to be resistance to the idea that their role should expand in the way Leggatt envisaged. One of the Commissioners, when asked whether the legal officers' role could be expanded to fit within the *Leggatt* notion of 'registrars', gave the following response.

> I'd like to be able to say, 'yes' unconditionally, but I don't think that's the right answer. Their real expertise is not in procedure. Their expertise is not being in a second-tier tribunal. Their expertise and experience is in social security and allied law. They've all been in it for many years. They have unbelievable experience in it, and in an area where very few people have the faintest idea what's going on in terms of the law, there's a huge amount of knowledge there. So I think their main purpose is not really traditional administration, it's in the more substantive law.

However, the White Paper (2004: 30) rejected the idea of a Divisional structure and did not make any reference to the possible role of registrars in a reformed system. Nevertheless, one of the main thrusts of the White Paper is to establish a tribunal system where there is active case management and the creation of 'proportionate dispute resolution'. This will involve making initial assessments on appeal cases in order to find more appropriate procedures to handle them, possibly referring them back to the initial decision maker, or advising mediation where appropriate. The idea is to create a new Tribunal Service with a far more creative role in *developing* new procedures to serve the users' needs. The legal officers at OSSCSC not only have the specialised knowledge in their particular jurisdiction but they also already have interlocutory powers and they link the judicial and administrative functions at several points in the organisation. Their role should be further developed, consistently with the government's other plans, to create the required linkages between the judicial and administrative elements necessary to create a more user-friendly and flexible system. An enhanced role for 'legal officers' or 'registrars' or perhaps some other appropriate title, in a reformed tribunal system, would also go some way to explaining to administrators the importance of judicial decision making and to judges the importance of good administration. With proper development, such a role could have a unique contribution to make in the establishment of second-tier appellate bodies.

Chapter 4

Access to Justice

Introduction

One of the most powerful, but strangely contradictory, messages to come from the Leggatt review is contained in the title of the report 'Tribunals for Users' (Leggatt, 2001). The sentiment that a reform of administrative tribunals, the scope of which includes the Commissioners, should be based on a bottom-up perspective from the users and potential users of tribunals is laudable and refreshing. This message is contradictory in the sense that little new and direct evidence from those users appears to have informed the Leggatt analysis.

This is not to say that such evidence does not exist. There is a literature on social security appeals stretching back at least 30 years, an impressive proportion of which has been based on empirical research involving social security claimants (as appellants) and their representatives.[1] However, within this otherwise comprehensive literature the experiences and views of people appealing to the Commissioners are, glaringly, missing. The empirical research that we have carried out as part of this analysis of the Commissioners' role was aimed squarely at redressing this imbalance. Not only were we interested in filling a gap in knowledge about appellate structures but we also wanted to add the voice of appellants to the policy making arena.

Of course, it will never be possible to reflect the desires and aspirations of all appellants in the design of appellate structures and processes. For one thing, there will never be a consensus about what needs to be done. However, it is important that the range of views is addressed and acknowledged, so that whatever policy decisions are made about reform are informed by the bottom-up perspective.

In this chapter therefore, we concentrate on the views and experiences of the sample of users who took part in a telephone-based study (described in Chapter 1). The respondents were asked about their motivations for appealing to the Commissioners, the main issue behind the appeal, their views on the independence of both tribunals and the Commissioner, their views on the handling of their paper or oral hearing, on the time taken, and on the role and contribution of external representatives (see Appendix 2). We also incorporate the views of Commissioners, particularly, in the light of Leggatt, on the important subject of representation.

---

[1] The bibliography in Adler and Gulland (2003) provides a useful guide to the literature.

The chapter begins by looking at people's motivations for pursuing their appeal from an unsuccessful tribunal hearing. We will argue that these motivations reveal different underlying conceptions of justice as developed by Miller (see Chapter 1). In the section on 'access' we explore appellants' conceptions of the independence of the Commissioner and some of the potential technical and psychological barriers that appellants face in getting their appeal started. The section on the experiences of appellants deals importantly with the issues of time, participation, dignity and transparency. Given the importance of representation in current debates we deal with this subject at length from the perspectives of appellants and Commissioners, and include consideration of Secretary of State representation. We believe there are some lessons to be drawn here for the development of the Commissioner role in the future.

Motivation to appeal and conceptions of justice

This section presents an analysis of people's motivations for appealing. In the research interviews people were asked why they appealed to the Commissioners and what the main issue of their appeal was. The subject of motivation is important because it is known from some studies of social security appeals that there is a degree of attrition at each level in the hierarchy of decision making (Sainsbury and Eardley, 1991; Sainsbury, 1999; Sainsbury and Corden, 2004). In other words, people who have been turned down for an initial claim to benefit, or on a review of a disallowance are more likely to accept or resign themselves to the decision rather than pursue it further. People who have lodged an appeal with the Commissioners have, in contrast, already come through the initial decision making level, possibly an internal administrative review, and through the tribunal level. The people in our sample had by definition not given way to the pressures of attrition. They might therefore be the source of useful lessons for those interested in promoting the greater use of appeal rights. When it seems that many people are put off pursuing appeal rights at all or give up at a later stage, why is it that some people persevere?

The accounts of our sample about their motivation for appealing generate some interesting findings. One finding that warrants a mention at the outset is that most people did not discuss their reasons for appealing in the overt language of 'justice'. Among our sample, only one person used the word directly. However, as we shall see below, what people did say can often be seen as expressions of one of the forms of social justice discussed by Miller (1976): see Chapter 1.

Another interesting finding was that some people's explanations of why they appealed to the Commissioners referred mainly, and often only, to the original decision on their claim rather than the decision of the tribunal. This was particularly the case with people who had not attended their tribunal hearing. An important additional point to make is that, for many people, there was not a single reason behind the decision to appeal. For some, there was a combination of factors, which taken together, appeared to provide the impetus to pursue their case further.

Motivation as an expression of 'rights'

Some people explained their motivation by reference to the decision of the tribunal or the original decision, which they described simply as being 'wrong'. For example they thought that some piece of evidence had not been taken into account or interpreted incorrectly. Their hope was therefore that the Commissioners could put things right for them. There was particular discontent expressed about information about them in medical reports written by examining doctors in connection with claims for incapacity benefits, disability living allowance and attendance allowance. It was seemingly self-evident to some people that the decision on their claim must be wrong if it was based on incorrect information in medical reports. For example, an appellant turned down for attendance allowance explained his dissatisfaction thus:

> I did say to this doctor, I said I have even attempted to play a little bit of golf … I went with my wife and we managed to cover three holes. Now I told him this, but I was in agony after I had done this and after each walk, I had to sit down, this is not playing golf, this is proving to me that golf was something I would never play again. That's all I was trying to prove. He's said in his report that I could play golf!

This was typical of a number of instances where information provided by third parties, frequently doctors, was criticised for being inaccurate. An additional criticism was often that medical examinations had been inadequate, in terms of the length of time they took or the types of questions asked.

At the heart of these appellants' appeals we can identify a concern that their entitlement to benefit, or their 'rights' to benefit, had been infringed because of a failure in the rational processes of decision making. This can be argued to be a reflection of a model of administrative justice based on 'bureaucratic rationality' (see Chapter 1). The correct process of applying social security law to the facts of the appellant's circumstances had broken down because the evidence from which the 'facts' were derived was flawed. What was required from the Commissioners therefore was a critical examination of the evidence, possibly taking into account fresh evidence.

Motivation as an expression of 'need'

Among our sample of appellants a number explained their decision to pursue an appeal initially in terms of the amounts of money that they felt they had been denied or that they had been asked to repay the Department of Social Security (DSS). The respondents did not offer any explanation for the decision being 'wrong' in the sense of being based on faulty or partial information. However, the amounts involved were sufficient for them to continue their appeal beyond the tribunal.

One man had been asked to repay an overpayment of benefit of several thousand pounds. This was a substantial amount of money for him and he felt unable to make any decisions about his future until the appeal was resolved. He was therefore pursuing his appeal in the hope of getting the demand to repay removed. Another respondent had an even larger overpayment that she was seeking to overturn. Interestingly both of these respondents also gave additional reasons for appealing later in the interviews. The first respondent explained that the overpayment, which he did not dispute had arisen, was incurred at a time when he was unwell and could not have been expected to know how to comply with his responsibility to inform the benefits office of his change in circumstances. The second respondent was able to pursue her appeal on the grounds that the tribunal mishandled the evidence before it.

What these two cases illustrate is how motivations to appeal might not initially be based on points of law but only lead to a legitimate appeal when a point of law has been identified. The question then arises of how that position is reached when most appellants are in ignorance of the closely defined limits on the powers of the Commissioners. The answer in some cases is that representatives, from for example Citizen's Advice Bureaux (CABx) or trades unions, construct grounds for appeal on behalf of their client in terms that will satisfy the conditions on leave to appeal. This role of representatives will be discussed more fully later in the chapter.

Motivation as an expression of 'desert'

Some social security claimants when their claim for a benefit has been turned down or a claim in payment has been stopped express their dissatisfaction in terms of 'desert' (see, for example, Sainsbury and Corden, 2004). They do not argue that their decision was wrong, i.e. that the information used was deficient or that the rules were applied incorrectly. Neither do they make reference to needing the money. Instead, they use language that reflects a sense of their own 'deservingness' to the benefit in question.

This might be expressed in different ways. For example, it is not uncommon for people to refer to what they have put into society, often over a lifetime of employment, in National Insurance contributions. When a claim for a benefit is perhaps made later in life they feel an acute sense of deservingness, that at a time when they cannot draw an income from working, they are entitled morally to at last receiving some support from the state. If such a claim is turned down a strong reaction of injustice can result, of feeling let down, or even degraded, which is sufficient to motivate people to challenge that decision. A different sense of deservingness derives from people's comparisons of their circumstances with those of people they know, particularly neighbours. If someone has been denied a benefit when, in their perception, someone nearby in the same (or usually better) situation has been successful, then again a deep sense of injustice can arise that can lead them to make an appeal. For example, one respondent explained that he was:

> ...angry when I see other people getting everything when there is nothing wrong with them, or very little wrong with them ... a member of my extended family who gets it, they get full disability; there is very little wrong with him.

In pursuing appeals based on feelings of desert, the fact that an eventual decision will be based on an impartial application of the law can be of little concern or interest.

Motivation as grievance

It is possible to argue that what unites all appellants who lodge an appeal to either a tribunal or to the Commissioners is that they have a sense of grievance. This grievance might be expressed in different ways and directed at different things. In this study of appellants to the Commissioners the range of grievances already discussed has included grievance at a perceived wrong decision, grievance that their needs have not been met or their well being threatened, and grievance at a social security system that treats them badly in comparison with what they see as their just deserts. And as we have seen, people do not always, or often, express a single sense of grievance.

In our interviews with appellants, two other types of grievances were also raised that related more to either the substance of social security law or the process by which their claims were decided than with the outcome of the process. For example, we heard 'process' complaints about the conduct of examining medical practitioners and of tribunal members, about representatives being excluded from the tribunal proceedings, about not being allowed to question a tribunal medical member, and about the long distances they were expected to travel to a tribunal hearing. The other type of grievance was against the substance of social security law, for example about the assessment of functional ability in the 'all work test' for incapacity benefit.

It was not often appreciated that these sorts of grievances are not within the remit of either tribunals or the Commissioners. The former type, about administration, can be pursued via complaints mechanisms and ultimately the Ombudsman arrangements, and the latter fall within the domain of political action. Appellants with either of these sorts of grievance are unlikely to find redress within the mechanisms and structures of social security appeal however.

Access to the Commissioners

One of the prime motivations behind reviews and suggested reforms of systems of redress in administrative law is to improve access to justice. There is clearly no point in setting up well-trained, knowledgeable and competent bodies to hear appeals if the perceived and experienced barriers to accessing those forums prevent people from taking up their appeal rights. Our sample of appellants, by definition, must have been able to deal with any barriers to making an appeal to the Commissioners but their accounts of the process can shed useful insights into what it takes to get through to the Commissioner level. In this section, we look firstly at perceptions about whether the Commissioners are independent, and the requirement that appeal must identify a point of law, as possible barriers to access to the Commissioners. Finally, we examine the relevance of the personal characteristics and qualities of appellants in pursuing an appeal.

Perceptions of the independence of the Commissioners and tribunals

Independence is an important principle that has consistently featured in debates about decision-making and appellate structures, and was famously endorsed by the Franks Report (1957) that laid the foundations for the modern structure of administrative tribunals. For the most part, it has become virtually axiomatic that appellate bodies should be independent of lower tier decision makers in state and other bureaucracies, and both the Appeals Service (AS) and the Commissioners' office have made efforts to stress this aspect to prospective and actual users of their services. The proposals emanating from Leggatt and the White Paper seek to emphasise and strengthen that independence.

In our study we were able to examine people's perceptions of independence and the importance of independence to them. This is important because one possible barrier to people unhappy with the decision of their tribunal pursuing their case further is a view that the Commissioners are not independent and therefore it would be a waste of time taking their case further. Within the constraints of our empirical project we were not able to interview people who did not appeal to the Commissioners but evidence exists from other research that tribunals are sometimes perceived as extensions of the social security administrative bureaucracy.[2]

In our study we asked appellants their views about the independence of both the social security tribunal and the Commissioners. It must be remembered that this was a qualitative study of the experiences of 26 appellants and so generalisations from the data to the population of appellants are not appropriate. However, we were alert to the possibility of an 'outcome effect' that has been reported elsewhere in research on social security administration (Sainsbury, 1992b). In short, the outcome effect suggests that people happy with a decision on their claim or appeal tend to have more positive views about all aspects of the decision making process. It was therefore interesting from this study that negative views about the independence of tribunals were common (though importantly not ubiquitous) among all our sample, who by definition had been turned down by a tribunal, regardless of the outcome of their appeal to the Commissioners. In contrast, views about the independence of the Commissioners were generally either positive or non-committal, including those whose appeal did not succeed.

---

[2] For example Eardley and Sainsbury (1993); Sainsbury and Corden (2004).

There were several aspects of their dealings with the Commissioners that, for the appellants, showed evidence of their independence. Some respondents referred to aspects of the Commissioners' decision. For some the fact that they received a favourable decision (usually a referral back to a tribunal rather than a substitution of a new decision) was enough to demonstrate independence. There may be something of an outcome effect here in the sense of *post hoc* reasoning – i.e. because the Commissioners made a different decision to the tribunal, they must therefore be independent. For some others though, whose case was heard only on the papers, a well-explained written decision that showed that the important details of their case had been taken into account was evidence of independence. This perception was increased when Commissioners either criticised some aspect of the law they were administering, or where, in an oral hearing, they expressed sympathy or solidarity with the appellant. One respondent appreciated the sentiment expressed by the Commissioner in a hearing that he 'was morally right' in his appeal even though the decision of the tribunal had to be upheld. Finally, one appellant attending an oral hearing said that she thought the hearing was independent because of the helpful way the Commissioner and 'specialist doctor' conducted the proceedings.

In answering the question in the research interview about the independence of tribunals, people in our study often said that what they did *not* like was a sense that tribunals were closely aligned with the interests of the (then) Benefits Agency or DSS. For example one respondent commented:

> I didn't think it was independent; it was just stacked against me. I mean they say they're independent, but I don't think they are really. I think they're more in sympathy with the Benefits Agency than being independent.

Another respondent struggled to articulate why he felt that the tribunal was not entirely independent:

> Difficult to say, to be honest, not one hundred per cent. It's one of those difficult things. I don't know who this guy holding the tribunal was, what position he held or anything. And if you're dealing with officialdom you're dealing with officialdom. I can't say I went there thinking the odds are stacked against me or anything like that but on balance I think, you know, you didn't exactly have the feeling it was one hundred per cent independent. Although you had the feeling it must be because…do you know what I mean?

Some respondents doubted the independence of the tribunal because they perceived it to be an instrument for implementing government policy to reduce the amount of money spent on benefits. Another group of appellants concluded that the tribunal was not independent because the members did not listen to them or their representatives, or seemed to have prejudged their case and were just 'going through the motions'.

In contrast, some appellants who said they had been treated fairly by the tribunal and had no complaints about the way their hearing was conducted, were happy that it was independent. One respondent commented that the varied membership of the tribunal (which in his case included a doctor and a carer) was an indication that it was independent.

In summary, several aspects of the Commissioners' and tribunals' practices and procedures were cited by our sample as evidence, in their eyes, of independence, including the people acting as tribunal members, of Commissioners, the decisions made and reasons for those decisions, and the expression of sympathy and support for the appellant. It was also interesting what was not mentioned however. There were no mentions of either of the principal administrative organisations, the AS or the Commissioners' office, as evidence of independence from the then DSS and Benefits Agency. On the contrary, some of the criticisms of tribunals especially were about being closely aligned with the interests and goals of government and the DSS.

Satisfying the requirement to identify a point of law

Having the motivation to appeal, wherever that motivation comes from, is of course not sufficient to get an appeal heard by the Commissioners. Leave to appeal must first be sought and allowed either by the tribunal chair or by a Commissioner (see Chapter 3). What is intriguing from the analysis of motivation above is that references to 'points of law' were rare. Where people did refer to points of law this was usually in the context of discussing their experiences after making the appeal and particularly in relation to their understanding of the Commissioners' decisions. Several respondents only became aware of the salience of this issue in the course of dealing with their representatives or from communications from the Commissioners' office. Obtaining leave to appeal on a point of law is therefore a hurdle that all potential appellants have to overcome, and yet the people in our sample only rarely constructed their appeal in such terms initially.

From some respondents' accounts it is clear that the appeal to the Commissioners relied on the intervention and help of a third party. These included CAB offices, local authority welfare rights offices, trades unions and solicitors. This, and the wider role of representatives, is considered later in the chapter.

Personal characteristics of the appellants

From the analysis of people's accounts of how they came to lodge an appeal, it emerged that one of the contributory factors was perseverance, a doggedness and resilience to pursue an appeal that seemed to reflect on them on as individuals rather than on any intrinsic merit of their case. As explained in our concluding chapter, there appear to be some appellants, particularly those relating to disability and incapacity related benefits, for whom adverse decisions in this area are perceived as reflecting badly on their character. Although our respondents did not describe themselves in such terms, their testimonies showed that a strong will and determination not to accept an adverse decision of a tribunal contributed to getting their case heard by the Commissioners.

Interestingly, this perseverance was demonstrated by seemingly very different people. Some of our sample were angry at not getting a favourable decision on their claim and often identified the object of their anger, for example, the medical reports of examining doctors. Other people showed a more quiet determination in pursuing their appeal, often linked to a sense of injustice based on their own view of their deservingness. While some people talked about being uncertain or unconfident about pursuing their appeal, others with either professional backgrounds or with experience of previous appeals were more confident and assertive and undaunted about the prospect of appealing. The latter type of appellant was more likely to pursue their appeal unaided, while the former were more likely to have had help from a representative organisation. Some respondents were clear that they could only have pursued their appeal with the help of a representative. Again, we return to the role of representatives in a later section.

The experience of appealing

Leggatt has rightly couched his proposed reforms to tribunals in the UK in terms of a service to potential and actual users. Hence if we want to consider what such a service should look like we need to take note of the views of users and what, for them, contributes to their satisfaction or dissatisfaction. In this section therefore we examine some of the major aspects of service raised by the appellants in our study, and by external bodies, such as the Select Committee on Social Security, and drawn from the theoretical and empirical literature. We begin with the difficult subject of *time*. We also look at *participation*, *dignity* and the *transparency* of decisions and processes.

Time

The question of the time taken to produce a decision is fraught with difficulties and probably incapable of satisfactory resolution. It is hard to argue with the simple and persuasive force of the old maxim 'Justice delayed is justice denied'. However, some things take time that is reasonable and justifiable, for example if a period of information gathering is needed. In the context of social security decision making and appeals what is arguably less acceptable is 'delay' by which we mean an interval of time where a case is receiving no positive attention within an administrative organisation.

As we have explained in Chapter 1, the Select Committee (2000) reported critically on delays in granting leave and in determining appeals by the Commissioners. The period in which our research took place, shortly before the Select Committee's report and ending just before the publication of the Leggatt review, was therefore fortuitous in that it enabled us to focus on the nature of what the Select Committee called the 'culture of delay' and also to observe some of the changes in the management of the appeals in the Commissioners' office which attempted to deal with these problems and provide a more user friendly timescale – one of the perceived objectives of Leggatt.

In our study we were able to examine a large number of case records (see Chapter 1) and calculate the time taken from the date of the tribunal hearing to the Commissioner's decision. Many of the respondents had experienced very lengthy delays in their appeals. The period of the appeal process from tribunal hearing to Commissioner's decision had fallen to an average of 488 days and within that total period the average time taken from receipt by the Commissioners' Office to Commissioner's decision had also fallen to 344 days. We need not dwell too much on the precise length of the time taken to process Commissioner cases, since the Select Committee has drawn attention to them and, as we have already noted, actions were taken after our analysis to speed up processing. The important point to note is the overall scale of the times taken in the context of the appellant's circumstances. Time taken, whether justifiable and reasonable or 'delays', has potential costs for the appellant that might be material (in money lost or expenditures incurred) or emotional and psychological.[3]

Among our sample of respondents, the time taken to resolve their cases at the Commissioners was a source of concern that left many confused, demoralised or angry. Even respondents who were generally quite well disposed to the appeal process and stated that they had been on the whole treated fairly simply could not understand the delay. Even some with experience of working in bureaucratic organisations who could understand that decision processes took time considered their waits unacceptable. Others made comparisons with other welfare institutions, for example, the response rate of letters from their local hospital, council and so on.

Most respondents had very little idea or no idea at all what the Commissioners' office was doing with their case; even some representatives were surprised at the lengths of delay encountered. A number of representatives were clearly advising their clients that their appeals would only be resolved within a long time-frame, no doubt to prevent appellants from forming too high expectations about the expedition of their cases. A number of respondents clearly felt that the onus was on them to follow up the case while it rested in the Commissioners' office. Some did mention 'one or two letters' that arrived to report on the progress of their cases, but also noted that their own phone calls to the office frequently elicited a brush-off reply and complained of being 'fobbed off', for example being asked to phone back at the end of the month.

Many respondents were able to articulate in some detail the financial effects of the delay, in particular where a benefit had been withdrawn or lowered in rate pending the outcome of the appeal. One respondent reported that the mistakes on his claim and the resulting delays while appealing against these had contributed to the accumulation of mortgage arrears and indeed he faced a repossession action after the conclusion of his appeal. Another complained of the expenses she had

[3] These latter costs are discussed by Mashaw (1983: 98) as 'psychic costs'.

incurred in photocopying documents to prepare for her appeal and paying for recorded deliveries.

Many reported high levels of stress as a consequence of the delays experienced. Some reported that they were going through a period of depression and the delay exacerbated this. Some respondents clearly perceived that the stress associated with a lengthy ongoing appeal would ultimately not be a price worth paying for pursuing the appeal. A respondent with depression stated:

> I got to the end of the road and I thought, look I've got to get rid of this, I've got to get rid of this thing off my shoulders. It's not the only thing I've done it with but it just took so long and was so involved that eventually I gave up, basically.

The length of delays in some cases made the task of dealing with the anticipation of a forthcoming hearing, even a paper hearing, much more onerous than it might otherwise have been. Other respondents reported being 'frustrated' or 'annoyed' about the delay and one that it had affected her general confidence in the social security appeal system. One respondent went as far as to describe the delay in her appeal as a 'human rights issue' and implied that the lengthy timescale and intervention of the Secretary of State's submission was intimidatory. One respondent's appeal against an overpayment allegedly obtained fraudulently by herself and her husband, was finally allowed by the Commissioner after four years. However, her husband had died by this time and the respondent clearly felt the stress of the process had contributed to his death.

Delay was not always negative however. There were respondents in our sample appealing against overpayment decisions who felt that the delay worked in their favour, putting off the day when they would be liable to repay it.

Participation: oral and paper hearings

In Chapter 1 we set out Fuller's argument for placing participation at the heart of adjudicatory processes. His assertion that 'whatever heightens the significance of this participation lifts adjudication towards its optimum expression' suggests that there is not a single paradigm manifestation of participation, but that there may be a number of ways in which to 'heighten the significance of participation'. Mashaw presents an additional perspective when he describes participation as an important but elusive 'process value' that enhances the dignity and self-respect of individuals (Mashaw, 1983: 95). Sainsbury has argued that participation can also contribute to the quality of decision making by allowing an additional means of exploring the issues in a case (Sainsbury, 1992a).

In our study we were able to explore views about participation from the perspectives of Commissioners and appellants. Of particular interest have been opinions about the relative merits of dealing with Commissioner cases by oral or paper hearings, a controversial issue in relation to social security tribunals.[4] The views of the Commissioners, set out in detail in Chapter 3, were generally positive about oral hearings, and there was some surprise that so few oral hearings were requested.

The views of the appellants in our study were, perhaps surprisingly, more varied. A number of respondents did not appear to put a very high value on the possibility of having an oral hearing. For some people the option of *not* attending a hearing was welcome. Some thought that other factors in their case, for example, the presentation of a key piece of evidence, would be more likely to affect the outcome rather than merely the fact of having an oral or paper hearing. Others thought that the outcomes of their appeals would probably be the same irrespective of the mode of hearing, including some respondents whose paper hearings had resulted in failure. Some respondents however, did feel that an oral hearing would mean the case would become 'public knowledge' and therefore would reduce the possibility of awkward cases being 'put under the carpet'. Others had initially thought that an oral hearing would simply be easier than filling in a form or sending paperwork. One man, who was initially relieved at not having to attend, regretted his decision:

> I felt relieved that I didn't have to go but it turned out not to have done me any service at all.

A number of respondents simply took the advice of their representative without reflecting upon that advice, and others said they were not aware that an oral hearing was even an option. One respondent reported that in his representative's view a paper hearing was preferable in that all that was required was to identify a clear point of law in order to get the case remitted back to a tribunal where it would have a better chance of a good outcome for the respondent. Some respondents, including one who described herself as liable to panic attacks in the presence of strangers, thought that an oral presentation would be preferable on the basis that you could 'put yourself over better in person' and gives a more accurate account of your situation.

Those actually attending an oral hearing before the Commissioners (see Chapter 3) generally reported that they felt they had had a fair hearing and the Commissioner had taken time to make them feel at ease and listen to their story. Another respondent who had an oral hearing held in a Crown Court venue agreed that the atmosphere had been quite informal and the case had been fairly conducted and all parties given a fair chance to speak: 'It didn't make you feel like you were in court'.

The research evidence from the appellants in our study is intriguing. Given that so few oral hearings take place, it is perhaps surprising that there is no discernible,

4 See Sainsbury (2000) for a discussion of how the reforms to decision making and appeals in the Social Security Act 1998 radically reduced the number of oral hearings in tribunal cases.

let alone strong, groundswell of criticism about lack of this form of participation even among those whose appeal on the papers failed or who were unaware that an oral hearing was possible. It is not possible at this stage to draw conclusions about the balance between oral and paper hearings. It is clear that for many people the paper-based appeal process at the Commissioner level is at least acceptable (even if some would still have liked to have their say in person).

Dignity

In our discussion of participation above we referred to what Mashaw[5] calls 'process values' which he describes as 'elusive' partly because how people view them and how much weight and importance they ascribe to them seems to depend on a person's personal preferences. Nevertheless, he emphasises, as do other writers on decision making and appellate structures, that for most people it is important to be treated with some degree of respect or dignity.

In our discussions with appellants it was clear that being treated with consideration and respect was important to most people. There were many references to officials, at tribunal and Commissioner level, who had impressed appellants with their kindness and personal treatment. In contrast, there were examples where people had become angry or upset at how they were treated. Many of the really strong grievances expressed by the respondents were often aimed at particular instances, either in the local tribunal hearing itself, or a telephone call with an official or an unfortunate phrasing in a tribunal decision or a brusque examination by an examining doctor, where the appellant had felt humiliated. Some people particularly disliked having the feeling that they were not believed, and were in effect being branded 'liars'. One woman described her tribunal experience thus:

> Well … they obviously didn't believe me from the minute I walked in. They were so horrible; they were just so degrading. I've never experienced anything so degrading in my life, ever … it was their attitude, the way they treated my answers. Just completely dismissive.

Another man was critical of a Commissioner at an oral hearing:

> It's not the fact that they … turn you down, it's the fact that they tend to give the air of disbelief every time that they talk to you. They tend to talk to you as though you are a second class citizen and because you're not wearing brogues and sitting around in a high chair as they are … they tend to look down on you…

Both these examples are drawn from unsuccessful appellants, once again suggesting a possible outcome effect. However, that does not mean that they should be dismissed. It is not surprising that people's sense of self-respect is particularly

[5] Mashaw (1983: 88 *et seq*).

vulnerable when they have lost (a usually long) struggle to get what they see as their entitlements.

There are probably no new lessons here. To treat people with dignity and consideration would seem to be a non-negotiable, axiomatic aspect of delivering appeal services. It remains the responsibility of individuals and the social security authorities to ensure that the highest standards of courtesy and tact are maintained.

Transparency: understanding decisions and processes

Transparency is another process value described by Mashaw (1983: 90-1) and encompasses the openness and comprehensibility of processes and particularly of outcomes, which in the case of social security appeals refers to decisions of tribunals and Commissioners. In Chapter 6 we discuss the arguments for the Commissioners as legal decision makers producing reasoned decisions. In this section, we examine the research evidence for levels of understanding among the appellants in our sample. The findings were in some ways difficult to interpret.

Some research on tribunals has suggested that people who win their appeals are not very occupied with the legal reasons their appeal succeeded.[6] The mere fact of winning is enough for them to put the experience behind them. People who fail at their appeal tend to be more likely at least to read the decision. Of course this should not be unexpected; favourable decisions from tribunals will lead, for example, to benefits being awarded or reinstated, or overpayment requests being rescinded. These are tangible results affecting the material well-being of the appellant. Unfavourable decisions will of course have equally tangible, but unwelcome results. There is little incentive for the winners therefore to be concerned with reasons for their success.

To a certain extent, the findings from our sample of Commissioner appellants are comparable. However, there is a difference between them and tribunal winners in that 'success' is more often a referral back to a tribunal rather than a substituted decision. There is therefore perhaps more incentive to read favourable decisions as there might be information that could assist in the re-hearing.

However, among all our small sample, we found that levels of understanding appeared to be generally low. Some people were able to explain their understanding in fairly broad terms but without much elaboration. One man whose case was remitted to a tribunal said of the Commissioner's decision:

> He says in his opinion that the judgment of the tribunal falls down because it was wrong in law. And therefore a new tribunal should be appointed with all new people.

Appellants whose appeal failed seemed to understand that a decision was based on the law even if in the research interview they did not go into details:

---

[6] For example, Sainsbury (1992b).

> I'm no expert on the law ... all he's said is the law and the 'all work test' does not provide for me. And that's all. Which leaves me nowhere.

Another unsuccessful appellant commented:

> There was no other explanation whatsoever. I mean they said, or words to this effect, that the job had been done correctly and he had no need to change the circumstances.

These comments were made in the context of overall dissatisfaction with the decision of the Commissioner and, importantly, from appellants who had had no form of help or representation in taking their case.

In one rare case, an appellant in our sample was well-versed in the relevant law and an important recent court case and was able to discuss the detail of parts of the Commissioner's decision. It was more common, however, for people to report a lack of understanding about the decision itself or about the powers of the Commissioner. One unrepresented appellant explained:

> I don't understand the decision. All the way through this I've had DSS quoting sections so and so, so and so, the DSS law, so and so year, and all this. I've not even had access to look at what the law means. And all the way through it's been quoted in a very non-usable terminology...

The evidence from unsuccessful appellants is that reasoned decisions do not often persuade them that they have received a correct decision. Dissatisfaction with the substance of the decision and its possible financial effects appears to dominate thinking, summed up colourfully by one angry appellant: 'I understand that the law is an ass...'. In contrast, another appellant explained that she understood and accepted the Commissioner's decision that the tribunal had acted properly in turning down her original appeal.

From the research evidence that unrepresented appellants are more likely to have difficulty understanding their decision we can perhaps deduce that there is a further role for representatives here, which also emphasises the potential difficulties for 'do-it-yourself' appellants.

Representation and self-representation

One of the more controversial aspects of the Leggatt report is the suggestion that more people should be encouraged, and enabled, to pursue their own appeals. This has attracted some early criticism (Machin, 2001; Adler, 2002) and appears to run counter to much evidence in the field of social security in recent years that representation overall is both necessary and desirable if members of the public are to be able to exercise their appeal rights effectively (Genn and Genn, 1989; Baldwin *et al*, 1992; Adler and Gulland, 2003).

In this section, we present the experiences and views about representation from the Commissioners, appellants and others interviewed as part of our study.

The value of representation

One recurring comment from Commissioners was the way in which very good representation, either from the appellant's side or from the Department, was greatly appreciated by them. There was little substitute for a good, experienced representative who had a detailed knowledge about the 'background' to the law's development. Less useful were representatives who seemed to have other agendas, 'axes to grind', in their support of appeals. Overall, most of the Commissioners mentioned that the quality of representation was very variable.

What seemed to be valued most highly by Commissioners was technical competence in presenting legal argument. One Commissioner pointed out that it was not helpful when representatives could not grasp the difference between arguing a factual point and a point of law. The Commissioners looked for and appreciated focussed representation from welfare rights advisers:

> You do not want 22 grounds of appeal, 19 of which are hopeless, because by the time you get to number 19 you start to flag, you know, and it's more difficult to spot a good point in lots of bad points.

Appellants also valued what they perceived as representatives' knowledge of legal terminology and familiarity with procedures. As one appellant who was accompanied to an oral hearing of the Commissioners, commented:

> I must admit I felt easier, knowing that I had somebody who was representing me that knew everything, the job, what she was supposed to do.

For some people, the processes and language of legal argument were effectively beyond their grasp. One appellant who said he could not have pursued his claim without help from a local CAB explained his difficulty thus:

> I found the whole thing … unfair on people who, for example, hadn't gone to Citizens Advice like I did. I don't see how you could beat this system. It's set up in a language which, to me, isn't very much in layperson's terms. It's … gobbledygook to me.

Another appellant eloquently summarised a layperson's perspective on how hard it can be to negotiate a way through legal argument, which led her to conclude that 'I need representing':

> You say one thing but they interpret it another. If I was to say I went to a shop once a month, it's interpreted as you go shopping. Well, I don't call popping in and out of a shop shopping. I call shopping like when my daughters go down and look all round the stores.

Another appellant made a similar point about his representative being able to engage with procedures in an oral hearing before the Commissioner, which he felt he would not have been able to do. When asked if he felt representation was important he responded with some admiration for the representative from a local advice centre (to the extent of inventing an evocative new word):

> Absolutely, they wind you round their little finger otherwise. The quotations he was having to make … he was just literally solicitoring them. So without the advisor … and he was really good, certainly I'd have got lost you know.

The value of representation often went beyond what might be thought of as functional, i.e. bringing competence and expertise. People talked about the reassurance and confidence they felt when representatives 'knew what they were doing' in a setting which was, for many, daunting and alien. Some people in the sample also commented on the 'moral support' of representatives (and others such as family and friends) that might offset their feelings of insecurity, nervousness and even fear. It was an aspect of representation that was valued by many appellants, particularly those with mental health conditions such as depression and anxiety. One appellant expressed with approval the feeling that her representative was able 'to take the pressure off' her. Often it was the input from representatives that transformed dissatisfaction with a tribunal's decision into the motivation to pursue the case further.

An interesting comment made by a number of respondents relates to their experience of their tribunal hearing and has possible implications for the way tribunals are handled. There was strong criticism of tribunal chairs who prevented representatives (and friends and family) taking an active role in the tribunal hearing. Some people took representatives purposely to speak for them for a number of reasons, including to argue their case, to act as witness and to allay their feelings of stress and tension. There was an almost incredulous tone to their complaints that tribunal members only addressed questions to themselves – why did the tribunal think they took someone with them?

The value placed on representation by appellants and Commissioners alike is a reflection of the wider issue of an 'inequality of arms' between the parties to a Commissioner's case, about which Commissioners themselves, DSS staff, and appellants all had views. It is an issue that gains salience in the light of the Leggatt recommendations on self-representation.

Handling an 'inequality of arms': is representation necessary?

The jurisprudence of the European Court of Human Rights[7] has developed the principle of 'equality of arms' that in a legal contest, the resources of the state should be properly balanced with those available to an individual person. Many appellants in our study were acutely sensitive to the imbalance between themselves

[7] In article 6 of the ECHR (fair trial/access to courts).

and the social security authorities. Principally they were aware of their limited knowledge of the law of social security and sometimes the guidance available to social security decision makers. Some also saw their own lack of confidence and feelings of nervousness as aspects of this imbalance.

Good representation is clearly one way in which this inequality can be addressed, but for those without the best or with no representation, the Commissioners themselves could make a contribution. One Commissioner informed us that one of his interview questions for the post of Commissioner was how he should react if he had a 'silk' (Queen's Counsel) on one side and an uninformed claimant on the other. Part of his answer was to try and keep the claimant informed of what the argument meant as the hearing proceeded. 'I just found myself really acting as a teacher rather than a judge and saying you probably don't understand that do you?' Most of the Commissioners agreed that though their role was, unlike the court, partly an 'enabling' role to bring out the claimant's arguments, in difficult and complex cases claimants ought to be represented by independent experts. A member of the DSS solicitor's branch held similar views about how an inequality of arms could be addressed:

> ... to some extent the problem is ameliorated by the fact that a Commissioner might be regarded as having an inquisitorial jurisdiction and … the representative is supposed to be operating in that capacity... One can say that the significance of the problem is diminished by those factors.

Some of the Commissioners commented specifically on the Leggatt 'do-it-yourself' advocacy approach,[8] which one Commissioner thought might be appropriate to the first-tier appeal, a robust fact-finding jurisdiction, but not appropriate to the second-tier.

Most of the people in our study had used some form of advice or representation at some point in the course of their journey through the social security appeal hierarchy. However, there were a few who had pursued their appeal on their own (thereby putting into action Leggatt's notion of 'do-it-yourself'). These divided into two types. Firstly, there were those who would have liked some form of representation but were unable to obtain any for reasons of cost, location or lack of knowledge. The second group knowingly decided to go it alone without representation. Again we must emphasise here the small scale of our qualitative study but nevertheless it is noteworthy that this group comprised articulate, assertive and confident individuals usually with professional backgrounds. They were not daunted by the prospect of engaging with either tribunals or the Commissioners.

Among those who had had some form of representation there were some strong views that it was not only helpful but essential. Most expressed these in simple, direct terms: 'I couldn't have done it alone'; 'without a representative I honestly didn't think that you would have any chance'; 'I wouldn't have been able to

---

[8] See Adler (2002) for a critique of this aspect of the Leggatt recommendations.

represent myself properly'. One man emphasised the importance he attached to representation by suggesting that advice about representation should be available very early in the appeal process:

> I feel that somebody should have said to me 'to make sure you get a fair hearing go and get advice from the CAB' or whatever it is ... and then as I see it, my case could be presented from an understanding of the way that the tribunal works...

Although there was a lot of support for the provision of representation for appeals at AS tribunal and Commissioner level, two alternative views were also expressed that came from different perspectives. One man suggested that the need for representation would not be as great if the tribunal process was fairer, and another seemed to reflect a belief in the rationality of the social security system and a faith in legally qualified decision makers:

> If all the documentation was in place, properly, and the medical evidence is all there, what else would you need to be represented? Why should the law be pointed out to people who know the law?

The tide of opinion among most of the participants in this study was, however, in favour of the provision of representation. There was little evidence that a Leggatt-style world of mass self-representation would be welcomed by most people who had encountered social security tribunals and the Commissioners.

Sources of representation

We can deduce from the views and experiences of appellants and Commissioners above that what constitutes good representation could be provided by a range of diverse bodies and organisations. However, in our study, Commissioners particularly singled out the Child Poverty Action Group (CPAG) as an example of quality representation, although they also mentioned other welfare rights bodies and law centres, comparing then with 'the highest standard that you get in the superior courts'.

In contrast to the generally high quality of representation from organisations such as CPAG, the Commissioners overall were less impressed by the contribution of many solicitors representing appellants.

> What you get from solicitors is very variable. Some that have the expertise are as good as the very best and better than the best welfare rights outfits. Others are just absolutely awful and you shudder to think they might be taking money from [claimants]...

It is likely that the lack of public funding has not encouraged the legal profession to develop an interest in this field, but there was a feeling that there were few solicitors in private practice having any experience or expertise in social security law. Some Commissioners described many examples of the inadequacies of solicitor representatives, such as poor preparation, apparent ignorance of relevant law and procedural rules, and failure to attend hearings.

These overall views are to an extent reflected in the experiences of the appellants in our study. Some respondents had approached solicitors but had not been able to afford to retain them or obtain Legal Aid. Several others had recruited solicitors at the tribunal stage but had not been impressed by their efforts. The criticisms of solicitors, including failing to make a contribution during a tribunal hearing or being of little help in preparing a case for the Commissioners, however were also levelled at other types of representative, and appeared to be more about competence rather than about any particular professional base.

Some of the Commissioners agreed that in an important minority of cases the outcome might have been different had better representation occurred. However, they thought that the majority would probably have been decided the same way irrespective of representation. This is an interesting observation that is shared by some of our sample of unrepresented appellants whose appeal was turned down by the Commissioners. When asked whether they thought the decision of the Commissioners would have been different had they received some form of help or representation, the perhaps surprising answer was often 'no'. What brought about this perception was often an acceptance, based on the written or verbal explanation of a Commissioner, that the decision was correct, as explained in the section above.

Representing the Secretary of State

Representing the Secretary of State in Commissioner cases takes on one of two forms: 'written submissions' and attendance at 'oral hearings' (see Chapter 3). It was not surprising therefore that our sample of appellants had little to say on the role and performance of the Secretary of State's representative. Few had experience of encountering one, and at oral hearings did not engage directly with them. In contrast, Commissioners had more to say.

As regards written submissions, the Commissioners perceived that there had been a general lowering in the quality of representation from the Secretary of State. There had been particular concern with the 'supported appeals', that is an appeal by a claimant that is supported by the Secretary of State. 'One got the impression it was a lot easier at one stage for them to support an appeal than to oppose it and they got fed up with being, with opposing things and not getting anywhere.' Some of the Commissioners had the impression that the Department did not really know how to argue 'inadequate reasons' cases properly. However, one of the Commissioners felt that the quality of written submissions had improved more recently because the Commissioners were giving a more focussed steer than used to be the case.[9]

---

[9] The Chief Commissioner, Judge Machin QC had issued a *Practice Memorandum* shortly before our interview work: 'Written Observations on Appeals in Social Security and Tax Credit Cases in England and Wales', 9 March 2001, reproduced in Rowland and White (2004: para 2.304).

As regards the quality of representation at oral hearings, most Commissioners remarked that it had been variable, such that they were not confident to go to a hearing and expect each side to explain clearly the legal issues and explain the authorities, which left them to make the determination. The Commissioners were keenly aware that they would have to do some thorough preparation in advance of an oral hearing and might have to take an inquisitorial approach to fully air relevant arguments. Also that an adversarial model would therefore simply not work in many cases. And they could not rely on both sides appearing with decent representation.

One of the long-serving Commissioners told us that in the past there was clear specialisation in the Department's representation. 'You used to get somebody from the Department who did nothing but disablement benefit. They all specialised and they were extremely good'. Some were regarded very highly, in particular the senior in-house solicitor for the Department's unit in London that specialised in providing their services for Commissioner hearings. However, the Commissioners noted that the good advocates from this unit were often moved on elsewhere in the civil service. In general, the Commissioners viewed the approach of the solicitors from this specialised unit as more even-handed, objective and that they came near to performing an *amicus curiae* function.

However, some of the Commissioners sounded greater caution on the quality of the representation. Some reported that the Department's solicitors had often not been fully instructed. One stated he often met the response 'I don't have instructions on that'. The Commissioner's view was that all lawyers owed a duty to the *court* in addition to their clients. One Commissioner thought that the Department's solicitors were often adequate on the narrow technical points, but might be out of their depth where a broader overview of social security policy was required. Equally, some Commissioners reported that the Department's solicitors on occasion made submissions based on a Departmental policy that the Commissioner was unaware of. One Commissioner had concerns about instructions from 'the policy people on particular points that are, and are not, to be argued, which simply get in the way of the sensible resolution of the case.'

Several Commissioners mentioned the importance of having quality representation, in particular, in cases that might have a wider significance than just the individual appellant. In such cases, it was important to have representatives who were experienced enough to know what the likely effects would be of the Commissioner's decisions. One Commissioner said that in a Tribunal of Commissioners' hearing, for example, it was often important to be able to put questions to both sides' representatives, such as, 'if we do this here, what happens there?' Only the really experienced advocates would be able to respond.

There was a general satisfaction by the Scottish Commissioners with the quality of legal representation at oral hearings in the Edinburgh office. We were informed that the Lord Advocate appoints about three juniors to be standing counsel for a government department. Such an appointment is regarded as quite a prestigious marker in an advocate's career. Juniors tend to stay as counsel for the Department for some years so their representation is usually quite good quality but some will move if they take 'silk'. There were one or two advocates who might be called in to do the work as a one-off task if standing counsel were not available but 'it is a small, small class'. One of the Commissioners informed us that 'a number of members of the Inner House [of the Court of Session] when faced with a social security case definitely pale!'

In Northern Ireland too the Commissioners were generally satisfied with the representation given on behalf of the Department for Social Development. They thought the Departmental representatives generally took a sound objective view and 'our colleagues in GB [Great Britain] are impressed by the standard of submission which we get'.

> … there's no doubt talking to my English and Scottish colleagues they envy us, the quality of the work the representatives put in they really understand the *amicus curiae* role. They are trying to get the right answer and in my view a tribunal system can only work when one side is trying to get the right answer.

Summary and discussion – creating a 'Commissioners for users'

As we have already mentioned, it is sometimes difficult to disentangle people's views and opinions about how their case was handled by the Commissioners from their feelings about the result achieved. In talking to some claimants it was clear that there was a strong 'outcome effect' in that almost every aspect of making their appeal attracted negative comments and criticisms. This is not unexpected. When the lengthy period from receiving an initial decision on a claim, through the appeal tribunal and eventually to the Commissioners finally ends in failure, negative thoughts are bound to dominate. In contrast, appellants who receive a decision they are happy with are more likely to gloss over or forget aspects of the process they were not happy with. This does not argue for dismissing the views of either contented winners or unhappy losers. Some winners had constructive critical comments, and perhaps reassuringly some losers made positive comments. In most of our interviews the respondents were reflective about the various stages and the various actors in their appeal and were able to differentiate between process and outcome.

It is not the intention here of reaching a conclusion about the quality of Commissioner appeals experienced by appellants or their levels of satisfaction. Reducing complex experiences to headline figures is neither justifiable nor useful. Rather we offer a range of observations on the research data that might serve as lessons for the future and which we draw on in our concluding chapter later.

First we consider what we can learn from our analysis of why people appeal to the Commissioners. It is probably fair to conclude that few people who pursued their appeals to the Commissioners had a clear idea early on that their right to appeal was limited to 'points of law' only. The motivation that prompted them to lodge an appeal in the first instance was maintained after their tribunal appeal had been unsuccessful for different reasons, which we have argued reflect different underlying conceptions of social justice as defined by Miller (1976).

It is interesting to reflect here on how the Commissioners compare with Mashaw's models of administrative justice, which as we suggest in Chapter 1 embody Miller's justice claims of 'rights', 'need' and 'desert'. The task of the Commissioners is to hear appeals from tribunals on points of law only. This can be interpreted as a *partial* expression of the bureaucratic rationality model, in that it is concerned with the accurate application of law to the facts of a case, but not with the adjudication of those facts. The Commissioners also display elements of the moral judgment model, in that they provide an independent forum for resolving disputes. However, given the constricting nature of many social security rules, they do not fully reflect one of the defining characteristics of the moral judgment model, the resolution of disputes based on the deservingness of the parties involved.

What the Commissioners (and tribunals, and front-line decision makers) do not embody however to anything like the same extent as bureaucratic rationality and moral judgment is the professional treatment model of administrative justice. They do not operate within the remit of deciding what is best for the claimant in their particular circumstances, in the way that a doctor, legal representative or advice worker might. They are not, in short, concerned with issues of 'need'. When appellants' motivation is based on their need for a benefit, either to enable them to do something or to prevent some harm coming to them, it is not surprising that some will be disappointed by the experience of appealing to the Commissioners (and indeed a tribunal). In some ways we have seen that Commissioners feel impotent in such cases when they express sympathy with appellants that they cannot help alleviate sometimes serious financial difficulties.

It is probably not feasible, in thinking about the development of the Commissioners in the future, to raise the possibility of trying to incorporate more of the professional treatment or moral judgment models of administrative justice into their remit, structures or procedures. What is needed perhaps more realistically is more attention to educating and informing potential appellants about the limitations on the powers of the Commissioners. Taking this point further it does seem that knowledge about the Commissioners, as evidenced by appellants' responses to questions about their independence, is generally fairly low. There is clearly a role here for representatives in filling gaps in knowledge and managing expectations. However, it is hoped that advisers are not drawn again into contributing to a 'culture of delay' as the Select Committee (2000) concluded.

The research evidence from appellants and Commissioners amply demonstrates the importance of representatives in the process of appealing decisions of tribunals. For some appellants they are instrumental in lodging an appeal in the first instance and afterwards in maintaining momentum in the face of the obstacles of complexity, lengthy delays and falling morale. In some ways, whether an appeal is lodged is something of a lottery, depending on a combination of knowledge, determination and perseverance, and external help. Determination may be enough to carry some people forwards, but our study suggests that for others representation at this early stage is a key contributory factor to an eventual successful outcome.

There are a few appellants confident and competent to pursue Commissioner appeals on their own, but they are a rare breed. Appellants in our study who used representatives at either or both the tribunal and Commissioner stages were mainly positive about their value to them. There were criticisms, but these point to deficiencies in the quality of individual representatives and do not provide arguments that representation is not necessary.

From this analysis questions about the future of representation move away from considering whether there should be more 'do-it-yourself' advocacy in the Leggatt mode towards thinking about how more representation could be encouraged, in both volume and quality. If we accept that more representation would be a good thing then we must address ultimately the question of resources, and in particular the case for more public funding of representation, a subject we consider further in Chapter 7.

The experience of pursuing a Commissioner appeal, for many people, can be characterised as not much happening for long periods of time. For some, whose cases perhaps are being handled by a representative, who have little or no contact with the Commissioners' office, and whose case is decided on the papers, there is often little direct experience of anything between lodging an appeal and getting a decision. This typical scenario poses challenges for satisfying the 'process values' of time, participation, dignity and transparency. The case for expediting Commissioner cases is unarguable and the response of the Commissioners and the improvements achieved are summarised in Chapter 7. The evidence about participation presented above leads to less obvious lessons. That there was no strong call among our sample for more face-to-face involvement with Commissioners through oral hearings suggests that it is possible to satisfy the process value of participation in a largely paper-based system.

It is probably fair to say that there are fewer opportunities for offending people's sense of dignity or self-respect in the system for handling Commissioner appeals compared with either front-line decision making or tribunals where contact with officials, examining medical practitioners, or tribunal members is much more likely. In our study, the most trenchant criticisms of impersonal, disrespectful or rude behaviour were associated with decision-making prior to the Commissioner appeal, in particular tribunal members and medical examiners. Indeed, as we have seen, for some people in our study it was a grievance about process values in general, and dignity in particular, that was the prime motivation for lodging an appeal. Hence, the value of dignity is clearly highly salient and needs to be recognised in the practices and procedures of the Commissioners' office and in the individual treatment of appellants.

From the experiences of the appellants in our study, we can probably infer that, for many people, the process of pursuing a Commissioner appeal engenders a feeling of powerlessness and remoteness, which can leave people bewildered at best or, at worst, with little or no faith in the integrity of the social security system and appeal structures. The evidence that some people have a starkly contrasting experience of being treated well and treated fairly shows that negative experiences are not inevitable. The lessons from both positive and negative sets of experiences can help inform the future development of the role and organisation of the Commissioners, themes that are taken up in our concluding chapter.

Chapter 5

Making Law: Constructing Case Law

Introduction

In 1946, James Griffith, the Minister in charge of steering the national insurance and industrial injuries legislation through Parliament, promised that decisions of the National Insurance Commissioner and of the Industrial Injuries Commissioner would be fully reported in much the same way as those of the courts. That promise was given in the context of a debate on whether to have Commissioners, courts, or both, dealing with these questions (see Chapter 2). Clearly he was using 'reported' in the conventional sense of 'published' and therefore more readily 'available' to the public. 'Reported', in that sense, is important as an aspect of accountability (see Chapter 6). It is also crucial as part of any system in which reasoned judicial decisions state, clarify, interpret and develop the law: in short, for any system in which such decisions have both a 'law-ascertaining' and a 'law-creating' function. In the Commissioners' context, however, the formal status of 'reported' has a more specialist meaning. It identifies it as more 'authoritative' than 'unreported' (but publicly available) decisions of individual Commissioners.

This chapter deals further with those aspects of access to justice concerned with the availability of Commissioners' decisions, which 'make law', and with issues about the process whereby decisions are selected from a larger mass of decisions, whether of single Commissioners or Tribunals of Commissioners, to be accorded the hierarchically superior status of 'reported'. Neither availability nor that process of selection have been unproblematic. Both general availability and the formal publication of 'reported' decisions have attracted criticism from users, from the Commissioners and from the Select Committee (see Chapter 1 and below). Clearly, in the period covered by our research, significant improvements have been made on both these aspects.

The chapter provides context by first considering the common law doctrine of judicial precedent and the importance and nature of law reporting in a common law system. It then considers the formal rules concerning the hierarchy of authority, both as regards the binding nature of court decisions on Commissioners, and as between Commissioners' decisions, noting that the Commissioner system, while having a hierarchy of 'authority' in terms of its decisions has a less strict element of *stare decisis* than in the general court system. It next surveys developments in the system of availability and the formal reporting of decisions adopted by the Commissioners since 1948. The chapter goes on to note criticisms by the Select Committee and others and to explore the rationale and policy underlying developments since the publication of the Select Committee's criticisms. In so doing it provides a unique, descriptive and critical account of the Commissioners' practice consequent upon the interview work with the Commissioners and the authors' own observation over a period of two years.

We observed a group of Commissioners who met regularly to decide which cases should have the formal authoritative status of 'reported' and which other decisions should be drawn specifically to the attention of lawyers, representatives and policy-makers as either 'starred' decisions or, latterly, 'highlighted' decisions. We observed this group, formerly known as the 'Star Chamber' (Chapter 1), develop its thinking and practice. It is now known as the 'Editorial Board' of the Commissioners.

This chapter also considers improvements in the general availability of decisions in the Internet age. Finally, against a backdrop of reporting practices in some other tribunal jurisdictions, the chapter considers, in the light of our critical analysis of the process of 'reporting', 'highlighting' and 'availability', the wisdom and viability of the Leggatt (2001) proposals that the Commissioner model on these matters be deployed across the broader range of second-tier appellate tribunals in the new Tribunal Service envisaged in the White Paper (2004).

Law reporting and the doctrine of judicial precedent

The doctrine of judicial precedent is a defining feature of the common law tradition. It has relied historically upon two pillars of support: a clear hierarchy in the court system and an effective system of law reporting. Clearly, a significant role of the higher courts is to produce authoritative decisions about contentious questions of law. Lower courts are generally said to be 'bound' by decisions of the higher courts on questions of law, but not fact. Reference to decisions being 'binding' means that where a similar point is raised in an indistinguishable later case before an adjudicating authority, that adjudicating authority must accept the interpretation of the law contained in the decision. So a decision of the House of Lords explaining what a term in a particular Act or regulation means, lays down the definition of that term in much the same way as if the term had been defined in the Act or the regulation in question. A court or tribunal decision that has this 'binding' precedental quality may also help in deciding what the same term means when it is used in a different set of legislative material, provided that the term appears to have been used in a similar context. However, it will not be the whole of the court or tribunal decision that has this 'binding' quality. Formally, it is only the core reason(s) for the decision on the question of law at issue that will bind the lower adjudicating authority. Lawyers often refer to this as the *ratio decidendi* or simply the *ratio* of the decision. Remarks in a case that are not strictly necessary to ground the decision, or are incidental to it, are referred to as *obiter dicta*.

Of course, lawyers and others will often disagree about whether any particular authority has the binding quality that covers a particular issue. The party desiring that it does not may often deploy counsel to argue strenuously that the (unfavourable) authority can be 'distinguished', that is, considered inapplicable. Counsel may argue, for example, that the point relied upon by the other side from a case is only an *obiter* statement and therefore lacks this binding precedental status. The other party will deploy counsel to bring forward argument to show why the (favourable) authority is indistinguishable and should apply. Furthermore, as will be seen, an *obiter dictum* statement can often be deployed creatively. In the social security jurisdiction, for example, where such *obiter* comments in a case have been fully argued and made expressly for the purpose of giving guidance, it is suggested that they should normally be followed by Commissioners.[1]

Law reporting has had a rich historical development, dating from the thirteenth century in England and Wales (see Smith *et al*, 2002). Sometimes judges, for example, Chief Justice Coke, produced and published their own decisions, but commentators produced most of them privately. The proliferation of various series of law reports in the latter part of the nineteenth century prompted the foundation of the Incorporated Council of Law Reporting (ICLR) for England and Wales in 1867.[2] The selection of cases for reporting was and is undertaken by members of the legal profession.[3] Nathaniel Lindley QC (who later became a Law Lord) had considered the selection criteria for reporting at that time and these are still adhered to today in the Council's production of the *Law Reports*, the *Weekly Law Reports* and other series of reports (Magrath, 2001). Lindley was clear that 'cases which pass without discussion or consideration, and which are valueless as precedents' or 'which are substantially repetitions of what is reported already' should *not* be reported. He thought the following categories of case *should* be reported.

> The subjects reported should include all cases which introduce or appear to introduce a new principle or new rule; or which materially modify an existing principle or rule; or which settle or tend to settle a question on which the law is doubtful; or which for any other reason are peculiarly instructive.[4]

The almost infinite storage capacity of legal and other information by means of electronic media and the Internet has, arguably, increased the need for selectivity in reporting. Some commentators have drawn attention to the threats posed to the common law tradition by over-reporting:

> Today, the tendency is increasingly to ignore the traditional filters and adopt a blanket policy of storing all the cases heard in the High Court and above. Despite the best efforts of the courts to discourage this development, the distinction between reported and unreported cases is being eroded to the point where it may soon cease to be meaningful. This inevitable over-reporting creates such a strain on our precedent based jurisdiction that surely it cannot be in the public interest. (Widdison, 2001)

---

[1] See *R(IB) 4/04.*

[2] Since 1970 the Council has operated as a registered charity and consists of members nominated by each of the four Inns of Court and by the General Council of the Bar. The two Law Officers and the President of the Law Society are *ex officio* members.

[3] In March 2005 there were 33 ICLR reporters (30 barristers and three solicitors).

[4] Lindley (1885: 143). Lindley originally produced these four criteria in a paper on law reporting in 1863 (cited in Magrath, 2001).

ICLR still maintains selectivity in its choice of reported cases from the superior courts. From around 5,000 decisions capable of being binding precedents the Council selects some 350 annually for the *Weekly Law Reports*. Of these, around 150 will appear in one of the four divisions[5] of *The Law Reports*. Widdison (2001) argues that one way to tackle the problem would be to take the *selection* function away from the lawyer-reporters working for ICLR and have the judges themselves deciding whether a case had precedental status by certifying it as falling within one or more of Lindley's four categories and additionally an 'unclassified' category. According to this view, cases could then be reclassified (and declassified) subsequently by courts of superior status to the original certifying court. The House of Lords, as final court, could reclassify its own decisions.

But, in addition to the *Law Reports* published by ICLR, which are now regarded as the 'official' reports, there are also other general reports of the superior courts published privately,[6] and there has been an increasing number of specialist reports published by government departments[7] and others and brief reports appear in the 'quality' daily newspapers. Technological development in the available media for reporting has had a significant impact. Indeed, 'neutral citation'[8] was introduced in 2001 in respect of superior court judgments to conform with the growing international practice and,

> ... to facilitate the publication of judgments on the World Wide Web and their subsequent use by the increasing numbers of those who have access to the Web. The changes should also assist those who use and wish to search judgments stored on electronic databases.[9]

In his *Practice Direction (CA: Citation of Authorities)*[10] the Lord Chief Justice welcomed the wider availability of transcripts and reports but restricted the citation of legal authority in all civil courts. A judgment relating to an application for permission to appeal, an ex parte application, or a county court decision (except to show *quantum* in personal injury cases or where no higher authority was available), could no longer be cited unless it either showed or expressly stated that it established a new principle or extended the law. Advocates were required to justify the citation of such cases by stating the proposition of law demonstrated.

---

5 'Appeal Cases' (AC) includes Court of Appeal, House of Lords and Privy Council; Chancery Division (Ch); Queen's Bench Division (QBD); and Family Division (Fam).

6 For example, the 'All England Law Reports'.

7 For example, the Inland Revenue's *Reports of Tax Cases* and the Patent Office's *Reports of Patent, Design and Trade Mark Cases*.

8 A unique number is given by the official shorthand writers to approved judgments, for example: Court of Appeal (Civil Division) [2000] EWCA Civ 1, 2, 3, etc; High Court (Administrative Court) [2000] EWHC Admin 1, 2, 3 etc.

9 Lord Woolf CJ, *Practice Direction (Judgments: Form and Neutral Citation)*, [2001] 1 W.L.R. 194, (11 January 2001). See also *Practice Direction (HC: Neutral Citation)* [2002] 1 WLR 346.

10 CA (Civ Div) [2001] 2 All ER 510.

A public committee examined Law reporting in 1940 (Law Reporting Committee, 1940) but it did not recommend any fundamental change. The criticisms then were not too distant from today's; the cost of the various series of reports, the difficulty of accommodation, the repetition of cases in the competing series and the difficulty of tracing cases in the multiplicity of reports. Furthermore, it was pointed out that the Law Reports, whilst accurate, omitted cases that should be reported, while other reports were not always accurate, and far too many cases were reported.

Given the recent trends in the development of comprehensive electronic databases, it is salutary to recall Professor A. L. Goodhart's (minority) view in the 1940 Committee in favour of the publication of the reports of *all* judgments by an official shorthand writer as passed by the Judge. He argued that this would reduce inaccuracy, would allow for the deletion of unconsidered phrases, and would make it necessary to consult only one source. However, while the doctrine of precedent and law reporting has developed along its own distinctive path in relation to the superior *courts*, there has not been an exact parallel in the development of both the doctrine and reporting practice in relation to *tribunals*. This is perhaps unsurprising given the piecemeal development of tribunals. One of the persistent criticisms voiced by the Council on Tribunals and others has been the haphazard way in which Parliament has established new tribunals and the low priority given in the legislative process to tribunal creation. Nevertheless, the Commissioners have had a reporting process in place since their inception in 1948.

Formal rules about reporting Commissioners' decisions: availability and 'reported' status

This section sets out the formal rules about reporting in relation to the Commissioners and the citation and availability of Commissioners' decisions. Figure 5.1 below sets out the essence of the precedent system, although the detailed rules are more complex as the lengthy quote on the page following the diagram shows. The commentary that follows expounds the formal legal rules, concentrating particularly on the hierarchy of authority as between Commissioners' decisions. The point of law, or *ratio*, on which the particular decision turns binds Appeals Service (AS) tribunals and decision-makers below Commissioner-level to apply that rule in an 'indistinguishable' case. There is a complex of formal rules on which decisions in that sense 'bind' individual Commissioners. While courts are not, strictly speaking 'bound' by Commissioners' decisions, being of higher status in the legal hierarchy than Commissioners, nonetheless, as is made clear in Chapter 6, Commissioners' decisions, especially a consistent line of them, are accorded great weight and respect. However, as regards all levels of adjudication and decision-making, it is important to be able to identify, particularly where decisions of Commissioners differ on a key point of law, which decision is 'authoritative', whether for the purpose of ascertaining which one is 'binding' (on those at or below Commissioner level) and which should be accorded most weight (for those above Commissioner level).

Figure 5.1 Precedent: (GB) Social Security and Child Support Commissioners

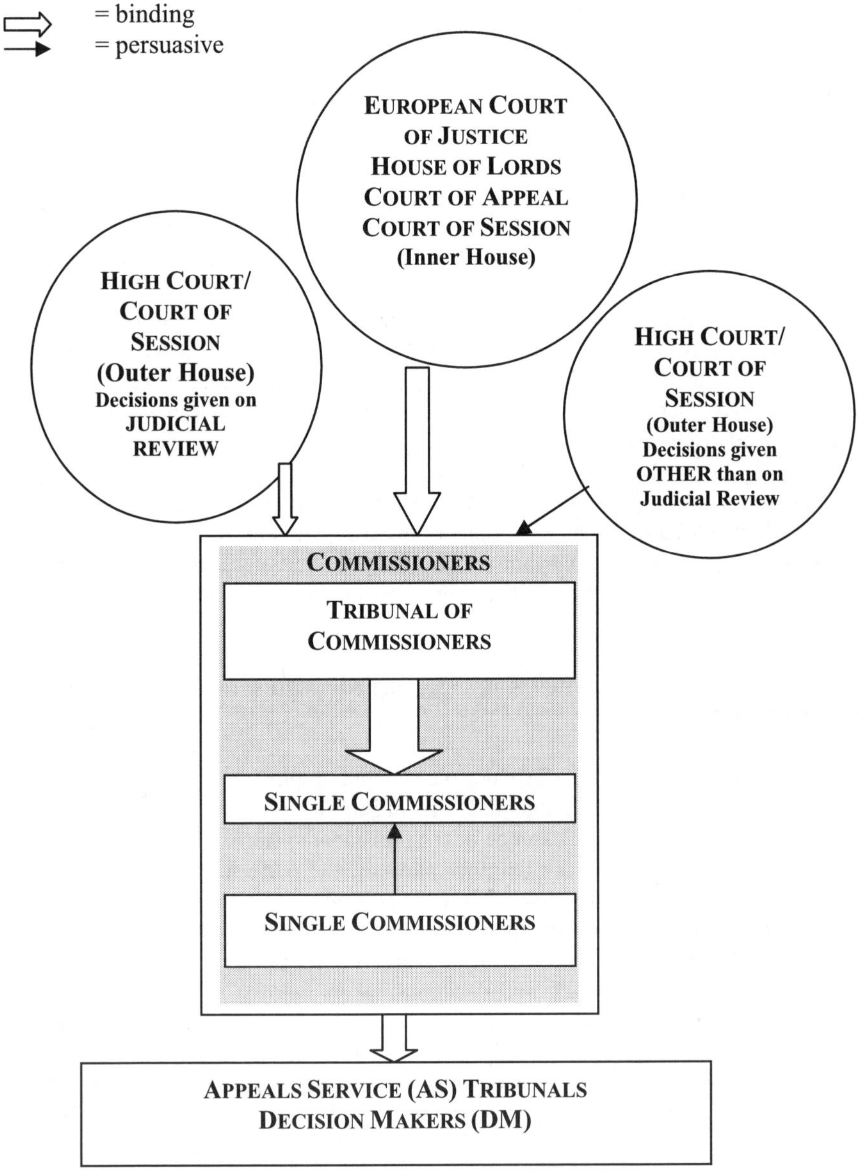

Without knowing the formal legal rules on these matters, it is impossible for those concerned as decision-maker, judge, adviser, or commentator, to be able to ascertain at any given time, just what is the law on a particular aspect of social security or child support. Decisions of the superior courts in Great Britain (GB) and Northern Ireland on questions of legal principle are almost invariably followed by decision-makers, inferior courts, tribunals and Commissioners, even when they are not strictly binding, because the relevant court was in a different part of the United Kingdom or exercised a parallel – but not superior – jurisdiction. The leading text, in commentary by Commissioner Rowland on section 14 of the Social Security Act 1998, expounds the position clearly.

> A Commissioner in England and Wales is bound by a decision of the High Court given on judicial review of a Commissioner's decision but otherwise is not strictly bound by a decision of the High Court, although he or she will rarely depart from a decision of a single High Court judge and will always follow a decision of a divisional court as a matter of comity (*R(IS) 15/99*, disagreeing with *R(S) 1/96*). A Tribunal of Commissioners may, on rare occasions, decline to follow a decision of a divisional court (*R(SB) 52/83*). Commissioners in England and Wales applying the law of England and Wales are bound by decisions of the Court of Appeal and will always, as a matter of comity and practicality, follow decisions of the Court of Session or the Court of Appeal in Northern Ireland that are not in conflict with decisions of the Court of Appeal, although they are not strictly bound by them (*Clarke v Frank Staddon Ltd* [2004] EWCA Civ 422, *R(SB) 1/90* and *R(IB)4/04*). Similarly, Commissioners in Scotland applying the law of Scotland are bound by decisions of the Court of Session and, subject to that, will always follow decisions of the Court of Appeal in England and Wales or the Court of Appeal in Northern Ireland. Should there ever be a conflict between decisions of the Court of Appeal and the Court of Session, Commissioners and tribunals in England and Wales would follow the Court of Appeal and Commissioners and tribunals in Scotland would follow the Court of Session and the Secretary of State's decision-makers would also have to make different decisions depending on which side of the border the cases arose. Presumably steps would be taken, by way of an appeal to the House of Lords or by legislation, to remove the conflict as rapidly as possible. All Commissioners are bound by decisions of the House of Lords. Strictly speaking, only the reasoning vital to the decision of a court is binding and other comments are not but, where those other comments are made after full argument and expressly for the purpose of giving guidance, they should be followed by Commissioners except in quite exceptional circumstances (*R(IB)4/04*). Similarly, a decision of the Court of Appeal refusing leave to appeal to that Court is not a full decision for these purposes and, while reasons given by the Court of Appeal for refusing leave are not to be disregarded lightly, their value as precedent must be assessed taking account of all relevant factors, in particular whether the Court heard substantial argument and whether the reasons were given fully (*CCS/2567/1998*, applying *Clark v University of Humberside and Lincolnshire* [2000] 1 W.L.R. 1988, and see also *R(IS) 15/96*). (Rowland and White 2004: 237)

The most recent *Practice Memorandum*, issued in December 2004 by the Chief Commissioner and his Procedure Committee, on *The Publication and Citation of Commissioners' Decisions*, like its predecessors, stipulates:

> Any decision of a Commissioner may be cited to the Commissioners in written submissions or at an oral hearing. However, reported decisions should be cited in preference to unreported decisions and, in general, unreported cases should be cited only if they decide some point of relevant principle. Citation of numerous unreported decisions that are merely illustrative of the application of a principle to similar facts is

unlikely to be of assistance. (*Practice Memorandum No 2*, para 7 – see Appendix 5 for full text)

Although the Chief Commissioner has thus directed that, so far as possible, reference should be made to reported decisions only, the legal position is that *all* decisions of Commissioners are binding on decision-makers and tribunals. A Tribunal of Commissioners (hereafter a 'Tribunal') gave the following ruling:

> Commissioners speak with equal authority. All their decisions whether unnumbered, numbered or reported [on the distinction between which see later] may be cited to Commissioners, local tribunals [now unified appeals tribunals] and insurance officers [now decision makers in the relevant department, agency or local authority]. Where they decide questions of legal principle they must be followed by insurance officers and local tribunals in cases involving the application of that principle, unless they can be distinguished. It should be borne in mind that similarity in underlying facts does not automatically give rise to similarity in the principle to be applied and questions of fact should not be elevated into questions of legal principle.
>
> If confronted with decisions which conflict, insurance officers and local tribunals must prefer the decision of a Tribunal of Commissioners (whether a unanimous or majority decision) to that of a single Commissioner. A reported decision, for the reasons given in paragraph 17(c) [the 'consensus test'], should prima facie be given more weight than an unreported decision. Subject to the foregoing insurance officers and local tribunals must choose between conflicting decisions and there is no obligation on them to prefer the earlier to the later or vice versa.
>
> In so far as the Commissioners are concerned, on questions of legal principle, a single Commissioner follows a decision of a Tribunal of Commissioners unless there are compelling reasons why he should not, as, for instance, a decision of superior Courts affecting the legal principles involved. A single Commissioner in the interests of comity and to secure certainty and avoid confusion on questions of legal principle normally follows the decisions of other single Commissioners (see Decisions R(G) 3/62 and R(I) 23/63). It is recognised however that a slavish adherence to this could lead to the perpetuation of error and he is not bound to do so.[11]

Where reported decisions differ on a point, then if one decision has been carefully considered in a later decision and not followed, that later decision should be applied.[12] Where there is a conflict, a reported decision should generally be preferred to an unreported decision, unless the unreported decision was the later decision and the Commissioner expressly decided not to follow the earlier reported decision.[13] A Tribunal will generally follow a decision of another such Tribunal but is not bound to do so, for example, if satisfied that the earlier decision is wrong.[14]

There are separate Commissioners in Northern Ireland considering legislation that is often indistinguishable from the legislation in Great Britain. Decisions of

---

[11] *R(I) 12/75(T)*, paras 19-21.

[12] *R(IS) 13/01*, applying *Colchester Estates (Cardiff) v Carlton Industries PLC* [1986] Ch 80.

[13] See the Northern Ireland decision, *R1/00(FC)*.

[14] *R(U) 4/88(T)*.

Northern Ireland Commissioners are not binding in Great Britain[15] but are of persuasive authority.

Citation and availability of commissioners' decisions

As the Tribunal noted in *R(I) 12/75(T)* cited at length above, there had, since 1948, been almost 60,000 decisions delivered by Commissioners. Of those, about 2,000 (3.3 per cent) had been accorded 'reported' status. The categories and citation of decisions had changed over the period, although the key distinction has always been between those accorded the most authoritative 'reported' status and those said to be 'unpublished' or 'unreported'.

'Reported' decisions These were printed by Her Majesty's Stationery Office (HMSO), made available for purchase by the public, and collected together in bound volumes. At the time of our interview work the bound volumes of reported Commissioners' decisions, published by HMSO, had not appeared since 1990.[16] There was a quarterly loose-leaf collection published by the Department of Social Security (DSS) from 1999/2000 but production of these was also delayed. The 'headnotes' for the loose-leaf collection were written by one of the legal officers and approved by Commissioners. A 'headnote', one of the classic advantages of law reporting, is intended to capture the *ratio* of a decision. The Stationery Office now publishes bound volumes, containing the decisions from both the GB and Northern Ireland jurisdiction. A 2003 volume has appeared and a 2004 volume will follow. Bound volumes will be produced annually. Reported decisions since 1990 are also now published in readily accessible format on the Department for Work and Pensions (DWP) website and on the Commissioner's website. Northern Ireland decisions can be found on the Department for Social Development website.

To preserve claimant confidentiality, unlike court decisions, Commissioners' decisions are not referred to by the name of the parties, but are anonymised with a mixture of numbers and letters. Reported decisions have always been accorded identifying letters according to the series (group of benefits) into which the decision fell: for example, 'U' for unemployment benefit, 'I' for industrial injuries benefits, 'IB' for incapacity benefit, 'DLA' for disability living allowance (for a full list, see Appendix 4). Before 1951, one referred to a reported decision simply

[15] *R(SB) 1/90(T)*.

[16] HMSO at the beginning of the 1990s published individual reported decisions on an *ad hoc* basis on behalf of the DSS to whom OSSCSC provided the material. This system petered out in the mid-1990s because OSSCSC's system for providing material broke down and HMSO's trading functions were privatised in 1996. It was agreed in 1999 that DSS would publish the decisions themselves to a quarterly timetable, backdated from 1991. The current volume was published first with the back volumes and further supplements of the current volume following. Delay in the volumes' appearance could occur when a case went through the courts. DSS did not want to pay for the bound volumes and eventually the Court Service agency, responsible for OSSCSC's administration, took responsibility for getting them published through the Stationery Office.

by its number and series initial, plus a suffix 'K' or 'KL'[17] (for example, the reported industrial injuries decision *CI 443/50 (KL)*), with the addition of 'S' or 'W' after the 'C' to indicate a Scottish or Welsh decision, respectively. Since 1951, the system has standardised using 'R' to indicate a 'reported' decision, so that *R(IB) 1/00* was the first decision on incapacity benefit to be accorded 'reported' status in 2000. Until 1999, the final digits identified the year the decision was *selected for reporting*. Since 2000, they have identified the year the decision was *published* by the Department. This change resulted from the fact that publication of decisions could be delayed if a case was in the courts for any length of time.

A Tribunal of Commissioners' decision is often denoted by adding 'T' in brackets after the reference, as in *R(I) 12/75(T)* referred to earlier. The referencing system in Great Britain does not specifically identify whether the decision is Scottish or English. For Northern Ireland decisions, since 1960 'R' has been the letter indicative of 'reported' status, but then follows number and year with series in brackets at the end, for example, *R1/00(IS)*. There are now some 40 or 50 decisions each year accorded reported status. This comprises around two per cent of the 2,260 Commissioners' appeals *disposed of* in 2004-05.

'Unreported' or 'unpublished' decisions These are available for inspection or purchase from the Commissioners' offices in London and Edinburgh. As noted in *R(I) 12/75(T)*, the system at that time distinguished between 'unnumbered' and 'numbered' decisions. The former comprised those in which well established principles of law had been applied to the facts as found or in which the sole issues had been of fact, and were decisions not thought by their authors to reflect any unusual circumstances or to contribute to the development of the law, except in some cases to reinforce accepted lines of authority. 'Numbered' decisions, in contrast, were those to which the Commissioner concerned had a number allocated with a prefix beginning with the letter 'C', so as to ensure a limited distribution of the decision as being of interest, either on its facts, or because it developed the application of some legal principle or because it was the first decision applying the provisions of some statute or regulation, or simply because the Commissioner for some reason wanted his decision to receive a wider distribution than that given to unnumbered decisions, which are identified by the number of the Commissioner's file (also prefixed 'C') at the foot of the decision. The practice developed that a decision thought by the Commissioner to warrant wider circulation would be 'starred' by him/her as worthy of such attention. From the end of 1998, the responsibility for 'starring' became that of the Chief Commissioner advised by a number of Commissioners in the 'Star Chamber' meetings, which was the subject of most of our observation work.

Many unreported decisions since 2000 are available on the Office for Social Security and Child Support Commissioners (OSSCSC) website, and some deemed by the Editorial Committee as being of special interest are 'highlighted' in the "What's New" section of the website only for a time. But 'highlighting', like the

[17] We understand these suffixes stood for 'key' and 'key law' respectively.

system of 'starring' it replaced, confers no added authoritative status on the decision.[18]

Each Commissioner's decision is given a file number in OSSCSC, which is a unique identification number. From 1997, cases have been registered consecutively by number within a calendar year, without a separate range of numbers for each benefit. Prior to 1995, there was a separate range of numbers for each benefit. So Commissioner's decision *CU 23/1992* is the 23rd case on unemployment benefit registered in 1992. The letters 'CU' indicate that the decision is that of a Commissioner (C) and that the benefit in question is unemployment benefit (U). Between 1995 and 1997, there had been a change of approach, reflecting computerisation. The system of numbering consecutively within benefits in a particular year ceased. The lettering system remained the same, but the number after the letters, as in *CU 7328/1995*, indicated that this was the 7328th case on any benefit registered since the beginning of 1995. Scottish decisions have an 'S' after the 'C' (for example, *CSI 26/98*) and, until the Welsh office of the Commissioners was closed, Welsh decisions could be identified as having a 'W' after the 'C'. From 2005, Welsh numbers are being reinstated, partly so that cases where the Welsh language should be offered can be easily identified.[19]

The Select Committee's inquiry and the availability of Commissioners' decisions

As stated in Chapter 1, the Select Committee (2000) reserved some of their strongest criticisms for this topic.[20] In our interview work with the Commissioners it was evident that the non-availability of the bound volumes of decisions for ten years was universally thought to have been an appalling state of affairs. The Select Committee viewed the problem, in combination with the lack of legal aid, as indicating a possible breach of the Human Rights Act 1998 that was to come into force in October 2000. There was common agreement that the availability of Commissioners' decisions was in a woeful state.

The Committee found that since 1991 when a DSS decision, seemingly motivated by purely commercial factors, ended the publication of bound volumes of Commissioners' decisions, there had been no readily available hard copy source of the information apart from the loose-leaf volumes compiled by and for the DSS, which were only available at Benefits Agency offices and a few voluntary organisations. The Select Committee was especially alarmed at this state of affairs because the lack of legal aid meant that many claimants who were already disadvantaged in many ways tried to represent themselves (Select Committee, 2000: para 34).

[18] To avoid perceptions that such decisions have a higher status, as wrongly happened with 'starring', a 'highlighted' decision is ephemeral and does not acquire an exrtra number.

[19] See also *Practice Memorandum No 3* 'Use of the Welsh Language in Commissioners' Cases', 31 December 2004, available on OSSCSC's website.

[20] See Select Committee (2000: paras 31-41).

The Committee's views on the state of electronic information was no less trenchant:

> Until very recently a claimant wanting information about the work of the Commissioners or needing to seek relevant decisions has been almost totally dependent on the website of one of the Commissioners who, presumably in his spare time and out of public-spiritedness, has created an unofficial website on the Internet [[21]] which gives a great deal of information and details of decisions which that Commissioner believes to be important. (Select Committee, 2000: para 35)[22]

The Committee noted that some progress had been achieved in the course of their inquiry. It also noted its expectation that LCD would make available necessary resources to ensure that the Commissioners and legal officers could identify decisions and prepare headnotes to fit in with the agreed cycle of publication by DSS. OSSCSC, in response to the Committee's recommendations, developed an effective website that carries reported and starred decisions.[23] The website currently carries (mostly in full text) reported decisions from 1991 to date, starred decisions from 1990 to 2001, a consolidated subject index[24] (1991-2000; 2001-03), a list of 'latest' decisions and a list of decisions 'highlighted' by the Editorial Board over the last 12 months. The 'unofficial' website was established in 1996 and, at the time of writing, was still available but now advises to go to the 'official' site for developments after the end of 2001. It also offered the following information:

> These pages will remain as they are for the time being in the hope that the improved arrangements on the official website at www.osscsc.org.uk will prove permanent.

One can now feel confident that they will.

Availability of decisions and according 'reported' status: the Commissioners' practice observed

The bulk of the interviews we carried out with the Commissioners occurred between October 2001 and November 2002. An account of the difficulties in finalising permission for the interview work and of the negotiation of the conditions under which the interviews were conducted is given in Chapter 1.

---

[21] Initiated by Commissioner Howell QC. See: http://www.hywels.clara.co.uk/commrs/index.htm

[22] See also the comments of Archy Kirkwood MP, the Chairman of the Select Committee, at Q.148, *Minutes of Evidence I*.

[23] See the official website of the Commissioners: http://www.osscsc.gov.uk/decisions/decisions.htm

[24] It should be noted that the production of quality 'indexing' and 'headnoting' will add value to the raw information contained in a decision. These are important benefits of the reporting function.

Stages in the process of according 'reported' status

At the time of our interviews, the 'reporting' procedure was carried out in four stages. Firstly, each Commissioner who had made a decision that he or she thought might warrant 'reported' status would autonomously put it forward for circulation by the 'Star Chamber'.[25] A process one Commissioner characterised as 'vanity publishing'. Secondly, the Star Chamber group would consider which of the circulated decisions should be 'starred' (see the section on 'unreported and unpublished decisions' above) and which 'starred' decisions should be considered for 'reporting', that is placed in a 'QR' (query reporting) file. Very occasionally, uncirculated decisions drawn to the group's attention by the Department, and less frequently, by welfare rights or a private individual, were also considered at the meetings.

Thirdly, the QR files would then be circulated (sequentially) to all the Commissioners and some of the legal officers in the London, Edinburgh and Belfast offices. The QR file asked recipients two questions: (a) did they agree with the law in the decision; and (b) should it be reported. The first question was intended to gather information in order to ascertain whether the majority of Commissioners agreed with the decision[26] (referred to here as the 'consensus test'). The second question elicited comments about the merits of having it accorded 'reported' status. Such comments often reflected differing views about the fundamental purpose behind the 'reporting' system. The process was also used to circulate a few unstarred decisions. One of the papers produced at a Star Chamber meeting stated, '[t]hese are usually decisions about which the Star Chamber have doubts but which are potentially important and on which the views of other Commissioners are sought before starring' (Star Chamber, 2001). We were also informed that the Department's Adjudication and Constitutional Issues Branch (ACIB) in Leeds commented on all starred decisions as regards their suitability for being accorded 'reported' status. The Star Chamber also considered their comments, along with the Commissioners and legal officers. The delays in the circulation procedure were condemned by many of the Commissioners. One remarked, 'it is humorously slow, by the time it's gone round us all, because of the mechanics of it, it very much sets back the actual having of reported decisions.' We were told that the circulation of the QR file was frequently delayed and could take as long as up to nine months. However, despite attempts to use electronic commentary this was abandoned. QR files are still circulated in the Edinburgh and Belfast offices, and in the London office they are placed in the library for Commissioners to complete. In practice, the circulation system now operates so that QR files are generally completed within the three months between meetings.

At the fourth and final stage the Star Chamber would consider the collective comments of Commissioners on the returned QR files. If the returns showed a clear

---

[25] It should be noted that the circulation system was also used to flag up decisions of interest irrespective of whether such decisions were to be 'starred' and/or reported.

[26] See *R(I) 12/75(T)*, para 17 and *Practice Memorandum No 2: The Publication and Citation of Commissioners' Decisions*, 31 December 2004, para 4. See Appendix 5 for full text.

majority in agreement with the decision, the consensus test would be satisfied, and the group would then consider whether to 'report'. In making that decision they would take account of the advisory opinions of the Commissioners on that question, which was also recorded on the QR file. Formally, until the *Practice Direction* issued in 2002,[27] the final decision rested with the Chief Commissioner, but our observation was that this had already become a collective decision of the group. The printing and production process could take at least another three months or so. In all, it was taking around 12 to 15 months for a decision to be signed off by a Commissioner until its appearance as a 'reported' decision. At the time of our interview work, OSSCSC was aiming to reduce this period to around six months.

The views of Commissioners on reporting practice

The Commissioners commented on a number of interlinked issues around the 'reporting system' that had been the subject of much discussion at the time of our interview work, not least because of the Select Committee's criticisms (see Chapter 1 and above). In addition, the then Chief Commissioner, Judge Machin QC, had undertaken a consultation exercise to seek views on the possible creation of an 'Editorial Board' to include persons from outside OSSCSC (Council on Tribunals, 2000: 23-4). Some Commissioners tried to separate out these issues more analytically. There was, on the one hand, the issue of the *publication* of decisions and their *availability* to the public. There were also questions about the *selection criteria* to be used in identifying cases for the higher 'reported' status. In addition, who should be responsible for applying those criteria? What did the Commissioners think about the consensus test? Alternatively, should the task of selection be taken away from the judicial body and given to an external one? If so, how should that body be constituted? These and other issues are considered in the following sections.

Publication of decisions As already stated, the bound volumes of reported Commissioners' decisions, published by HMSO, had not appeared since 1990. The Commissioners were acutely aware of these failures, and the role of the Select Committee in prompting action to remedy the situation. As one Commissioner, we interviewed, noted, 'following the Select Committee report, amazingly, they found that these [volumes] were all suddenly produced.' One of the Chief Commissioners commented:

> Oh, it was a scandal. Between 1992 and whenever it was there were no reported cases. I mean an absolute scandal! And then the idea that Commissioners could then think that they have authority in the field, when their decisions are not being reported. I mean, it completely undermined the point of having Commissioners.

---

27 *Chief Commissioner's Memorandum No. 1: The Publication and Citation of Commissioners' Decisions*, 25 March 2002, para 4.

In the words of one Commissioner, these past failures had been 'an absolutely disgraceful, dire, hopeless mess'. Although much of the responsibility for this state of affairs belonged to the Department's decision to cease publication on the basis it was 'uneconomic', the Commissioners' delays in operating their reporting system internally had undoubtedly contributed further to the problem. The Stationery Office now publishes bound volumes, containing the decisions from both the GB and Northern Ireland jurisdiction, annually.

Criteria for affording a decision 'reported' status As already seen, the formal criteria for giving some Commissioners' decisions an enhanced authoritative status are that the majority of Commissioners in Great Britain (or Northern Ireland, as the case may be) agree with the decision and in essence it decides a point of legal principle or otherwise provides useful guidance for decision-makers, tribunals and claimants. This is set out in a *Practice Memorandum* of 1987 by Chief Commissioner Bromley and has been substantially replicated in the *Practice Directions* of 2002 and 2004 by Chief Commissioners Harris and Hickinbottom respectively.

In our observations of the Star Chamber/Editorial Board meetings (see below) we discovered a very lively debate occurring about the application and reach of the selection criteria. This interest was also apparent in our separate interview work with the Commissioners (see Chapter 1 for 'methods'). Indeed, during the interviews the Commissioners often identified the different needs of different users of the reporting system. One Commissioner remarked, 'if we saw more of the concerns of the people in receipt of our decisions the selection would be better really.' Consistent with our findings in the observation of the Star Chamber meetings, the interviews with Commissioners also revealed a lack of clarity about the overall purpose and criteria for reporting. The Commissioners were aware of the different constituent users of their decisions and the different interests involved. One Commissioner reported that the vast majority of decisions cited to him/her were neither starred nor reported 'so clearly the decisions that the professions find helpful are neither of those and that should in my view raise questions.' Another Commissioner pointed to two key functions underlying the reporting system: a way of providing material for welfare advocacy, and a means to generate decisions that would have 'precedent' value.

The process of conferring 'reported' status: the consensus test or an external body? The 'Star Chamber' system had been initiated by Judge Machin QC towards the end of 1998. He had not been comfortable with the idea of the Chief Commissioner having the final decision and was keen on the idea of an Editorial Board containing at least some people external to OSSCSC; for example, representatives from both the Department and from welfare rights groups, perhaps chaired by an academic.

There were several Commissioners who expressed misgivings about the value of the 'consensus test' as a matter of principle. One Commissioner thought a case might need to be given 'reported' status because it was the *only* authority on that point without necessarily satisfying the consensus test. Others thought they might have been persuaded the consensus test was correct in principle but were concerned that its viability was threatened 'given the process by which the support of the majority of the Commissioners is ascertained' which had resulted in the problem of 'waiting for consensus to emerge'. However, other Commissioners remained supportive of the consensus test principle. 'I think the idea that the assent of the majority of the Commissioners, is quite a good idea, if reported decisions are going to continue to carry this slightly higher status.'

The alternative principle was for the Commissioners to give up their own control over the selection of cases and establish an external body to perform this function. While quite a few Commissioners favoured this solution, there was far less agreement as to the process and particular form it could take. One Commissioner strongly disagreed in principle with idea of taking selection outside of the Commissioners.

> If you had a body outside which was not a judicial body, not the superior court but a body outside which included people not being Commissioners saying, … 'Commissioner May is the precedent' or 'Commissioner Rowland is the precedent' then that strikes at the very root of the independence of the Commissioners. I mean, it means somebody else is actually determining the law not the Commissioners.

However, another Commissioner very much approved the external editorial board idea and thought the sooner this function was undertaken by a body, like the ICLR, with an independent, professional editor, the better. Another thought an editorial board, perhaps chaired by an academic and representatives of the publishers, could do the job. One Commissioner thought that OSSCSC was trying to do too many things, namely, devising systems to keep the Commissioners informed of possible conflicts and selecting decisions for 'reported' status. The two functions s/he thought could in fact be kept quite separate.

Restricting the volume of decisions The three Chief Commissioners interviewed and others expressed concerns about how the 'reporting' system could address inconsistencies between the decisions of different Commissioners. One of the Chief Commissioners preferred to have just 'reported' and 'unreported' decisions and nothing in between, but to be 'a little more relaxed about what gets reported [status]'. He favoured changing the system so that there were fewer, but clearer, 'reported' decisions in order to sharpen the consistency element.

> I mean we still have a lot of trouble, there's one Commissioner's decision saying one thing and another saying another, which can't be good for business!

There appeared to be several Commissioners who also shared the concern that there had been a sort of 'decision inflation' experienced, though one Commissioner thought the increase in 'starred' decisions was partly a result of the Commissioners working their way through the complexities of SSA 1998. One Commissioner warmed to the Court of Appeal's *Practice Direction*, noted earlier, that had had the effect of curtailing the prolific citation of authorities.[28] S/he expressed concern that those involved in social security adjudication might have a tendency to 'confuse information with knowledge'. On balance, however, s/he thought the 'starring' system was quite a good way of alerting Commissioners to significant points arising. In his/her view, it was essential to remain aware of what colleagues were doing. 'I don't mind *thought-out* division of opinion, but *unthought-out* division of opinion is disastrous, because it destroys coherence.' The discussions within OSSCSC about restricting the material that would be available to the public also had its detractors. One Commissioner had been very troubled by these discussions.

> The suggestion that there should be some means of suppressing publication of all but an approved selection of reports, particularly from Tribunals of Commissioners, over which the opposition is controlled by the Chief Commissioner. That's a bureaucrat's idea, that is. Departmental decision makers who say we want a mechanised system – and we want to know which ones we should follow and which ones we shouldn't.

The discipline of a system of 'precedent' The Commissioners' experience had clearly made them aware that some of their decisions might well create a legal 'precedent' that other Commissioners and AS tribunals would normally have to follow. They were also aware that sometimes their decisions might be utilised by others in unforeseen ways. Working in that environment imposed its own discipline on their decision writing; an infelicitous phrase could have damaging consequences. One Commissioner reported that on commencing the job a very helpful piece of advice was given by a more experienced Commissioner.[29] S/he advised, 'never let a kind of casual sentence go, because six months later the place will be littered!' One of the Commissioners took issue with the principle that Commissioners' decisions can establish 'precedents' at all. S/he thought the common law doctrine of *stare decisis* might not apply in a *statutory* jurisdiction where neither Commissioners nor AS tribunals were formally 'courts of record'. 'I doubt whether it strictly is "precedent" in the common law sense, because I don't think the common law bites.'[30]

Reporting and IT OSSCSC has only had a proper system for storing all decisions electronically since 2001. Several Commissioners referred to various implications for their reporting system that IT development posed. But there was less clarity on how these issues should actually be addressed. One Commissioner remarked, 'the whole theory of reporting decisions dates from a bygone age when making information available was a decision taken by a few for the benefit of the privileged.' The rapid developments in IT had, in his/her view, overridden the original aims of the reporting system. On the other hand, others pointed out that the electronic availability of a much larger quantity of decisions required greater

---

[28] *Practice Direction (CA: Citation of Authorities)* [2001] 2 All ER 510.

[29] On appointment, Commissioners and Deputy Commissioners are usually allocated a more experienced Commissioner to act as 'mentor'.

[30] But the 'stayed appeals procedure' in SSA 1998, s.26 (see Chapter 3, p 70) implies their precedental status.

attention to selecting decisions to be accorded the more authoritative 'reported' status. Nevertheless, the greater availability of cases and the private development of databases[31] were appreciated and appeared to meet the need for accessibility by all users.

Northern Ireland practice In Northern Ireland, decisions were referred to the Star Chamber committee for consideration. One of the Northern Ireland Commissioners regularly attended these meetings in London. If the group recommended starring, such decisions would be circulated to the GB Commissioners in the usual way and returned for further consideration. If the group did not disagree with the decision and the comments returned from the GB Commissioners indicated a clear majority, the Star Chamber would recommend to the Northern Ireland Chief Commissioner that the decision be reported in the Northern Ireland volumes. The Northern Ireland decisions appear on the Department for Social Development website,[32] which has a comprehensive electronic version of the bound volume containing decisions selected by successive Chief Commissioners in Northern Ireland during the period 1978 to 1999 for publication, and cases from 2000 to 2004 are also now available electronically from the Northern Ireland Digest of Cases.[33] Strictly speaking, GB decisions in Northern Ireland are only persuasive,[34] as it is a separate jurisdiction established under separate (though practically equivalent) legislation. One of the Northern Ireland Commissioners described GB decisions as 'strongly' persuasive but we were told it rarely posed any problems. The jurisdictions have been drawn further together by the regular presence of a Northern Ireland Commissioner at the meetings of GB Commissioners in London. One consequence of this has been to increase the numbers of Northern Ireland decisions that are circulated to the GB Commissioners and they are more routinely taken into account than in previous years.[35]

As there are only two Commissioners in Northern Ireland the consensus test is not very helpful[36] and this was given as one reason why they thought it was useful to put their decisions 'through the hoop' of the GB Commissioners. Both of the Northern Ireland Commissioners were pleased with the way Northern Ireland decisions had become easily available. One of the Commissioners said that a written decision would take about 10 to 14 days to get onto the website. They were also reported in some of the legal journals and Queens University in Belfast produced a monthly bulletin of Northern Ireland law and summaries of the Northern Ireland Commissioners' decisions.

[31] For example, Ferret Information Systems Ltd.

[32] http://www.dsdni.gov.uk/index/law_and_legislation.htm

[33] *Ibid.*

[34] See *R(SB) 1/90(T)*.

[35] Prior to the establishment of the Star Chamber, GB Commissioners were not even provided with reported Northern Ireland decisions.

[36] Strictly speaking, the majority rule contained in *R(I) 12/75(T)* has never directly applied in the Northern Ireland jurisdiction.

The Star Chamber/Editorial Board in action

An account of our methodology in respect of the observation of these meetings has been given in Chapter 1. The identity and powers of this small group of Commissioners and a legal officer changed over that period. Until March 2002, it was known colloquially by Commissioners as the 'Star Chamber',[37] and in formal terms, merely made recommendations to the Chief Commissioner who retained the final say. From March 2002 onwards the body became known as an 'Editorial Board', again usually chaired by the Chief Commissioner, but under the terms of the *Practice Direction* issued in 2002, the formal decision lay with the Board not the Chief Commissioner alone. This remains the position in the latest *Practice Memorandum* governing the publication and citation of decisions issued in 2004.[38] We observed six meetings of the Star Chamber[39] and two Editorial Board[40] meetings and were usually sent the agenda and minutes of the previous meeting in advance of each meeting.

Observations of Star Chamber/Editorial Board meetings The participants at the meeting usually included the Chief Commissioner (chair), a Scottish and Northern Ireland Commissioner, three senior London-based Commissioners and one of the legal officers. They came to the meetings in varying states of preparation. As with most committees, those who had obviously prepared well in advance of the meetings tended to influence its final deliberations more than other members of the committee.

Each participant had seen the Commissioners' responses to the QR file. The chair of the meeting would invariably try to ease out a consensus view on the two classes of decision it had to make: (i) whether to report decisions in the light of commentary; and (ii) whether to circulate starred decisions for commentary. In a small minority of cases, where no consensus emerged, a vote was taken by show of hands. It was understood that the Chief Commissioner had a casting vote. Where an appeal to the courts was pending, the case would not be selected for reporting until the appeal had been heard. The QR files of cases taken on appeal to the courts were considered by the Star Chamber without the views of Commissioners having being obtained. It was generally assumed that a case that had reached the appellate courts was correct without having to meet the Commissioners' consensus test. However, it did not always follow that it would be reported. One Court of Appeal decision was deliberately not reported on the basis that it contained no new

[37] See Chapter 1, pp 9-10, n 8.
[38] See Appendix 5 for full text.
[39] Variously, Trevor Buck and David Bonner: 9 January 2001; 21 March 2001; 9 May 2001; 21 June 2001; 20 September 2001; 19 November 2001 (minutes only); and, 14 January 2002.
[40] 12 March 2002 and 13 May 2002.

substantial point of law but was largely concerned with the credibility of evidence given at a local tribunal.[41]

A typical meeting lasted about two and half hours and considered around 20 cases for 'starring' and circulation and around ten for formal reporting. The Chief Commissioner would generally go around the table seeking the views of participants in turn. A different order was adopted for each case. Initial views expressed on the merits of cases for starring and reporting were frequently altered as the discussion progressed.

Passing the consensus test was always a necessary but not invariably a sufficient condition for gaining 'reported' status. We found no decision falling short of the consensus test obtaining it. However, the group did look to the degree of consensus numerically and to the quality of that consensus. For example, it would often take a view about the level of 'enthusiasm' or 'support' as evidenced by the various returned commentaries (some related *verbatim* to the meeting) to make the case for, or against, 'reporting'. Equally, even where there was agreement amongst Commissioners on the 'correctness' of the decision, the group would also take account of Commissioners' answers to the question about *whether* to accord 'reported' status. For example, there might be agreement with the correctness of the decision, but no desire to accord it that status because it was a straightforward application of a court decision or an accepted line of Commissioners' authority, or it concerned regulations since revoked or which were merely transitional. On the other hand, if transitional regulations were seen to be raising significant practical problems for decision makers or tribunals, that might equally be seen as a ground for giving it 'reported' status.

There were a range of factors informing the decision making of the group and the context of the decision at issue was determinative. In one meeting the group decided to 'report' two incapacity benefit cases. It took the view that these cases provided 'guidance' decisions in an area that was frequently visited but devoid of previous authority. One of the Commissioners had strong reservations, but the meeting nevertheless decided to 'report' each case. A family credit case was thought to be 'useful to have on the record' and was 'reported' despite some division in the commentary on the QR file. Another case gained 'reported' status despite some concern that parts of the decision were *obiter*. In one case there was clear agreement with the point of law, but no majority in favour of reporting it and the Department's view was that it should not be reported. However, the group decided to report it. Sometimes, cases arose where the point of law, though agreed, had been outdated by recent regulations. Generally, these were not 'reported', but in one such case, it was on the basis that the decision contained a 'proper point of law'.

Quite a few cases involved lengthy debate and fine decisions whether to 'report'. In one case there was much discussion about the Department's input, which had not favoured reporting. The case had concerned 'practice points' rather

---

[41] *De Silva v Social Security Commissioner* [2001] EWCA Civ 539. The Court held that the Commissioner's decision was wrong in law, but it would not in any event have made a difference to the outcome and the appeal was dismissed.

than substantive questions of law and some Commissioners took the view that the point in question probably affected more people than the Department would like to admit. The chair of the meeting called for a show of hands and it was decided to 'report' it. In another closely contested case, two members were for 'reporting', two against and two abstained. The Chief Commissioner used his casting vote in favour of giving it the more authoritative status of a 'reported' decision.

There were a number of reasons, other than simple failure of the consensus test, responsible for the group's decisions *not* to give 'reported' status. A 'similar fact' case was generally unlikely to be 'reported'. There were a few cases that, while they met the consensus test, were simply thought to be too lengthy. Sometimes, the comments returning from the QR files were impressionistic and uncommitted. In several cases, the consensus test was met on the point of law and supported by ACIB, but the QR file revealed no particular enthusiasm for reporting by the Commissioners. Where the Commissioners' responses were only 'lukewarm' it was not usually 'reported'. Where the cases involved arcane procedural points they were not 'reported'.

We observed a very lengthy discussion about one Tribunal of Commissioners decision, in which a member of the group was strongly *against* reporting it. S/he thought the decision was wrong in law and noted a number of reservations voiced in the Commissioners' commentaries on the case. S/he reminded the group that not all Tribunals of Commissioners cases were necessarily 'reported 'and thought that the majority of Commissioners had agreed to 'report' on the mistaken assumption that such cases must all be afforded such status. Another member of the group however, noted that the decision was 'pro-claimant' and uncontested by the Department, so therefore, on balance, ought to be reported. It seemed curious, at first sight, that such decisions were not *automatically* reported, given the criterion for selecting a case to be heard by a Tribunal of Commissioners was a 'question of law special difficulty' (SSA 1998, s.16(7)). However, it was clear that the group were looking at considerations other than pure legal principle to inform their determinations whether to give 'reported' status or not.

In several cases, though not invariably, it was decided not to confer such status on a single Commissioner's decision on the basis that the particular regulation in question had been later amended. In one case, the view was that the decision was an obvious application of *Cockburn*.[42] In another decision, though there was consensus that the decision was 'right', the group were concerned that there was insufficient analysis, or as one Commissioner put it, 'not enough meat'. 'Reported' status would not usually be conferred where the group could not easily identify some new issue of law and/or practice.

One matter that became quite clear was that the process of discussion, a) could result in one or more members changing their initial views, and, b) saw the deployment of a range of advocacy skills. Sometimes the atmosphere and form of particular discussions became quite 'adversarial', especially where one or more members seemed bent on burying a decision they thought wrong or not worth

---

[42] *Cockburn v Chief Adjudication Officer; Secretary of State for Social Security v Fairey; Secretary of State for Social Security v Halliday* [1997] 3 All ER 844 (HL).

reporting. There were some dominant personalities who emerged in sometimes quite vigorous discussions about individual cases, but no indication that others were necessarily restrained from making their own contribution.

Other tribunal jurisdictions

Immigration

Unlike the Commissioners whose quality of decision making has been generally well regarded (see Chapter 6), the Immigration Appellate Authorities (IAA) have been criticised for a history of poor quality and inconsistent decisions. As one means to rectify such inconsistency, the Leggatt report noted the development of 'a new system of selecting decisions by the IAT [Immigration Appeal Tribunal] that would normally be treated as binding on the whole IAA' (Leggatt, 2001: 152, para 20). In contrast to the open invitation in the social security jurisdiction[43] for the parties to submit decisions for consideration in the reporting process, a *Practice Direction* issued by the Chief Immigration Adjudicator[44] in 2003 expressly stated that the 'decision whether to report a case is that of the [Immigration Appeal] Tribunal and is not perceived to be an issue in which the parties to the appeal have an interest'. From May 2003, the Immigration Appeal Tribunal (IAT) ceased reporting and publishing *all* its determinations. Like the Commissioners it now also has a bifurcated system of 'reported' and 'unreported' cases. A selection of (anonymised) decisions are reported and made available to the public and the rest are sent to the parties involved but remain 'unreported' and unpublished. The *Practice Direction* attempts to exert much tighter control over the citation of unreported cases than has been seen in the social security jurisdiction. It states that no unreported determination of the IAT, or any determination of an Adjudicator, may be cited in proceedings, subject to a proviso that allows citation where the claimant or relative was a party to proceedings in the unreported case, or the Tribunal or Adjudicator gives permission on the basis of some detailed criteria.[45] However, 'starred' determinations of the IAT continue to have a special status. They are binding on all Adjudicators and the IAT unless inconsistent with any binding appellate court decisions. Part of the explanation for this more constrained control over citation was the increasing numbers of cases at both levels of the IAA. The criteria for the selection of reported decisions can be gleaned from the following note appended to (but not formally part of) the *Practice Direction*.

---

43 *Practice Memorandum No 2: The Publication And Citation Of Commissioners' Decisions*, para 5, issued by the Chief Commissioner on 31 December 2004.

44 Immigration Appeal Tribunal *Practice Direction No 10*. Office of the Chief Adjudicator, *Practice Direction CA3 of 2003*, 'Citation of Determinations', 16 May 2003.

45 Furthermore, '[p]ermission will be given only in exceptional cases, and even more rarely in relation to Adjudicator determinations.' *Ibid*, para 5.

> Determinations will not, however, be reported if in the Tribunal's view they contain no new principle of law or matter of real and generally-applicable guidance to parties, Adjudicators or the Tribunal, and no assessment of facts of such generality that others ought to have regard to it.[46]

The perceived problem in the immigration tribunal sector of 'selective citation' is that the process, it is claimed, is often misleading, as there is no proper effort to survey the whole of the tribunal output on a particular issue. The rationale for restricting the material available is ultimately that the tribunal will be able to maintain a more consistent level of decision-making. These arrangements are being kept under review.

VAT and Duties

The VAT and Duties Tribunals hear appeals by traders and organisations against decisions of the Commissioners of HM Customs and Excise relating to amounts of tax or duty to be paid, against penalties imposed upon them and against certain other decisions. There are permanent centres in London, Manchester and Edinburgh and the Tribunals' website states that it tries to arrange hearings within 50 miles of the appellant's place of residence.[47] An appeal against a decision of the VAT and Duties Tribunal is available to the Chancery Division of the High Court[48] or the equivalent in Scotland and Northern Ireland. There are currently 41 legally qualified chairmen of whom only a few are full-time; a President heads the Tribunal. The Tribunals dispose of around 3,500 cases per annum.[49] The practice of the VAT and Duties Tribunals is that the chairman will indicate whether in his or her view it should be reported. These recommendations are then considered by the (five) full-time salaried chairs and the President[50] makes the final decision.

> Only 35-40 cases a year are reported, these being cases which involve issues of principle and new questions of statutory interpretation. The objective is to have the leading Tribunal decisions readily available to chairmen and practitioners with a professionally produced head note.
>
> Among factors which enter into the selection are the quality of representation in the appeal, whether the decision raises new issues or merely applies existing principles,

---

46 See note 3 of Practice Direction No 10 cited at n 37 above.

47 http://www.financeandtaxtribunals.gov.uk/aboutus/vattrib.htm

48 A direct appeal route to the *Court of Appeal* was supported in Leggatt (2000: 201).

49 Leggatt (2001: 195) states it disposed of 3,207 cases in 2000. The Council on Tribunals (2004) tabulates an 'existing' caseload of 3,419 and 'received' caseload of 2,496 for 2003-04. Judicial Statistics (2003: 85) reports a total of 3,293 cases disposed of in 2003.

50 Currently Stephen Oliver QC, who also heads the other two tax tribunals; he is the Presiding Special Commissioner and the President of the Financial Services and Markets Tribunal.

whether there has been an appeal to the High Court, whether it is being cited in later cases and the amount of comment in the professional press.[51]

We were informed that Tribunal decisions are not binding on other Tribunals but are regarded as 'persuasive'. Chairmen will normally follow the principles established in earlier Tribunal decisions unless there is a clear reason why they should not do so.[52] Similarly to the Social Security Commissioners, the decisions of the VAT and Duties Tribunals are not infrequently followed in the courts.

Special Educational Needs

Where there is currently only one tribunal tier in a particular sector, for example the Special Educational Needs and Disability Tribunal (SENDIST) the usual arrangement is that their decisions will *not* set any binding precedent. Concern over the consistency of SENDIST's predecessor tribunal had been expressed in Leggatt but it was noted that summaries of decisions were prepared by the President 'to provide general guidance' (2001: 189). However, formally one SENDIST panel will not be bound by the decision of a previous case. In keeping with the picture of many tribunals, there is an appellate route to the superior courts and SENDIST panels are of course bound by High Court decisions. At the time of writing, SENDIST had a fairly good collection of decisions on their website and were aiming to publish all decisions. A lack of resources had resulted in a backlog of decisions that had not yet been made available. However, we were told that there was no selectivity in terms of publishing some but not others, and that no 'informal precedents' had arisen amongst tribunal panels.[53] Nevertheless, the Education Law Reports, a series subject to academic editorship, have carried a selection of SENDIST decisions for some years.

Evaluation of Commissioner reforms on 'reporting'

Clearly, the wider and speedier availability of Commissioners' decisions on their official, relatively 'user-friendly' and informative website has essentially addressed the Select Committee's criticisms on availability. Basically, if a Commissioner wishes his/her decision to appear there, it will, although the decision whether to include it in the 'highlighted' decisions part of the 'What's new' section – the modern equivalent of 'starring' – is one for the Editorial Board. Decision-making on the quite complex question of according a decision the more authoritative 'reported' status has, since Micklethwait, moved out of the hands of the Chief Commissioner to become the collective decision of the Commissioners' Editorial Board. A number of suggestions for reforming that process are considered below in

[51] Personal communication to the authors from the VAT and Duties Tribunals organisation, 1 April 2005.

[52] *Ibid.*

[53] Personal communication from SENDIST official, 18 March 2005.

the context of the broader question of the system for reporting decisions of all second-tier appellate tribunals in the post-Leggatt era, something for which the Commissioners' procedures and approach provided Leggatt's preferred 'model'.

Tribunal reform and reporting

Leggatt acknowledged the problem of achieving consistency of decision-making in the tribunal sector (2001: 71-4, paras 6.16-6.26). However, it suggested that *first-tier* appeal tribunals should retain their role to examine each case on the merits. Consequently, it stated that it would be inappropriate for them to generate decisions having precedental value. However, the position of the *second-tier* appellate tribunals (like the Commissioners and the IAT) was recognised as distinguishable. In these areas, the law had become ever more complex and voluminous providing a stronger rationale for the provision of guidance and precedent to develop the law in a more coherent fashion.

The Leggatt report noted four possible options for the future. The first option – that appellate tribunals' decisions should *not* be binding – was rejected, as it would 'weaken the prospects for clear and consistent decision-making across the System.' The second option – appellate tribunals should be constituted 'superior courts of record' – was jettisoned on the basis that contempt powers would be inappropriate to a jurisdiction which is axiomatically informal and reliant on full and frank disclosure of facts and would blur the desired distinction between the tribunal and court systems. A third option – express (and novel) statutory provisions making decisions of appellate tribunals binding on inferior tribunals – was not preferred though it was recognised as creating 'the closest analogies between the new Tribunals System and the way in which the appellate courts work.' It was thought this option 'would require users to be aware of all relevant decisions, to know what law would apply to their case'. The final (preferred) option – express (and novel) statutory provisions making only a *limited selection of decisions* of appellate tribunals binding – was thought to have two methods of implementation. One (unfavoured) method would be to select, before listing, cases identified as raising 'particularly important or general questions of principle' and have larger panels to decide such precedent-setting cases, as happens, for example, with a Tribunal of Commissioners case:

> The advantage of this is that it reduces the risk of arbitrary or improper selection of decisions which might take precedent in the direction favoured by a selecting authority. The disadvantage is that it would be difficult, perhaps impossible, to sift out effectively the best precedent-setting cases, except in the case of interpretations of very new legislation. Also, it would be resource-intensive both in selection of cases and in hearings, and could be used only rarely. (Leggatt 2001: 73, para 6.25)

However, the final recommendation was 'that the system of designating some cases as binding (or limiting the cases which can be cited in argument), as used by the Social Security Commissioners and the IAT [Immigration Appeals Tribunal], should be adopted throughout the appellate Division.' (Leggatt 2001: 222).

> The advantages of this are that the selectors will have before them all appealed decisions as the pool from which to select the most analytically powerful precedents. Some control over the number of precedents is also possible, to give users greater certainty. There is a theoretical disadvantage in that it allows the selectors a power that is potentially open to abuse. This could be removed by making the final adoption of precedents a collective decision. (Leggatt 2001: 73, para 6.26)

The Commissioners did not accept that Leggatt's description of their system was accurate.[54] The Leggatt report made three clear recommendations about 'precedent' (2001: 222). Firstly, the decisions of first-tier tribunals should *not* set binding precedents. Secondly, '[t]he system of designating binding cases (or limiting the cases which are permitted to be cited in argument) as used by the Social Security Commissioners and the IAT should be adopted throughout the appellate Division.' Thirdly, the President of each appellate tribunal should take responsibility for decisions about binding precedents, with the approval of the Tribunal Board.

However, the government's White Paper (2004) following the Leggatt review of tribunals has done little further to clarify the details of what future arrangements will be made in relation to selective reporting and precedent in the tribunal sector. In its White Paper the government has sensed how precipitous change in this area could be disruptive and has left the details of the problem to be worked out at a later date in the tribunal reform programme.

> To enable the appellate tier to properly fulfil its role in achieving consistency in the application of the law and so as to encourage the development of precedent across tribunals, a series of common principles with regard to precedent will be developed in partnership with the jurisdictional Presidents. This will promote a common view of how these issues should be tackled across jurisdictions, but leave scope for a flexible approach in particular jurisdictions. To prevent uncertainty, it will have to be clear whether and how existing precedents are affected by any change. (White Paper, 2004: para 7.20)

The Tribunal Service Programme (TSP) established in the DCA after Leggatt and the White Paper (2004) is, at the time of writing, considering the drafting of legislation planned to appear later in 2005. A Chief Executive for the new Executive Agency of the DCA, Peter Handcock, was been appointed in 2004.[55] An announcement was made in November 2004 that the Lord Chief Justice, with the agreement of the Lord President of the Court of Session and the Lord Chief Justice

---

[54] See Chapter 6, pp. 192, 195.

[55] A former adviser on criminal justice to Lord Falconer the Lord Chancellor.

of Northern Ireland, had appointed Sir Robert Carnwath[56] (a Lord Justice of Appeal from 2002) to act as the Senior President-designate.[57]

Prior to the appointment of Lord Justice Carnwath, Lord Justice Brooke had initially advised the tribunal reform programme in the DCA and the question of reporting practice was considered briefly. It quickly became apparent that different tribunals had slightly different approaches and that the new appellate tribunals would need to be flexible. It appears that at the time of writing the TSP 'definitely envisage the appellate tribunal having a precedent function and the collective view is that it should be used selectively to ensure only the cases which help clarify particular points are cited.'[58]

The reporting model for a reformed tribunal sector?

There are a number of interlinked issues to be considered. Firstly, is it right that Commissioners' decisions (a prime example of a 'second-tier' appellate tribunal in the new Tribunal Service) should have *any* binding value other than on the parties concerned? Secondly, assuming they should, is it right that some decisions are more binding than others? Thirdly, if one assumes a hierarchy in the status of decisions, how is the selection of cases best organised, by whom, and on what principles? Finally, assuming we have settled the previous questions coherently, what publication arrangements are best suited to make the decisions – 'reported' and 'unreported' – of an appellate tribunal generally available?

The main argument in favour of the principle of judicial precedent is that it provides an authoritative voice that clarifies the law. Judicial precedent also supports the coherence of a system required to accommodate decision-making from the initial decision of a departmental official through two tiers of tribunal scrutiny and possibly beyond to the courts. In the social security and other tribunal jurisdictions there are particular arguments to retain the principle based on the complexity of the law itself. Despite occasional initiatives aimed at simplifying the law,[59] it would seem that the likely future refinements of state support in the form of welfare benefits will continue to demand high levels of complexity and difficulty. The sheer numbers of discrete benefits and the volume of recipients has continued to increase over the past 50 years. The authoritative statement of law provided from a judicial source, separate from Executive control, remains a key feature of British constitutional arrangements and a method of enhancing public confidence in the integrity of the legal system as a whole.

---

[56] Lord Justice Carnwath had a mixed practice at the Bar comprising Parliamentary, Planning and Local Government, Revenue and Administrative Law. He was Attorney General to the Prince of Wales from 1988 to 1994. He has sat in the Chancery Division of the High Court since 1994 and was also a Judge in the Administrative Court. He has been Chairman of the Law Commission 1999-2002 during the period of the Leggatt review.

[57] Ministerial speech, Lord Falconer, 25 November 2004.

[58] Personal communication from TSP, 21 March 2005.

[59] The National Audit Office, in co-operation with RAND Europe, is currently working on a project entitled 'Managing the Complexity of Benefit Regulations'.

The system employed by the Commissioners that we have looked at in some depth provides a classic example of how 'reported' decisions are regarded as being more compelling and important than 'unreported' ones. There are other tribunal sectors that, in essence, also operate selectivity in reporting cases. The IAT is the prime example in the United Kingdom. The rationale for a hiearchy in their legal status is partly principled and partly practical. As a matter of principle, higher status is likely to be awarded to a decision that sets out a relevant general principle of law coherently and can be easily applied to similar cases with similar facts. Such similar cases will naturally 'follow' the precedental decision. From a practical viewpoint, the Commissioners and many of the other tribunal jurisdictions are producing an increasing quantity of decisions that, without some kind of management, threaten to stupefy users of the system and undermine any consistent development of the law. A smaller set of 'leading' cases, having the imprimatur of 'reported' status, provides a clearer signpost to the Commissioners, the AS tribunals, the relevant 'department' and to appellants and their representatives and other users of the tribunal system.

However, while it may be generally agreed that *some* type of selective process is necessary, there is less agreement as to the nature of the particular mechanism that can deliver it. Our observation of the Commissioners' selection process was conducted at a time when this issue was being actively considered and debated by the Commissioners and legal officers at OSSCSC. Underlying their concerns was the dilemma of who or what type of body ought to be responsible for the selection exercise? Some of the Commissioners did indeed favour the option of establishing a body independent of the Commissioners, though possibly having Commissioner representation. As it turned out, a policy decision was finally made to keep the selection process as an in-house activity. The only formal change was to recognise that the Editorial Board now had collective authority to select reported cases rather than the Chief Commissioner alone. There has also been a nod made towards wider user participation by making it clearer that the parties are invited to send their contributions forward to the Editorial Board for consideration.[60] A position that can be contrasted to the thinking in the immigration sector, as already pointed out, in that it is only the tribunal, and not the parties, that has an 'interest' in reporting.

It may be that the decision at OSSCSC to keep reporting decisions as an in-house activity was affected by the prospect of the oncoming tribunal reforms. Perhaps it was thought unwise to alter practice on this issue too radically until the outline and details of those reforms had been further advanced. The move to a collective rather than individual decision-making authority on selection of cases was also consistent with the indication given in Leggatt (2001: para 6.26). Ultimately, the question of what *type* of body controls the selection process ought to be rationally related to an agreed understanding of what *interests* are actually served by having precedental case law in this arena. One of the Commissioners colourfully identified some of the interests at stake.

---

[60] See the Commissioners' official website: http://www.osscsc.gov.uk/

> We have a vested interest in stopping maverick decisions and everyone from time to time gives maverick decisions. … we want decisions reported which basically have the assent of most commissioners. Welfare rights of course just want a decision that favours them, or they think favours them. And academics want decisions which provide handy examination questions or that can be turned into articles. Of course, the DSS wants to suppress decisions that it doesn't like.

Certainly the Commissioners and other tribunal appellate judges ought to have an interest in providing consistency in the development of the law and leadership on questions relating to the interpretation of the law. Our interview work confirmed that the Commissioners did indeed have such concerns. The Department's submission to the Select Committee (2000) also highlighted the need for a structured development of the case law. It pointed out that sound decision-making by the Secretary of State's staff depended upon clear guidance on the interpretation of statute law and noted that the '[c]larification of the law is one of the main reasons why the *Department* will seek leave to appeal a tribunal decision.'[61] The Department supported greater consistency in Commissioner decision-making and the greater use of the Tribunal of Commissioner arrangements.

Welfare rights organisations also have much to contribute. Their interest in identifying reported decisions is to provide suitable argument to advocate on behalf of claimants. Academics too have made their contribution and have an interest in observing and commenting upon the law's development. Their wider perspective on the law's development, for example, on the influences from European law, Human Rights legislation and developments in public administration and policy, can be a useful standpoint from which to view the 'bigger picture'. Academics have also made a sustained contribution in many tribunal jurisdictions to training activities, a critical role especially at the outset of developing a new ethos in a reformed Tribunal Service.

The way forward is probably to devise representational 'Decision Boards' in each jurisdiction to select cases for reported status. In many ways this may be a natural development following the establishment in some of the tribunal jurisdictions of 'user groups' (see Chapter 6). If that is to be the right direction, the process must be, and must be seen to be, one in which all participants have confidence. In the social security jurisdiction, for example, the Board could comprise of, say, three Commissioners, one legal officer, two Departmental officials, two welfare rights representatives and two academics. The Commissioners' consensus test should probably be retained though there is clearly room for experimentation in the process of how it is actioned. The availability of electronic commentary can surely eliminate the kinds of delays experienced in the past. It should be possible to devise a more sophisticated QR file, in particular an electronic equivalent, which could direct Commissioners' attention to a more detailed exposition of the relevant selection criteria. Without some such shared

[61] Select Committee (2000), *Memorandum submitted by Department of Social Security (APP 15)*, Minutes of Evidence, The Social Security Committee, Wednesday 16 February 2000, para 14.

approach, the use of criteria for awarding 'reported' status will remain opaque and variable.

Membership of the Board could rotate every, say, two years.[62] The chair could be elected by the Board and have a casting vote. The Commissioners themselves would continue to advance their own decisions for consideration but also more active steps could be taken to encourage the parties and others to do so. Such decisions would then be sent to OSSCSC for circulation and commentary. That information could be summarised and made available to Board members.

If our observations of the Commissioners' meetings are anything to go by, it is likely that the decisions of the Board would arise consensually in most cases, but, where necessary, could be taken to a vote and loyally supported. It is likely that a considered participation in this activity would deepen the analysis of all participants of the importance of the reporting function in achieving a structured and consistent development of the relevant law. It would not be difficult either for each individual jurisdictional Decision Board to develop and refine written selection criteria guidance under the supervision of the Senior President. Lindley's fourfold categorisation in 1863 (see above), which is to some extent reflected in current tribunal practice memoranda, is still not a bad starting point from which to devise such criteria. Lindley's fourth 'sweeping' category ('all cases which for any reason are peculiarly instructive') invites discussion of what is instructive about potentially key decisions in each individual jurisdiction.

Finally, in devising any such system as suggested above, the proposed 'Decision Board' ought to have the responsibility for ensuring that the whole process of identifying reporting status through to publication runs appropriately, and in particular that electronic files of reported cases are made available on the tribunal website as soon as practicable.

---

[62] The position formalised in 2001 was that GB Commissioners of the Editorial Board rotate every two years, except for the Chief Commissioner and Commissioner Mesher, who are permanent members of the Board.

Chapter 6

Accountability of the Commissioners

Introduction and overview

Decision-making by the Commissioners has obvious affinity with Mashaw's (1983) third model in his taxonomy of possible justice models, although it is not the only one applicable (see further, Chapter 7). That third model is the 'moral judgment' model, which stresses the resolution of conflicts by an independent decision-maker in a process that has 'fairness' as its legitimating value, and, it will be recalled from Chapter 1, this model also implies a *just process* of proof and decision. Of course, the judgments made by Commissioners are 'legal' not 'moral' ones; the 'fairness' of the resource distribution reflected by social security provision is hardly their particular responsibility as Commissioners. However, a responsibility does rest with the Commissioners to produce 'procedural fairness' in their appeal work, a consistent theme in the development of the tribunal ethos since the Franks Report (1957).

Moreover, under this model of justice independence of decision-making does not necessarily mean lack of accountability. Without detracting from the principle of judicial independence in terms of rendering their own decision in individual cases, individual Commissioners, and the Commissioners as an entity, are accountable in a number of ways to a variety of bodies and to the public they serve. A number of facets of accountability and supervision are examined in turn in this chapter:

- the requirement to give reasoned, published decisions open to critical scrutiny
- supervision and correction by the courts
- the role of the Lord Chancellor
- the role of the Council on Tribunals
- scrutiny by the House of Commons' Select Committee
- the Leggatt review of tribunals
- the expectations of the peer group – 'collegiality'
- the role of, and responsiveness to, 'user groups'
- the demands for statistical data

The chapter finishes with consideration of possible changes to the system of accountability in a reformed tribunal structure.

While such scrutiny and accountability has clearly identified flaws in the process by which the Commissioners seek to deliver justice to litigants and to make sense of complicated legislative provisions, a clear and consistent theme emerges in terms of the immense respect among these disparate scrutineers for the calibre of the Commissioners and the quality of their decisions in developing social security law. Of these scrutinising processes and institutions, two were very much 'one-off' interventions (the Select Committee and Leggatt), though they have had a pervasive influence on the Commissioners over the past five years. The remainder relate to the forms of ongoing accountability provided by the institutional structures surrounding the Commissioners. Only two of these deal directly with decisions in individual cases: reasoned published decisions; and the changing modes of supervision and correction by the courts.

The importance of reasoned, published decisions

In this Human Rights Act era, in which public authorities, including the Commissioners as a court or tribunal, are required to respect Convention rights,[1] it is apposite to begin with article 6(1) of the European Convention on Human Rights (ECHR):

> In the determination of his *civil rights and obligations* or of any criminal charge against him, everyone is entitled to a fair and public hearing within a reasonable time by an independent and impartial tribunal established by law. Judgment shall be pronounced publicly but the press and public may be excluded from all or part of the trial in the interest of morals, public order or national security in a democratic society, where the interests of juveniles or the protection of the private life of the parties so require, or to the extent strictly necessary in the opinion of the court in special circumstances where publicity would prejudice the interests of justice. (Emphasis supplied)

Social security benefits – whether insurance based or social assistance – and the payment of social security contributions fall within the concept 'civil rights and obligations' (see further, Rowland and White, 2004: paras 4.53-4.64). We have already seen in Chapter 4 that an 'inequality of arms' between the parties to a dispute is potentially a breach of the right to a fair hearing. Likewise, a duty to give a reasoned decision is inherent in the notion of a fair hearing or trial, although the level of reasoning need not be detailed.[2] There has never been a *general* duty to give reasons at common law, but, since 1991, the common law notion of 'fair hearing', while not imposing in all cases a duty to give reasons, has been developed so as to require reasons to be given where a decision has significant impact on important rights and freedoms (e.g. personal liberty, employment status) or legitimate expectations and is aberrant or such as to call for explanation.[3] From

[1] Human Rights Act 1998, s.6(1), (3).

[2] *De Moor v Belgium* (1994) 18 EHRR 372; Rowland and White (2004: 1146).

[3] *R v Civil Service Board, ex parte Cunningham* [1994] 1 All ER 310; *Doody v Secretary of State for the Home Department* [1993] 3 All ER 92; *R v Higher Education Funding Council, ex parte Institute of Dental Surgery* [1994] 1 All ER 651.

their inception in 1948, Commissioners were under no legal duty to give reasons, although generally reasons were given for their decisions (Micklethwait, 1976: 71), as the Minister in charge of the national insurance and industrial injuries legislation (Mr Griffiths) had made clear during its passage in 1945-46 (Chapter 2). Following the Franks Report (1957: paras. 98, 351) the Tribunals and Inquiries legislation, overseen by the Council on Tribunals, has from 1958 stipulated that generally tribunals listed in Schedule 1 of the legislation – and the Commissioners and a Tribunal of Commissioners are so listed – had to provide oral or written reasons if requested to do so, unless reasons were required by another statutory provision. Only since 1975 have the Commissioners been under a specific statutory requirement, to give reasons for decisions, other than in respect of leave to appeal (Micklethwait, 1976: *ibid*). From 1958 to 1975, the self-same duty to give reasons presumably flowed from the Tribunals and Inquiries legislation,[4] but was, in any event, established practice. The current specific requirement is set out in the relevant regulations.

> The decision of a Commissioner on an appeal or reference shall be in writing and signed by him and, unless it was a decision made with the consent of the parties or an order setting aside a tribunal's decision under section 14(7) of the Act, he shall include the reasons.[5]

These regulations impose no requirement to give reasons in decisions on leave to appeal and, until the advent of the Human Rights Act 1998, the Commissioners were, as regards such decisions, exempted by the Lord Chancellor, in consultation with the Council on Tribunals, from the duty to give reasons otherwise arising under the Tribunals and Inquiries legislation. That exemption was presumably grounded on the authorised heading that the subject matter, or the circumstances in which the decision was given, rendered the giving of reasons 'unnecessary or impracticable'.[6] The imminence of the entry into force of the Human Rights Act 1998 rightly saw the lifting of that exemption order as unlikely to be 'Convention compliant', and since October 2000 reasons have been given for refusing leave to appeal.

The giving of reasons is valuable in a number of respects. It lets the claimant know what has happened to his appeal. This is both an important protection of his human dignity (Resnick, 1977: 217) and an antithesis of arbitrariness (Rabin, 1976: 77-8). Being told why something has happened may also enhance participation in decision-making. The goal is, of course, to make things clear to the claimant, to the department, and to the relevant appeal tribunal, both the one which made the decision and the tribunal to which the case may be remitted for rehearing. Micklethwait (1976: 72-3) stressed the value of stating the outcome in the opening

---

[4] Tribunals and Inquiries Act 1958, s.12, Sched 1, paras. 11(b) and 11(c) and 18(d). Tribunals and Inquiries Act 1958, s.12, Sched 1, para 18(d).

[5] The Social Security Commissioners (Procedure) Regulations 1999, SI 1999/1495, (hereafter 'SI 1999/1495') reg 28(2).

[6] Tribunals and Inquiries Act 1992, s.10(7), Sched 1, paras 7 and 41.

paragraph of the decision; a practice inherited from his predecessors and something that now seems invariable. He saw it as 'helpful to the many claimants who cannot take in more than a paragraph or two' and doing so for all avoided an invidious task of deciding which claimants could absorb more and which could not. This concern for clarity for the claimant continues, but the task of achieving it has become the more difficult as social security law has become increasingly legalistic and complex. As we have seen in Chapter 4, even the small number of articulate, educated appellants who represented themselves at Commissioner level, had difficulty in doing so; hardly an encouragement for the Leggatt philosophy of 'do-it-yourself' tribunal representation. At several user group meetings, Chief Commissioner Machin floated the idea of following a model used by social security tribunals in the United States of expressing the outcome in simple language on a separate front sheet to the decision, although other Commissioners expressed concern that this was too prescriptive.

Requiring reasons to be given is valuable on instrumentalist and non-instrumentalist grounds (Committee of Justice, 1988: 69-70; Akehurst, 1970). As with all decision-makers, a key rationale of requiring the giving of reasons is that – especially where the decision can be subject to another level of scrutiny by a superior decision-maker – it concentrates the decision-maker's mind on the key issues and the evidence. This may result in detailed reasoning in appropriate cases. That can sometimes result in language that is impenetrable to users of the system. However, the process does ensure that relevant points that are put to the appellate body will have to be dealt with and not ignored. The healthy discipline this imposes should make for decisions that are better thought-out. A reasons requirement as an aspect of natural justice (the duty to act in a procedurally fair manner) may help enhance objectivity and impartiality by making for 'open justice', the principle embodied in the terms of article 6(1) ECHR, quoted earlier. As Bentham put it,

> Publicity is the very soul of justice. It is the keenest spur to exertion and the surest of all guards against improbity. It keeps the judge himself, while trying, under trial ...[7]

Most cases that go to the Commissioners are disposed of on paper. The attendance of members of the general public at oral hearings would be unusual, though as mentioned earlier,[8] one Commissioner referred with enthusiasm to the interest shown by the attendance of observers from local welfare rights organisations and local departmental staff. Nor can it be said that Commissioners' decisions are widely read or even noted in the Press. The fact that reasoned decisions of Commissioners are publicly available is the key manifestation of the open justice principle in this area. It is important to recall that the decisions not only dispose of the individual case. Crucially, they lay down rules of law, which may bind others lower in the hierarchy, and which can influence other

[7] Cited in *Scott v Scott* [1913] AC 417, at 447.
[8] See Chapter 3, p 90.

Commissioners and the courts. Hence the vital nature of systems of reporting and access to decisions considered in the previous chapter.

Commissioners decisions will not, however, only be keenly scrutinised by the claimant and his/her representative to understand what has happened and why, and to consider whether to take the matter further through review or appeal. They will also be scrutinised by academic and welfare rights' researchers in a variety of journals, and by the professionals in welfare rights' or other relevant agencies and in government departments. These may seek to use the decision in argument in other cases before other Commissioners and, where there is a division of view among Commissioners, perhaps before a Tribunal of Commissioners, the decision of which – hopefully resolving the conflict of view – is more authoritative than the decision of a single Commissioner. Someone, moreover, can challenge the decision, in the courts so long as s/he has (for want of a better term) a 'sufficient interest' in the case. This may be the claimant, or his/her trade union or the Secretary of State, the latter perhaps concerned to reverse the decision as an alternative to or supplementing the device of changing the statutory rules for the future. In some situations, a challenge to the rules might be mounted by a pressure group such as the Child Poverty Action Group (CPAG), either directly or by aiding the claimant to take the matter further. The modes of further challenge must now be considered.

Supervision and correction by the courts through review and appeal

As Chapter 2 has shown, those who framed the Commissioner model of second-tier appellate adjudication desired to keep matters out of the courts. No right of appeal from Commissioner to the courts was provided in the legislation coming into force in 1948, and, since rights of appeal are solely creatures of statute, no right of appeal existed. It was realised that the supervisory jurisdiction – the inherent, common law, jurisdiction of the High Court to review and correct the actions of inferior tribunals, a term which embraced the National Insurance and Industrial Injuries Commissioners – would not be excluded, despite provisions about the finality of Commissioners' decisions. But that supervisory jurisdiction was only anticipated as regards lack or 'excess' of jurisdiction. Those examining the matter could not foresee the revival of review for 'error on the face of the record' in and since *R. v Northumberland Compensation Appeal Tribunal, ex parte Shaw*.[9] The Commissioners were amenable to *certiorari* (a 'quashing order'), and, until statute provided a right of appeal on a point of law from the Commissioners to the Court of Appeal, judicial review was the only way to take a matter to the courts. Since that conferment in 1980 of a right of appeal, with leave of the Commissioner or the Court of Appeal, the role of judicial review in relation to the Commissioners has effectively been confined to challenging their refusal to grant leave to appeal an

[9] [1952] 1 KB 338.

appeal tribunal decision to Commissioner level. Throughout, the courts, whether on review or appeal, have accorded Commissioners and their decisions a very high degree of respect.

The approach of the courts on review prior to the conferment of appellate jurisdiction on the Court of Appeal

In 1957, the Court of Appeal in *R v Medical Appeal Tribunal, ex p Gilmore,*[10] had to consider whether, given a finality clause, the decision of a medical appeal tribunal or medical board was subject to *certiorari* and to judicial review. The court decided that those bodies – like the National Insurance and Industrial Injuries Commissioners – were amenable to judicial review by way of that remedy; the clause stating that 'any decision on a claim or question shall be final' meant only that the decisions specified could not be the subject of appeal or reference; they did not suffice to prohibit applications for *certiorari*, whether on the ground of error of law on the face of the record or excess or lack of jurisdiction.

A long line of authority showed that the remedy by *certiorari* could not be taken away except by clear and express words in an Act of Parliament. The court here considered an earlier decision *R v National Insurance Commissioner, ex parte Timmis,*[11] in which the matter of the effect of the finality clause on reviewability of Commissioners' decisions had been left open by the Divisional Court since it was clear in any event that on substantive grounds (no error of law) the orders of *certiorari* sought had to be refused. In *Gilmore*, Denning LJ (as he then was) stated:

> The word "final" is not enough. That only means "without appeal." It does not mean "without recourse to certiorari." It makes the decision final on the facts, but not final on the law. Notwithstanding that the decision is by a statute made "final," certiorari can still issue for excess of jurisdiction or for error of law on the face of the record.[12]

However, while the National Insurance and Industrial Injuries Commissioners were thus also in principle amenable to review, he stated categorically that,

> … they are so well versed in the law and deservedly held in such high regard that it will be rare that they fall into error such as to need correction.[13]

A recent *Westlaw* search indicated some 80 judicial review cases in respect of the Commissioners prior to the 1980 right of appeal. *Certiorari* for error of law was, of course, on occasion granted, and decisions made by the court have been influential in the development of social security law. But, even where, intervening to correct a majority decision of a Tribunal of Commissioners, Lord Parker CJ

10 [1957] 1 QB 574.
11 [1955] 1 QB 139.
12 [1957] 1 QB 574, at 583.
13 *Ibid*, at 585.

expressed hesitancy granting *certiorari.*[14] On the whole, however, the courts did not prove keen to exercise those powers of review, on occasion expressly deferring to the expertise of the Commissioners as a specialist jurisdiction. For example, in *Culverwells* case, the Court of Appeal had to consider the meaning of the phrase 'in the course of employment' as a condition of entitlement to industrial injuries benefit. Lord Denning MR opined that:

> This is one of those questions which, as it seems to me, the legislature has decided should not be brought up to the courts of law for decision, but should be entrusted to the specialised statutory authorities for determination. It may occasionally be of use, if there is a real error of law, for a case to be brought before this court, but not in such a case as this. No error of law is shown here.[15]

Davies LJ echoed those thoughts saying that he deprecated:

> ...the practice, and [hoped] it would not continue, of attempting to magnify or inflate questions of fact into questions of law and of trying to obtain decisions from the courts on matters which the legislature would appear to have thought suitable for decision by the various bodies and authorities set up under the Act of 1946.[16]

In *R v National Insurance Commissioner, ex p. Stratton*,[17] the Court of Appeal made clear that, where there was a consistent line of decisions in this field of national insurance by specialised tribunals over a large number of years, a court should be slow to depart from them.

The approach of the courts under appellate jurisdiction

The Social Security Act 1980 conferred a right of appeal on a point of law from the Commissioners to the Court of Appeal. This greater legitimacy for court intervention thus sanctioned by Parliament, enables courts to correct any error of law, no matter how technical or trivial; they are no longer limited by the narrowness of grounds of judicial review (Wikeley, Ogus and Barendt 2002: 206). Nevertheless both the House of Lords and Court of Appeal have continued to express great respect for the Commissioners and their expertise, without deferring to a degree that would render pointless the right of appeal conferred by Parliament. Indeed the period since 1990, 'has witnessed a number of landmark decisions in

[14] See *R v Industrial Injuries Commissioner, ex p. Ward* (DC) [1965] 2 QB 112, at 121.
[15] *R v Industrial Injuries Commissioner Ex p. Amalgamated Engineering Union (No 2)* (CA) [1966] 2 QB 31, at pp 48-49.
[16] *Ibid*, at 50.
[17] [1979] QB 361. See Lord Denning MR at p 369 and Bridge LJ (as he then was) at p 374.

test cases by both the Court of Appeal and the House of Lords',[18] although opinions will inevitably differ as to whether judicial intervention has always been helpful.

In *Presho v Department of Health and Social Security (Insurance Officer)*[19] a trades dispute disqualification case coming to the courts via the new appellate route, Lord Brandon endorsed those earlier expressions of opinion on Commissioners' decisions, and regarded them as applicable to that case, noting that the approach he adopted to the substantive question accorded with that which had been adopted since 1926 by a substantial number of Commissioners (or their earlier equivalents) after the expression concerned – 'directly interested in the trade dispute' – had first appeared in this class of legislation in 1911.

Chief Adjudication Office v Brunt[20] was a case on the notorious 'full extent normal' rule preclusive of entitlement to unemployment benefit (see Buck, 1987; 1989). For the claimant who has a chequered history of full employment, unemployment and part-time employment, that rule, set out in regulations, bristled with ambiguity and doubt. The commissioners invented the rough and ready *prima facie* rule that after a claimant had worked part-time for a year, he became 'a person who does not ordinarily work on every day in a week' and is debarred from claiming benefit because he is 'employed to the full extent normal in his case.' The obscurity of the statutory language compelled the Commissioners to invent, by a process of judicial legislation, tests which were not to be found in the words of the regulation and were therefore hedged around with qualifications, some introduced by the Commissioners themselves and others by the Court of Appeal. The House of Lords dismissed the appeal showing 'unwillingness to probe too deeply into the subtleties of social security law' (Wikeley, Ogus and Barendt 2002: 206). In the Court of Appeal, a departure from the accepted way of approaching the regulation embodying the rule was rejected, in part because, applying the statements in *Presho* and *Stratton* noted above:

> …this court would have to set aside a construction of the regulation which has been followed and acted upon for a long time in a large number of decisions by Commissioners, and by Adjudication Officers ['departmental' decision-maker] in reliance upon those decisions; and that is a course which we should not take save in exceptional circumstances and for compelling reasons.[21]

That same approach to a consistent line of Commissioners' decisions on a point had been taken by Slade LJ in the earlier *Riley* case[22] on the 'full extent normal' rule. In *Cartlidge v Chief Adjudication Officer*,[23] the question for the Court of Appeal was whether a Tribunal of Commissioners had erred in law in deciding that

---

[18] Wikeley, Ogus and Barendt (2002: 206), citing *Mallinson v Secretary of State for Social Security* [1994] 1 W.L.R. 630 (HL).

[19] [1984] AC 310.

[20] [1988] AC 711.

[21] *Ibid*, at 720, per Ralph Gibson LJ.

[22] *Riley v Chief Adjudication Officer (Note)* [1988] A.C. 746.

[23] [1986] QB 360.

Mr Cartlidge was disqualified from receiving unemployment benefit because he had lost his employment by reason of a stoppage of work due to a trade dispute at his place of employment. It was argued for him that disqualification ceased where, although originally caught by the preclusion, his original employment was recovered and then terminated for reasons unconnected with the stoppage or trade dispute. Although Ralph Gibson LJ concluded, with regret, that this argument had to be rejected, reject it he did because the construction of the Act applied by the Tribunal of Commissioners which produced that result was in accordance with the ordinary and natural meaning of the words and with a line of decisions as to construction of those words which it would not be right for the court to overturn.

Someone refused leave by a Commissioner to appeal to the Court of Appeal can apply directly to that court for leave to appeal. In *Cooke v Secretary of State for Social Security*,[24] Hale LJ (as she then was) advocated for the court a cautious approach to such applications, encapsulating once again and very graphically the view that the Commissioners are generally the best judges on social security law. Deputy Commissioner Hereward had dismissed Mrs Cooke's appeal from a disability appeal tribunal and Commissioner Rowland had refused her leave to appeal. Hale LJ, on 4 December 2001:

> ...adjourned the application for an oral hearing with both parties to attend, and the appeal to follow if permission was granted. Among my reasons for doing so was that the question arises as to whether an application such as this, from a second and highly expert judicial tier of appeal, should be regarded as akin to a second tier appeal from the High Court or a county court and thus, although not technically within section 55(1) of the Access to Justice Act 1999, subject to a similar threshold test.

The grant, on 25 April 2001, of permission to appeal was made, in part, so that the Court of Appeal could consider that question of their approach to applications for leave to appeal Commissioners' decisions. The court decided eventually that there was no error of law in the decision appealed against, but the comments on this wider question of approach are illuminating. Section 55(1) of the Access to Justice Act 1999 stipulates that:

> ...where an appeal is made to a county court or the High Court in relation to any matter, and on hearing the appeal the court makes a decision in relation to that matter, no appeal may be made to the Court of Appeal from that decision unless the Court of Appeal considers that-
>
> (a) the appeal would raise an important point of principle or practice, or
> (b) there is some other compelling reason for the Court of Appeal to hear it.

That envisaged something more than the standard test for permission to appeal, that the appeal had some prospect of success. The section clearly could not apply in this case. But Hale LJ, giving the judgment of the court, considered that many of the reasons underlying the provision applied equally, if not indeed more strongly, in

[24] [2002] 3 AER 279, reported as *R(DLA) 6/01*. See also Chapter 3, p 94.

the context of the relationship between the Court of Appeal and the Commissioners:

> Firstly, this is a highly specialised area of law which many lawyers, indeed, I would suspect most lawyers, rarely encounter in practice. Secondly, there is an independent two-tier appellate structure. [Indeed, under the system as it was when this case was decided the adjudication officer had a degree of independence from the Secretary of State]. After the initial decision there is a fresh hearing before a specialist tribunal which is chaired by a lawyer and has an appropriate balance of experience and expertise amongst its members. After that there is an appeal on a point of law to a highly expert and specialised legally qualified body, the social security Commissioners. Thirdly, it is essential that that tribunal structure is sufficiently expert to be able to take an independent and robust view, particularly in cases where the government agency has gone wrong. It must be in a position to see through what the relevant sponsoring department is saying when it is arguing the case.
>
> It is also important that such appeal structures have a link to the ordinary court system, to maintain both their independence of government and the sponsoring department and their fidelity to the relevant general principles of law. But the ordinary courts should approach such cases with an appropriate degree of caution. *It is quite probable that on a technical issue of understanding and applying the complex legislation the social security Commissioner will have got it right.* The Commissioners will know how that particular issue fits into the broader picture of social security principles as a whole. They will be less likely to introduce distortion into those principles. They may be better placed, where it is appropriate, to apply those principles in a purposive construction of the legislation in question. They will also know the realities of tribunal life. All of this should be taken into account by an appellate court when considering whether an appeal will have a real prospect of success.
>
> In my view the Court of Appeal should take an appropriately modest view, especially when it has heard only one side of the argument, of how likely it is that the Commissioner will have got it wrong. *Obviously, however, that will differ according to the nature of the problem presented and the arguments in issue. In my view this case is a good example.* The principle which was advanced on paper in support of the appeal is common ground between the parties. On examination of all the relevant material, which is now before us and was not before, it becomes plain that the tribunal and the Commissioner did not err in law. One reason for that was the sensible and considerate approach of the Secretary of State and the adjudication officer in advancing the case for review. It would not be in the overall interests of this claimant or any other for this court to take a line which encouraged the Secretary of State to argue the alternative ground for review when there was no need to do so. Hence, I agree with Mr. Forsdick for the Secretary of State that, although section 55 does not apply, a robust attitude to the prospect of success criterion ought to be adopted in these cases. (Emphasis added)

This approach has been followed in a good number of cases both in England and Wales and in Scotland. But, as Hale LJ indicated in the passages given emphasis above, the degree of respect and deference is also dependent on the subject matter. So, in *Gillies*,[25] the Court of Session, allowing the Secretary of

[25] *Secretary of State for Work and Pensions v Gillies*, 2004 SLT 14.

State's appeal against a finding by a Tribunal of Commissioners of disqualification of a medical member of a tribunal under the apparent bias rule, stated:

> It was urged upon us that, in view of their accumulated experience of the working of tribunals, their members and the evidence provided to them, we should be slow to interfere with a decision of the Tribunal of Commissioners. We would see the force of that submission in a case which was concerned intimately with the Social security legislation and the practice and procedure of tribunals. However, the present case presents a specific example of a general point relating to public confidence in the process of adjudication. In these circumstances, while we do not hesitate to accord respect for the view of the Tribunal of Commissioners, we do not consider that, because of their familiarity with the Social Security scene, we should on that account defer to their view of the matter at issue. Having considered the factual circumstances we are of the view that the fact that Dr. A. carried out examinations and provided reports for the Benefits Agency as an EMP would not be sufficient to raise in the mind of the reasonable and well-informed observer an apprehension as to her impartiality as a member of a disability appeal tribunal. The mere fact that the tribunal would require to consider and assess reports by other doctors who acted as EMPs would not be such as to raise such an apprehension.

The incidence of appeals to the courts

The fact that cases might be taken further appears, from our interview work, to have an impact on how Commissioners write up their decisions, and is a factor, among others, contributing to careful and quality decision-making.

It is generally thought that for most claimants, Commissioner-level is in practice the end of the road. The judicial statistics published by the DCA in respect of the Court of Appeal support that: see Table 6.1 below. An analysis of social security cases in 2004 on the *Casetrack* database for the Court of Appeal and the Administrative Court gives an interesting snapshot. The Court of Appeal determined 12 appeals against Commissioners' decisions. Five were successful, six unsuccessful. Four appeals involved housing benefit (unsurprising given the newness for Commissioners of this jurisdiction), one concerned child additions to Jobseekers allowance and a claim of discrimination under the Human Rights Act 1998, two raised child support issues, one concerned disability living allowance (DLA) and the other covered disabled person's tax credit. In a further two cases, the court reserved judgment. The court also disposed of 12 applications for leave to appeal Commissioners' decisions. All but two were refused. Six applications involved DLA, three concerned income support, and the other three embraced child support, housing benefit and incapacity benefit, respectively. The court also dealt with three appeals on refusal of the High Court to grant judicial review of a Commissioners' refusal to give leave to appeal to the Commissioner from a tribunal.

As regards Scotland, a search of their court opinions webpage in March 2005 produced only 11 decisions of their higher courts between March 1999 and September 2004 (both dates inclusive).

Table 6.1 Appeals from the Commissioners to the Court of Appeal and total cases disposed of by Court of Appeal (1998-2003)

Year	Allowed	Dismissed	Dismissed by consent	Otherwise disposed of	Total	Total appeals disposed of by Court of Appeal
2003	8	7	4	2	21	1075
2002	5	4	5	3	17	1088
2001	6	5	2	3	16	1120
2000	4	4	1	1	10	1065
1999	5	8	6	3	22	1127
1998	115	10	5	2	132	1243

Source: Judicial Statistics (2004)

Of those, four were seeking judicial review of a Commissioner's refusal to grant leave to appeal to Commissioner level from a tribunal, four were full appeals and three sought leave to appeal. A *Westlaw* search found only four reported Court of Session decisions from 1995 to date.

The Northern Ireland judicial statistics (see Table 6.2 below) show no more than a few cases going to the Court of Appeal in Belfast each year.

Table 6.2 Court of Appeal in Northern Ireland: appeals from the Northern Ireland Commissioners

	Pending at the start	Set down	Disposed of	Pending at end of period	Total set down in Court of Appeal (NI)
2003	0	2	0	2	86
2002	1	2	3	0	89
2001	4	1	4	1	70
2000	1	4	1	4	54
1999	1	7	7	1	67

Source: NI Judicial Statistics (1999-2003).

As for the House of Lords, the DCA's judicial statistics classifying the subject matter of civil appeals disposed of as being social security reveal only one case in the period 1998-2003, and that in 1999. This is clearly misleading, suggesting that 'social security' may have been dropped as a classification after 1999, since in the period since its decisions were reported online on the House of Lords' website (part way through 1996), a search identified the following as social security cases, showing approximately one case each year.

Table 6.3 Social security cases reaching the House of Lords, 1999-2005

Date	Name	Citation	Subject Matter
3 March 2005	*Hinchy v. Secretary of State for Work and Pensions (appellant)*	[2005] 2 All ER 129	Overpayments
6 May 2004	*Kerr v Department of Social Development (appellant) (Northern Ireland)*	[2004] 4 All ER 385	Social Fund: funeral payment
31 July 2003	*Moyna v Secretary of State for Work and Pensions (appellant)*	[2003] 4 All ER 162	DLA cooking test
28 June 2001	*Chief Adjudication Office v Stafford and Banks (appellants)*	[2001] ELR 729	Income support & JSA
5 July 2001	*M (appellant) v Secretary of State for Social Security*	[2001] UKHL 35	DLA
11 May 2000	*Chief Adjudication Office (appellant) v Faulds*	2000 SC (HL) 116	Industrial accident
21 Oct 1999	*Nessa (appellant) v Chief Adjudication Office and another*	[1999] 4 All ER 677	IS – person from abroad
27 Nov 1997	*Chief Adjudication Office v Wolke (appellant)*	[1998] 1 All ER 129	Income Support
21 May 1997	*Cockburn (appellant) v Chief Adjudication Officer; Secretary of State for Social Security (appellant) v Fairey*	[1997] 3 All ER 844	Attendance Allowance; DLA

The use of judicial review since conferment of a right of appeal

Giving a right of appeal to the Court of Appeal on a point of law means that the Divisional or Administrative Court level is bypassed. So that while there has been a burgeoning of judicial review cases in other areas of governmental life or public law fields, it has but limited use in the fields of social security and child support within the jurisdiction of the Commissioners (Wikeley, Ogus and Barendt 2002: 205; Robson, 1998), essentially being a means of challenging a Commissioner's refusal to grant leave to appeal from a relevant tribunal to Commissioner-level. Analysis of the *Casetrack* database for 2004 cases reveals that the Administrative Court disposed of seven applications to review a Commissioner's refusal to grant leave to appeal to him or her from a tribunal.

Figures provided by the Office of the Social Security and Child Support Commissioner (OSSCSC)[26] show 26 applications for permission for judicial review

[26] Personal communication to the authors, 14 March 2005. It should be pointed out that these figures were only the cases OSSCSC knew about, i.e. where the Commssioners were served with papers.

of Commissioners' decisions in (calendar year) 2003, 25 applications in (calendar year) 2004 and three applications for January and February 2005. Only four of the 26 applications in 2003 were given permission to proceed by the Administrative Court and only two of the 25 applications in 2004 got past the permission stage.

The role of the Lord Chancellor

Any exposition of 'accountability' would not be complete without a discussion of the power to appoint and remove Commissioners. The appointment of a Commissioner or a Chief Commissioner is a Crown appointment exercised (by convention) on the advice of the Lord Chancellor.[27] Historically, this arrangement was a means to win support for the exclusion of the courts in favour of this specialist jurisdiction (see Chapter 2). Commissioners are appointed from those holding a 10-year general qualification (barrister or solicitor) or those who are advocates or solicitors in Scotland of at least 10 years standing.[28]

The Lord Chancellor also has three direct statutory powers and s/he must consult with the Secretary of State prior to exercising them.[29] Firstly, a power to appoint a Deputy Commissioner, likewise selected from those with the 10-year qualification, 'for such period or on such occasions as the Lord Chancellor thinks fit.' The overall purpose of Deputy appointments is prescribed as being 'to facilitate the disposal of the business' of the Commissioners.[30] Secondly, the Lord Chancellor has a power to remove a Commissioner or Chief Commissioner from office 'on the ground of incapacity or misbehaviour'.[31] Thirdly, the Lord Chancellor has a power, exercisable by regulation, to provide for legal officers 'to make any determinations that fall to be made by Commissioners'[32] (see Chapter 3 on the role and function of the 'legal officers'). Commissioners must retire when they reach 70 years.[33] The Lord Chancellor is responsible for paying the Commissioners' salaries, remuneration and expenses. S/he is also responsible for paying the travelling and other allowances (including compensation for loss of earnings) of the parties attending a Commissioner's appeal hearing. The independence of judges has for several centuries been supported by secure conditions of tenure. Security of tenure of judicial office has been regarded as a cardinal constitutional principle. Wade and Forsyth comment:

---

27 It has been 'a long-standing constitutional practice that the Lord Advocate is [also] consulted in the appointment of the Chief Commissioner and Commissioners' (Walker, 2001: para 14).

28 SSA 1998, Sched 4, para 1(1).

29 *Ibid*, para 8.

30 *Ibid*, see para 1(2).

31 *Ibid*, Sched 4, para 5(1).

32 *Ibid*, Sched 4, para 6 and the Social Security SI 1999/1495, reg 7.

33 The Lord Chancellor has a discretion to extend tenure if s/he 'considers it desirable in the public interest'. See Judicial Pensions and Retirement Act 1993, s. 26(4)-(6).

> The tenure of the judiciary of all ranks, however, is as firmly protected in practice as it could be by positive law. Any undue interference with it would raise a political storm. Fearless judicial impartiality is the indispensable basis of the rule of law, and has been respected as a constitutional principle since the revolution of 1688 put an end to the abuses of the Stuart kings. (Wade and Forsyth, 2000: 75)

Judges of the High Court and above are protected by statutory provisions derived from the Act of Settlement 1700 which provide that they hold office 'during good behaviour subject to a power of removal by Her Majesty on an address presented to Her by both Houses of Parliament.'[34] Circuit judges, like the Commissioners (and sharing the same judicial pay grade, see Chapter 2, Table 2.3), are subject to removal by the Lord Chancellor for incapacity or misbehaviour.[35] Only one circuit judge has ever been removed. In 1983, Judge Bruce Campbell was sacked after having been convicted of smuggling spirits, cigarettes and tobacco into England in his yacht. No doubt there have been instances where, to avoid public scrutiny and scandal, a judge may be asked by the Lord Chancellor to 'resign'. One Commissioner informed us that:

> It's a problem but as Lord Hailsham [a former Lord Chancellor] said, nobody really anticipated problems because when Bruce Campbell and the district judge were sacked, one for smuggling the other for a drink driving offence where he was sent to prison. And Hailsham said, when we put that section in we never anticipated that it would ever be used. We never anticipated that we would ever have to sack a judge.

The fact that the Commissioners held a 'Crown' appointment was perceived by some of the Commissioners to be an important indication not only of the independence of the office but also of the required *status* of the job within the judicial hierarchy. One Commissioner remarked.

> As far as the 'Crown appointments' are concerned they are desperately important from two points of view. One is the fact that a Crown appointment really does give the maximum security of tenure and that is essential if it is perceived to be independent. ... Second thing is that the Crown appointment carries with it a status. I have to tell you that if it had been a Lord Chancellor's appointment or any other appointment other than a Crown appointment I certainly would not have contemplated this job at all.

However, though the Crown appointment of a Commissioner is like that of other judges in terms of security of tenure and the limited power of removal, it has been pointed out that 'there is no judicial oath attached to the office and the inherent powers, privileges, and immunities of other judges are lacking' (Walker 2001). Though the statutory provisions only specify the formal legal qualifications of the office of Commissioner, the Lord Chancellor's Department (LCD) had a

---

[34] See Supreme Court Act 1981, s.11(3) and Appellate Jurisdiction Act 1876.
[35] Courts Act 1971, s.17(4).

policy that a candidate should have served two years but at least a minimum of 40 days as a Deputy Commissioner. That policy has not been without its critics.

> This can provide a substantial bar for a candidate from private practice who may have acquired or be in the process of acquiring judicial experience in a part-time appointment of equivalent or higher status – none of that service apparently goes towards his qualifying period. Thus able candidates from private practice who may have served for example in England as recorders, in civil matters or as Deputy High Court Judges, and in Scotland as Temporary Judges of the Court of Session or as Sheriffs, may be deterred or effectively barred. (Walker, 2001: para 11)

One of the Commissioners interviewed thought that building in this requirement for the post of Commissioner was not doing any service to the system; in fact it was tending to *restrict* the pool of suitable applicants.The Commissioners will no doubt have a weather eye on the forthcoming changes to the constitutional arrangements, that is the legislative modifications to the office of Lord Chancellor and the involvement of a new 'Judicial Appointments Commission', which will change the way in which judicial Crown appointments are made in the future. When the Constitutional Reform Act 2005 is implemented the Lord Chancellor will be under a duty to make a recommendation to fill Crown appointment vacancies, unless s/he agrees with the Lord Chief Justice that the vacancy can remain unfilled. Normally, the Lord Chancellor will make a request to the newly established Judicial Appointments Commission to select a person for appointment.[36] In addition to these quite far reaching constitutional changes, the government's acceptance of the core principles of Leggatt and its intention to legislate on tribunal reform also present the prospect of a changing relationship with the Secretary of State for Constitutional Affairs as the Minister responsible for 'redress policy', to use the White Paper (2004) terminology.

The Council on Tribunals

One of the central recommendations of the Franks Report (1957) had been to create 'openness, fairness and impartiality' in the tribunal sector. Franks also recommended the establishment of a Council on Tribunals to provide a monitoring function in respect of the various tribunals that had been generated by the post-war welfare state. The Tribunals and Inquiries Act 1958 which reflected many of Franks' recommendations established the Council and it currently consists of not more than 15 and not less than ten members appointed by the Lord Chancellor and the Scottish Ministers.[37] However, the Council does not have any executive functions. Its principal role is 'to keep under review the constitution and working of the tribunals specified in Schedule 1' and to make annual reports to the Lord

---

[36] See Constitutional Reform Act 2005, sections 85-93 and Schedule 14, Part One.

[37] See now the Tribunal and Inquiries Act 1992.

Chancellor and the Scottish Ministers that must be laid before Parliament.[38] The Schedule currently lists around 70 tribunals, (including the Appeals Service (AS) tribunals and the Commissioners)[39] under its direct supervision. The power of Ministers and others to make procedural rules in relation to a ('scheduled') tribunal is only exercisable after consultation with the Council.[40] The Council is usually consulted on draft legislation intending to create tribunals though there is no statutory requirement to do so. It can initiate its own 'special' reports on matters of interest.[41]

In 1980 it recommended that its own role ought to be expanded to cover the whole area of administrative adjudication and that it should have a statutory right to be consulted on draft legislation. The government rejected most of these recommendations though a consultation code of practice emerged to restate the obligation on departments to consult the Council on proposals for procedural rules and to suggest the desirability of consulting them on proposals for certain other primary and subordinate legislation. The Council, however, has always been hampered by its weak political position. Unlike the Parliamentary Ombudsman, for example, it has not had a Parliamentary Select Committee to support its aims and agendas. Wade and Forsyth (2000: 904) state that the Council has only been successful 'in a miscellany of minor matters'. However, there have been some isolated successes, for example, in persuading the government to add an independent element of adjudication to discretionary social fund decision making, originally conceived as a purely internal management review (Buck, 2000: 29).

Given the importance and volume of social security tribunal cases, at least at the AS tribunal level, the Council has frequently commented on the details of procedural regulations. It supports its supervisory role with a comprehensive visiting programme. The social security legislation specifically prescribes the right of Council of Tribunal members to attend AS tribunal and Commissioners' oral hearings irrespective of whether the chair of the hearing has specified a private hearing.[42] There are usually several members of the Council who have some expertise in relation to the social security and child support jurisdiction. The Council's annual reports refer on occasion to meetings by Council members with the Chief Commissioner on policy and other matters and to Council members' visits to Commissioner hearings. However, the limited number of Council members and the total size of the tribunal sector mean that such visits are exceptional. Furthermore, oral hearings, as has been seen, only represent a very small minority (4 per cent) of cases dealt with by the Commissioners. As a form of accountability the Council of Tribunal's impact on the Commissioners has been weak and sporadic, owing mostly to its lack of resources and distance from the

---

[38] Tribunals and Inquiries Act 1992, sections 1 and 4(7).

[39] *Ibid*, Schedule 1, para 41.

[40] *Ibid*, section 8.

[41] For example, *School Admission and Exclusion Appeal Panels* (May 2003, Cm 5788).

[42] See respectively, the Social Security and Child Support (Decisions and Appeals) Regulations 1999, SI 1999/991, reg 49(9)(e) and SI 1999/1495, reg 24(8).

political centre of strategic planning. The brief commentary in the Council's annual reports on the Commissioners too often merely repeats initiatives and developments that other bodies have taken and usually falls short of formulating a distinctive Council position.

For example, in their 1999-2000 annual report the Council notes the Chief Commissioner, Judge Machin's 'consultation exercise' on how decisions were 'starred' and later selected for reporting (see Chapter 5). The Council concluded:

> We stressed the need for proper reporting and publication of relevant decisions. Although we did not consider that the practical arrangements for identifying the relevant decisions for publication were a matter for us, we said that dissemination of at least the key decisions should be seen as part of the Commissioners' judicial functions. (Council on Tribunals, 2000: para 15)

The Council had a good opportunity to make its voice heard following the Commons' Select Committee inquiry into the Commissioners (see Chapter 1 and below) but decided instead merely to report this fact and noted the government's response to conduct a review at some future date. The Council concluded, '[w]e endorse the Committee's recommendation and welcome the Government's response' (Council on Tribunals, 2000: para 18).

The following year (2000-01) improvements in the publication of Commissioners' decisions were noted. 'Starred' and 'reported' decisions were then being made available on the Court Service and DWP websites. It also reported efforts to include information on the Commissioners in the Court Service website and advised that '[i]t might also be helpful to users if the Commissioners were to follow the example of the Immigration Appellate Authority and acquire their own domain name, rather than use the Court Service site as a vehicle' (Council on Tribunals, 2001: para 10). The Council noted that the average delays (which peaked to 64 weeks in 1998) had been reduced to an average of around 36 weeks by June 2001 and the government's response to the Select Committee report had announced a new target of 26 weeks, 'but as we have seen in other tribunals, this figure is skewed by the effect of older cases coming onto the list for disposal' (Council on Tribunals, 2001: para 11). Finally, the Council noted developments in the setting up of the user group.

> Our Chairman attended the inaugural meeting of the User Group set up by the Commissioners, and we have been represented at the two further meetings this year. We welcome this development, which has generated a valuable dialogue with user representative groups and interested organisations on a range of issues, including the reporting and publication of decisions, procedural changes, and issues generated by the new system for Housing Benefit and Council Tax Benefit appeals. (Council on Tribunals, 2001: para 12)

In its 2001-02 annual report the Council reported the launch of the Commissioner's website in April 2002 ('a significant development') under its own domain name (www.osscsc.gov.uk) (Council on Tribunals, 2002: para 8). It also briefly noted the new case management arrangements 'to encourage improvements in the quality of written submissions and to remove unnecessary delays' (para 9) and their impact on waiting times:

> The Commissioners' office advise that, as at December 2001, the average waiting time stood at 25.3 weeks. This would suggest that the Commissioners are well on track to meet the April 2002 target of 26 weeks from receipt of an appeal to the despatch of a Commissioner's decision. (Council on Tribunals, 2002: para 10)

In the next annual report (2002-03) the commentary provides further encouragement about waiting times:

> We are pleased to note the continuing efforts being made to reduce waiting times for bringing cases to a hearing before the Commissioners, which in the past year has reduced from 39 to 16.9 weeks, which is well within the Lord Chancellor's target of 26 weeks. This reduction has been achieved through the introduction of new case management procedures, focussing on the end to end appeals process, and clearing very old cases. (Council on Tribunals, 2003: para 16)

This annual report also notes briefly Chief Commissioner Harris' proposals to abandon the Commissioners' long-standing practice of omitting the identity of appellants and others from the body of their decisions, apart from child support cases. The Council concluded:

> We broadly supported the proposals but suggested that Commissioners might wish to retain a discretion to preserve the confidentiality of certain groups of persons. We thought it should be for the Commissioners to decide whether, in certain cases, confidentiality would best be protected through anonymity or through limited disclosure of information, or a combination of both. (Council on Tribunals, 2003: para 16)

As it turned out, the Commissioners decided not to change their existing practice on this issue.

In the following year (2003-04), the Council were able to report that the Lord Chancellor's target of 26 weeks had been bettered with an appeals disposal rate of 19.7 weeks in 2003-04 (Council on Tribunals, 2004: para 16) though it is noted that case numbers had reduced overall by about ten per cent in that year, in part reflecting the reduction in the numbers of appeals to AS tribunals. The report also noted the difficulties of having the Commissioners' administrative staff in a separate building but that 'the arrangement is likely to remain until the expiry of the lease on the Commissioners' present building' (Council on Tribunals, 2004: para 17). Finally, the Council conducted a survey of all scheduled tribunals in this year to evaluate their compliance with the access to goods and services provisions of the Disability Discrimination Act, which came fully into force in October 2004. The following information in relation to the Commissioners is noted.

- An accessibility audit has been carried out and hearing premises are now fully compliant. There is wheelchair access and adapted toilets. There is no provision for parking at Harp House or assistance for those with visual impairment. An induction loop is being installed. Ad hoc hearings take place at either Crown or County Court venues, which are compliant.
- Leaflets include advice about accommodating the special needs of those with disabilities. Large print copies of leaflets are available. Requests are dealt with on an individual basis. Interpreters are provided on request.
- Users can make contact via e-mail and the website. Minicom facilities are available at the administrative centre in Newspaper House.
- All appellants have their travel expenses refunded, including the expenses of companions for those who cannot travel alone.
- All staff and Commissioners have received in-house equality and diversity training. Specific requests are referred to managers.
- User groups meet regularly, including representatives from various disability groups including RNIB and RNID. Feedback is routinely collected from users. (Council on Tribunals, 2004: 34)

As regards the exemption order[43] referred to above, which authorised the Commissioners to refrain from giving reasons on applications for leave, the reasons for the order were explained thinly in one of the Council's annual reports:

> The order was made originally to help maintain swift resolution of social security appeals and to offset the workload implications of additions to the Commissioners' responsibilities and their increasing volumes of appeals. (Council on Tribunals 1999: para 2.221)

The Council had questioned the policy in their 1992-3 annual report. However, it would appear there was no general use made of the exemption in any event.[44] In our interview work, some of the Commissioners mentioned that they had continued to give reasons in suitable cases during the period when the exemption order was in force. One of the Chief Commissioners referred to his discussions with the Lord Chancellor in which he recommended that this exemption order be lifted. No doubt the impending Human Rights Act legislation was also a prompt for this action and the renewed practice of giving reasons on applications was formally confirmed in a *Practice Memorandum* issued in March 2001.[45]

---

43 See the Tribunals and Inquiries (Social Security Commissioners) Order 1980, SI 1980/1637, reg 2. See also *R v Secretary of State for Social Services, ex parte Connolly* [1986] 1 WLR 421.

44 Wade and Forsyth (2000: 917).

45 See *Practice Memorandum* 'Written Observations on Appeals in Social Security and Tax Credit Cases in England and Wales', 9 March 2001, reproduced in Rowland and White (2004: para 2.304).

Scrutiny by the House of Commons' Select Committee on Social Security

The Select Committee on Work and Pensions (formerly Social Security), following a resolution of the House of Commons in May 2002, is encouraged to perform a number of 'core tasks'. These are to carry out inquiries into (a) government policy proposals, (b) areas seen to require examination because of deficiencies, (c) departmental actions, (d) associated public bodies (of the Department), (e) major appointments, and (f) implementation of legislation and major policy initiatives (Select Committee, 2004: 6).

The Select Committee's inquiry into the Commissioners, although occurring prior to this procedural guidance, undoubtedly fell within category (b). The Select Committee (2000) came to scrutinise the Commissioners, apparently inspired by a Parliamentary Question on 9 November 1999,[46] that had revealed the waiting times for an appeal to the Commissioners as having risen to 64 weeks in 1998. The Committee's terms of reference were 'to examine the operation of the current [Commissioner] system and to consider the scope for improvement.' An outline of the four main areas of concern to the Select Committee (2000) – delay, the publication of Commissioners' decisions, the impact of DMA changes and judicial independence – has been given in Chapter 1. The issue of 'judicial independence' arose in the Select Committee's intervention in two ways. Firstly, there was concern about the propriety of judges being interviewed by a Parliamentary Select Committee. Secondly, the report of the Select Committee found that there was a too 'cosy' relationship struck up between OSSCSC and the Department of Social Security (DSS). The Select Committee's report explained the sensitivities about the constitutional issues:

> As far as the constitutional position is concerned, the Chairman at the opening oral evidence session made it clear that it was never proposed to question the judgments of Commissioners or to affect the judicial independence of the post-holders. The Chief Commissioner [Judge Machin QC] quite willingly gave oral evidence to the Committee and at no stage did he or the Lord Chancellor's Department question the probity of our inquiry. For our part we recognise and value the independent role that the Commissioners play and the esteem in which they are held. (Select Committee, 2000: para 8)

In response perhaps to these concerns, the Committee's oral questioning of the Chief Commissioner and Mr Walker QC, the then Senior Commissioner for Scotland, was largely confined to process issues. On the point about the Department's relationship with the Commissioners, the Select Committee report had this to say:

> This included regular meetings and the pressing of issues both ways. For example, the DSS discussing their desire for more consistency of decision making; and seeking the

[46] Hansard, *Written Answers*, 9 November 1999, cols 503w-504w.

> Commissioner's agreement not to do a submission in every case; and the Chief Commissioner making representations that the Department make more use of section 13(3) of the Social Security Act 1998. There is also the Commissioners' practice of giving priority to DSS appeals; and the consultation with the Department as to which decisions should be reported. The Chief Commissioner has already hinted that he recognises that he needs to be more even handed in his dealings. (Select Committee, 2000: para 42)

The Commissioners, as will be seen, were mostly (but not unanimously) offended by the allegation from the Select Committee about the nature of their relationship with the DSS. One Commissioner interviewed, for example, noted that the Committee had totally misunderstood that the reason for expediting Secretary of State's appeals was that claimants were, pending such appeals, often kept out of benefit until the matter had been resolved.

It should be remembered that the Select Committee was taking evidence in February and March 2000 and produced its report in May 2000, while the Leggatt review team was appointed in May 2000 and reported in August 2001. It is undoubtedly the case that the quick sequence of both these interventions had a significant impact on the development of OSSCSC. Our interview work (mainly carried out between October 2001 and November 2002) picked up the Commissioners' own responses and views to the accountability provided by the Select Committee's intervention.

Select Committee: the views of the Commissioners

Most of the Commissioners interviewed commented directly or indirectly about the impact of the Select Committee's intervention. In addition to the constitutional issue – the propriety of senior judicial figures being interviewed by a Parliamentary Select Committee – they also provided a broader picture about how they viewed the increasing forms and intensity of 'accountability' applied to them. Some focussed too on the particular administrative and other changes that the Committee's intervention had prompted. Others were moved to discuss their security of tenure as judges and how that was important to preserve judicial independence.

We observed the Commissioners at a time of significant change within the organisation and at a time when radical reform of the wider tribunal sector was being actively debated. Change is threatening and intimidating to some, welcomed over-optimistically by others, and perhaps regarded with some interest combined with a reserved caution by the remainder. A range of such responses was detected.

Nearly all of the Commissioners agreed that the Committee had justifiable, critical points to make about the past delays and the lack of accessible publication of Commissioners' decisions. On the constitutional issue, most of the Commissioners were reasonably comfortable in drawing a line between questions about the *administration and management* of Commissioners' appeals and the core *judicial function* of the Commissioner. In the former case, they thought that the

Committee not only could, but also, ought to be able to ask what questions they thought fit. One Commissioner said:

> I don't have a problem with it provided [the Select Committee] don't start asking why we decided certain cases as we have or even why we have the procedures that we do. What I do find much more objectionable constitutionally is an MP writing in and saying 'Why has this person's DLA claim has been refused?' I mean that really is difficult.

Another Commissioner thought that the Committee had not really got the distinction clear at the outset about what was proper to investigate, but that 'once they got that clear then I personally welcomed their intervention. There were bureaucratic and administrative problems that needed searchlights focused on them.' One Commissioner stated that the Committee 'made it undoubtedly clear that they weren't going to investigate our decision-making.'

Chief Commissioner Machin, who appeared before the Committee, had sought guidance from both the Lord Chancellor and the Lord Chief Justice on whether he should appear. His view was that judges should not be seen to be isolated and he therefore agreed to appear.

The Committee's criticism that OSSCSC had conducted a 'cosy' relationship with departmental officials had certainly struck home. One Commissioner was 'annoyed' at this allegation and could not find any justification for it. In fact, he said, officials 'were kept very much at arm's length'. Another Commissioner implied however that it was the officials who had tried to cosy up to the Commissioners, not the other way around.

The background to this was that during the introduction of SSA 1998, which represented wide-ranging organisational changes, there had been an especial need for a series of rolling consultations between departmental officials, AS and the Commissioners. It was thought that at some of these meetings the remit of individual participants was not sufficiently clear. Nevertheless, some of the interviewees were quite defensive on behalf of the Chief Commissioner:

> I think the Select Committee criticised the Chief Commissioner, I think unfairly, for cosying up too closely to the Department. That upset him a lot. And I think it was unjustified actually because it is absolutely essential to have discussions about certain things. …
>
> Unfortunately … I suppose they've got their agenda, but I think focusing on the Chief Commissioner being over cosy with the Department was desperately unfair.

However, one Commissioner voiced a strong concern about the dangers of mixing judicial and administrative functions without clear demarcation lines.

> I think there is absolutely nothing wrong in an open consultation process as being contributed to by the judiciary as long as its on the table and, for example, welfare rights organisations and CABs and so on are also involved in the same process. What's dangerous and what was rightly criticised by the Social Security Select Committee is the administration here having cosy behind-the-scenes discussions with the Department

> about litigation or potential litigation in which the Department is a party before us. You simply can't have that.

The same Commissioner, when asked about the propriety of having pre-legislative consultation with the judges, provided the following response:

> I wouldn't have thought that it would be right for the specialist experience of the Commissioners to be deployed in a behind-the-scenes 'stitch up' with the Executive if that was the aim of [such consultation].

The Commissioners frequently gave broader pictures of how the Select Committee's intervention had made them address *generally* questions of accountability relating to their office. One Commissioner stated:

> Commissioners are certainly being defensive and have bristled at the idea of anyone asking any questions. I think that is one of the things that has contributed to us being a backwater. I've said this to other Commissioners – not comments that have made me very popular!

The same Commissioner thought that the diverse (and relatively numerous) appointments of Commissioners made in the previous three years had contributed to 'the broader view' of the outside world that was emerging at OSSCSC. Though many of the Commissioners welcomed the Committee's intervention, some qualified this by questioning whether the Committee was forearmed with sufficient knowledge to understand what the Commissioners' role actually was.

> I can't see why I shouldn't be looked into, as long as someone looks into me with proper knowledge and understanding of what it is that I am supposed to be doing.

Another Commissioner thought that all judges nowadays simply had to expect a series of spotlights on their work.

> I mean I don't mind being under the spotlight as long as those applying it are given the right sort of information and make a representative and balanced judgment. I'm not so sure that the Select Committee did that because I don't think they appreciated what an appeal to the Commissioners and what an appeal to the tribunal – what it really involved. I think they were really interested in 'how many cases are you're deciding' and a number-crunching attitude, and the delay issues.

In general, most of the Commissioners understood that there was little reason for them to have immunity from being analysed by a Select Committee or the Leggatt review or other such forms of accountability so long as their area of judicial decision-making was not usurped.

There were different views expressed about the application of 'key performance indicators' and 'appraisal' to the work of judges. Some very much supported these initiatives; others viewed them with great caution. One Commissioner drew an important distinction between 'management controls' and 'appraisal by one's peers', the latter having nothing whatsoever to do with any infringement on the merits of judicial decision-making. Judicial independence was in any event protected by the security of tenure of the Commissioner's office, but, it was argued, that was no reason for Commissioners to think they had nothing more to learn after being appointed.

> 'I wouldn't want to go to a doctor or a dentist who had never ever after he/she was appointed had anybody look at them'.

Other Commissioners pointed to positive outcomes of the Committee's intervention in detailed terms. Several Commissioners, for example, saw a clear causative link between the appearance of the Select Committee report in May 2000 and the establishment in the Autumn of that year of an internal 'case management committee' within OSSCSC consisting of the Chief Commissioner, a legal officer and a few senior Commissioners to address the problems of delay by undertaking a fairly radical review of their case handling procedures. One Commissioner thought that the strength of the Select Committee's comments and their commitment to follow up action provided 'a very conducive backdrop to the introduction of the case management procedures'. The 'case management committee' put proposals forward at the end of 2000 and these were adopted at the beginning of 2001. One Commissioner pointed out that:

> The [case management committee proposals] have been very successful. If they had been put into effect well in advance of the Select Committee's investigation, the first of those criticisms, of delay, would not have been made.

In addition to the case management initiative, it also appeared that the 'user group' (see below) had been, at least in part, prompted by the Select Committee's interest in the Commissioners' operation. The Committee had recommended its establishment, to an extent, as an antidote to the formation (or perception) of covert links with the Department.

The Leggatt review intervention

An outline of Leggatt (2001) and the White Paper (2004) is given in Chapter 1 and there are some evaluative comments on the broad policy points contained in Chapter 7. This section discusses briefly what the Leggatt team made of the Commissioners. It then goes on to explore the Commissioners' own views about the Leggatt review, drawing both on their formal written responses and our own interview work with them. Leggatt's review suggested reforms of the framework for accountability. Some, but not all, of these have been taken up in the White Paper and are examined at the end of this chapter.

Members of the Leggatt review team visited the London office of the Commissioners and talked with some of the Commissioners, legal officers and administrative staff. An oral hearing was observed. There is a brief pen picture of the Commissioners recorded in the Leggatt (2001: 183-6) report based on the information they gathered from their visits and the written consultation reports received from the Commissioners in all three offices (see Machin, 2001; Walker, 2001 and Martin, 2001).

Leggatt's view of the Commissioners

Precedent This issue has already been explored in detail in Chapter 5. Suffice it to say here that the Leggatt report recommended that '[t]he system of designating binding cases (or limiting the cases which are permitted to be cited in argument) as used by the Social Security Commissioners and the IAT [Immigration Appeals Tribunal] should be adopted throughout the appellate Division' (Leggatt, 2001: 73). However, as the Commissioners reminded us repeatedly in our interviews with them, Leggatt had misunderstood some of the details of the Commissioners' reporting system. There is no system, as suggested in Leggatt (2001: paras 6.20, 6.26), for the separate designation of certain cases as compulsorily binding or for the restriction of cases that might be cited in argument. The Commissioners' position was that reported decisions should *normally* be preferred to an unreported one, a position only justified by the 'consensus test'.[47]

Supervision and correction by the courts through review and appeal The overall divisional structure proposed in Leggatt would have resulted in the formation of a new appellate body, a 'Social Security and Pensions Appeal Tribunal'. It was intended this body would take appeals from the first-tier bodies: the Appeals Service, Pensions Appeal Tribunal, Fire Service Pensions Appeal Tribunal, the Police Pensions Appeals Tribunal and the Criminal Injuries Compensation Appeal Panel (Leggatt, 2001: 78). The Leggatt report also recommended that the availability of legal challenge by way of judicial review should be eliminated, and that there be a statutory exclusion of second-tier tribunals from the supervisory jurisdiction of the Administrative Court (2001: paras 6.34-6.36).

Crown appointments and the role of the Lord Chancellor Leggatt recommended, as outlined in Chapter 1, that appointments to tribunals currently in the hands of the Minister in charge of the tribunal's 'sponsoring' Department, should go. It was recommended that the Lord Chancellor should become responsible for all appointments to tribunals that would otherwise be made by Westminster Ministers (Leggatt, 2001: 31). The then Lord Chancellor, Lord Irvine, announced in March 2003[48] that the government had accepted the general thrust of the Leggatt

[47] See Chapter 5, p 149.
[48] Lord Chancellor's Department, 'Government Announces Modernised Tribunals Service' *Press Release, 106/03*, 11 March 2003.

recommendations. The new Tribunal Service would bring together the ten largest tribunals (including the Commissioners), with other tribunals joining later, and the new Service would be accountable to the Lord Chancellor. It was ambiguous in Leggatt whether the recommendation that appointments should be for a renewable period of five to seven years was to be applied to *both* first-tier and second-tier tribunal judges. There was an ominous absence of any reference to the future of Crown appointments for Commissioners or members of the Employment Appeal Tribunal who also hold Crown appointments.[49]

The Commissioners views of the Leggatt report

The two sections below explore, respectively, the Commissioners' collective, formal, written responses to the Leggatt review team and their individual views as expressed in their interviews with our research team.

Commissioners' written responses to Leggatt The Commissioners from the London, Edinburgh and Belfast offices provided their reports in response to the Lord Chancellor's consultation on the Leggatt report: see respectively Machin (2001), Walker (2001) and Martin (2001).[50] The 'agreed collective response' from the London office generally approved the commitment demonstrated in Leggatt to improving service to users and to independence and approved the Commissioners becoming part of a unified second-tier appellate body. However, it did have criticisms to make of Leggatt's assumption that appellants were able to represent themselves satisfactorily.

> [T]he Report assumes that tribunals deal with issues on which the appellants are able to present their own cases. This overlooks the nature of the issues that now come before tribunals in social security and child support cases. Many of those issues are technical and complex. They have become increasingly so since the overhaul of benefits in 1988. Even with good submissions from the Secretary of State and an inquisitorial and enabling approach from an experienced tribunal, a lay person can be at a disadvantage. (Machin, 2001)

Furthermore, while acknowledging that public funding of legal representation was available on an exceptional basis, it was pointed that the current procedures for obtaining legal aid for Commissioner cases had led to delays. It was specifically proposed that a specialist (second-tier) body such as the Commissioners ought to have a power to be able to certify a case as suitable for public funding. Indeed, Micklethwait had also proposed this. He thought the Commissioners 'would be far better equipped than anyone else to discriminate between cases and decide whether legal aid was necessary' (Micklethwait, 1976: 56).

---

[49] Employment Tribunals Act 1996, s.22(1)(c).
[50] These documents were available on Commissioner Howell's website: http://www.hywels.clara.co.uk/commrs/leggatt.htm

The London Commissioners agreed that only complete severance of tribunals from their 'sponsoring' Departments would convince users of the appeal body's independence. The Belfast office response gave an example of a problem that might otherwise arise 'that staff may hold back appeals for the administrative and financial convenience of the sponsoring department.' It did not consider 'that there should be any forum for departmental control of the judicial function in the tribunal system' (Martin, 2001). The London office response generally supported the structure of a new Tribunal Service envisaged in Leggatt, though it pointed out that '[a] unified structure does not require uniformity' (Machin, 2001). The Edinburgh office response however, saw Leggatt as fundamentally flawed. It argued there would be no 'unity' in the system; there would be constitutional difficulties in abrogating Crown appointments (if that was the intention) and the proposal for a 'Tribunals Board' smacked of an administrative body that, it was argued, would usurp judicial functions.

The London Commissioners thought that the second-tier should be a part of the Administrative Court. It provided a convincing analysis of the advantages of creating a unified second-tier body.

> The appeal to the second-tier should be to a single body. That body would need to sit in separate specialist divisions with the members ticketed according to their interests and experience. This has numerous advantages. It would allow the concentrated acquisition of expertise that makes a contribution towards the efficient and effective disposal of cases. It would replace the existing various appellate bodies at our level and be more easily understood by users. It would allow a more coherent development of the 'unlawfulness' ground of appeal – at present the bodies to whom appeal lies on error of law have developed their jurisdictions differently. It would allow more efficient and effective adjudication of issues that cross the boundaries of the present system. For example, a claimant's immigration status can determine entitlement to a social security benefit. Those cases could be heard by someone ticketed in both jurisdictions. It would also allow coherent development of common areas. For example, the new Tax Tribunal will have jurisdiction over working families' tax credit which operates on rules that have been interpreted by us in relation to income support and family credit and which also apply to benefits within our jurisdiction. It would allow easier movement of judicial personnel to take account of fluctuating work loads in different jurisdictions. It would allow greater diversity in what can become narrow specialities. (Machin 2001)

All the Commissioners' responses supported the idea of importing more court-like and 'judicial' nomenclature into any reformed system in order to enhance the user's confidence in their independence and they all supported the retention of Crown appointments for Commissioners. The appellate body itself should be designated a 'court'. Indeed, the Edinburgh office response specifically argued for the Commissioners to be constituted as a 'superior court of record' in order to equip them with powers to enforce interlocutory orders. The London Commissioners agreed that the body should be a 'court':

> … since it will be concerned with the lawfulness of decisions under appeal and will exercise a supervisory jurisdiction, equivalent to that of the High Court, over the tribunals within its jurisdiction. The term 'tribunal' is likely to cause confusion when used to describe a judicial body dealing with appeals from other tribunals, whilst the term 'court', on the other hand, appropriately describes a judicial body which is concerned with developing and applying legal principles common to different areas of decision-making (such as adequacy of reasons), and whose decisions constitute binding authority. (Machin 2001)

The London Commissioners were concerned that the separate system envisaged for tribunals was in danger of becoming inferior to the court structure, rather than enhancing its image. In particular there were concerns about the proposed titles of bodies and personnel, the possible removal of Crown appointments and the fixed term nature of judicial posts.

> These are not matters of empty nomenclature and status. They have an impact on the perception and understanding of the public for the work of the bodies. This in turn has an impact on the extent to which the public has confidence in a body and respect for its decisions. (Machin 2001)

The Scottish Commissioners were more strident in their criticisms on this issue and argued strongly for retaining Crown appointments.

> It appears to us that in preparing their report Sir Andrew Leggatt's Committee have discounted opportunities to enhance the status and independence of the Commissioners and have made proposals which would be likely to both diminish independence and potentially affect the quality of the judicial work of the Commissioners. (Walker, 2001: para 4)

They were also very concerned about other aspects of Leggatt which, in their view, threatened judicial independence. For example, their response states, '[t]he introduction of performance appraisals is inconsistent with the security and judicial independence afforded to Crown office holders. (Walker, 2001: para 5). The Scottish response also pointed out the inadequacies of Leggatt in addressing devolution issues, and robustly defended the current arrangements whereby administrative staff were provided by the Scottish Executive, and, opposed any change that would bring about a more distant command structure (see Walker, 2001: Appendix).

The Commissioners' responses pointed out the mistaken representation of the Commissioner system of reporting in Leggatt. 'Just for the record, the starring of a decision is a preliminary stage in identifying cases that may be worth reporting. The Report misunderstood our system' (Machin 2001). The London Commissioners specifically opposed the selection of decisions for binding status, otherwise than by a body that is directly exercising a judicial appellate function.

As regards the role of the legal officers, the London office response acknowledged that the Commissioners' system works quite well and its extension to other comparable appellate tribunals might usefully be considered.[51]

The Commissioners' individual responses to Leggatt There was a mixed response. On the one hand, there was general support, as in their written responses, for a rationalisation of what Commissioners regarded as a fragmented tribunal sector. There was also broad support for the distinction between first- and second-tier tribunal bodies. On the other hand, many of the Commissioners referred to the 'missed opportunities' of Leggatt. One Commissioner thought that Leggatt had produced confusion between an overall strategic vision of the tribunal sector and detailed proposals for procedural reforms of individual tribunals. Some, but not all, Commissioners thought the proposals should have been more robust in unambiguously advocating an integrated tribunal system. There was also a general feeling that the new system would result in the undervaluation of tribunals. One Commissioner thought that Leggatt had viewed the tribunal system as 'some second class judicial set up'. Another Commissioner stated,

> One word that seems to appear very little is 'justice' in the whole of the Leggatt report. That I am concerned about – an underlying theme in Leggatt which seems to be – that the Tribunals are different from the Courts, largely on what seem to be social reasons more than anything else. And I don't think that Leggatt has defined adequately or properly the ways in which one can develop coherent consistent principles of adjudication applicable over the whole of the field. And I think that is a missed opportunity in Leggatt.

Very clear comments were given criticising Leggatt's 'do-it-yourself' philosophy of representation. One Commissioner pointed out that Leggatt had failed to reconcile the basic contradiction between the 'enabling role' of tribunals and the lack of legal representation where that would obviously be appropriate. Another Commissioner said:

> … saying as they do that tribunals should enable claimants so that they can present their own cases is just batty. I mean you know some of them can and some of them clearly can't. No matter how clearly you present materials they don't read them, we know that they don't read them, because they don't understand the whole concept of reading things. And they don't understand the concept of trying to get help, even though I think the Department gives them a list of places that they can go for help they'll still say, you know, that's just silly.

---

[51] However, the London office response disagreed with Leggatt (2001: 186, para 18) that there was no objection to registrars/legal officers setting aside decisions if the parties are agreed. 'There is an objection in principle to decisions of a judicial body being set aside, solely on the statement of the parties, without judicial authority' (Machin 2001).

An important point not picked up by Leggatt, according to one of the Commissioners, was that many tribunals were very under-funded by their sponsoring Departments, for example, Mental Health Review Tribunals, but 'administrative justice shouldn't be dependent on the type of decision being challenged'. This Commissioner took the view that the allocation of funding should be a judicial not a political responsibility in order to provide resources on broader justice grounds rather than specific political grounds.

Most of the Commissioners agreed that a rationalisation of a second-tier appellate body was good in principle, and they acknowledged that OSSCSC could form the 'natural core' of such a new body. However, there were concerns by some of the Commissioners that the system of 'ticketing' appellate tribunal judges might prove difficult in practice. Some of the Commissioners simply did not see how one could adequately cope with doing a social security case one day and, say, an immigration or employment case the next. The specialisation required for all of these areas was too demanding. However, others saw distinct advantages of linking up with other comparable jurisdictions. Indeed, one Commissioner pointed out that this was already occurring within OSSCSC given its various jurisdictional requirements.

The expectations of the peer group – 'collegiality'

Like most professionals, the Commissioners are particularly responsive to the views and opinions of their peers. Many of the Commissioners referred to a notion of 'collegiality' to describe the informal framework of their interaction with each other. In fact the research team heard this word used by Commissioners so much in our informal discussions with them that it soon found its way as an 'add-on' in our interview question schedule (see Appendix 1). One Commissioner, when asked what he understood by the term 'collegiality', responded as follows.

> Well in this context, what I think is meant is that you have a group of individuals who meet regularly who exchange views regularly and so that, not on everything, but on a wide range of topics, you get a common view emerging. So that people don't speak, at any rate on most topics, with disparate voices.

As made clear in Chapter 2, the wider base of appointments over the last decade had provided a stronger collective pool of expertise, but arguably at the expense of 'collegiality'. We gathered the perception that over the years the increasing number of Commissioners in the London office may have changed the nature of Commissioner collegiality.

On the other hand, a more informal (but no less efficient) organisation is perhaps more appropriate where there are smaller numbers of Commissioners, as in the Edinburgh and Belfast offices. A Commissioner in the Belfast office, when asked what was particularly distinctive about the Northern Ireland jurisdiction replied, 'I think it is really the degree of collegiality that we can have here.' The mid-morning coffee/tea break in the London office appeared to be an occasion when Commissioners regularly gathered and discussed matters of common interest, including the cases they happened to be working on at the time. Some Commissioners regularly lunched together.

Collegiality: the Commissioners' views

Most of the Commissioners, in discussing collegiality, would point out that a collegiate environment was conducive to achieving *consistency* in their approach to decision-making. The initiatives being taken at the time of our interview work on training were, in one sense, a way in which common approaches to problems could be ventilated in a more structured fashion. However, some of the Commissioners were keenly aware of how such 'training' might shade into management control. One Commissioner commented:

> I personally would be quite in favour of us having a formal discussion session using one of our training days and involving the legal officers as well to discuss, rather like the criminal judiciary do with regard to approaches to sentencing. … I can't see anything wrong with that at all because to ventilate the way one would approach it and listen to the way other people would approach it, it would only be beneficial for general consistency which is a prime concern in a jurisdiction that has so many cases coming in. But that's not happened so far and any form of central directive as to how individual cases should be decided I would be violently opposed to. That's not to say that those kind of ideas aren't being suggested at the moment.

One of the Scottish Commissioners based his own concept of collegiality on the model of the Court of Session, a 'collegiate court'. A London-based Commissioner thought that their informal collective discussions were much the same as would happen in a set of chambers. The Commissioners who viewed the Chief Commissioner's role as being limited to a spokesperson for the Commissioners, a *primus inter pares*, tended to have a stronger sense of the Commissioners as a collegiate body.

One of the Chief Commissioners appeared to recognise the advantages of utilising this type of informal contact. A small group of five Commissioners was selected to do housing benefit cases in order to produce greater consistency in the early stages of their introduction to the Commissioners' jurisdiction. The Chief Commissioner commented,

> …at least it's a small group and they can talk to each other. I'd like them to talk to each other and suggested that they have a constant conference, 'I've just met this problem, what do you think the answer might be?'

One of the Commissioners took the view that they were collegiate as regards reporting decisions which required the assent of the majority and, 'collegiate also in so far as we're a body of specialised lawyers and we can air common topics at meetings or at coffee in the morning and get to grips with what is troubling the Office generally.' However, several Commissioners were eager to point out that 'collegiate' did not mean that Commissioners necessarily *agreed* with each other. They said they were not in the business of coming to some kind of anodyne collective response. One Commissioner noted that collegiality, if it did exist, was 'not an evenly spread thing'. There were clearly some Commissioners who kept more on the fringes of the mid-morning coffee sessions and for whom this type of 'accountability' to one's peers was arguably weaker.

User groups

The Select Committee (2000: Q197) had questioned the Chief Commissioner whether a 'user group' consultative arrangement – that is, consultation with a range of organisations that campaign on behalf of and advise and represent individuals at tribunals – had been established in relation to OSSCSC's activities. Judge Machin QC replied that such an arrangement had not yet been established and that one of the difficulties had been that there were a large number of welfare rights organisation, but that was not an insuperable obstacle and he favoured setting one up.

The Leggatt review team were clearly impressed by the way in which user groups generally had responded to their own consultation exercise and noted the support there had been for some kind of formalised ongoing consultation with such groups (2001: 49-50). The model of the national forum of user groups with an interest in AS, that had already been established, was also noted as an example of best practice.

> We support the idea of user groups. It would be a useful mechanism to identify practical problems, to get feedback on the users' perspective, to test out drafts of new documentation and to act as a quality feedback mechanism. The group structure should meet two needs – to provide a forum for discussion on particular matters in specific tribunals or Divisions and to enable those running the Tribunals System to discuss with user representatives issues relevant to the System as a whole. Those running the Tribunals System should have the benefit of a strategic view across all tribunals in order to share best practice and help achieve consistency and cross-fertilisation of ideas for improvements. (Leggatt, 2004: 50)

In response to the prompts provided by both the Select Committee and the Leggatt review, the Chief Commissioner, Judge Machin QC, convened the first meeting of the OSSCSC user group towards the end of 2000. It was soon argued that amalgamation with the existing AS user group consultative committee would be beneficial. Following the 'double' appointment of Judge Harris to the Chief Commissioner's post in addition to his existing role as President of the Appeal Tribunals, the two consultative bodies were combined. Judge Harris was in favour of amalgamation, there was a large amount of overlap between issues raised at both forums and it was reported that representatives attending OSSCSC meetings had found them of limited value 'chiefly because representatives drew a much smaller proportion of their workload from commissioners' cases'.[52] In addition, representatives outside of London felt one body would be easier to attend. The first *joint* consultative meeting was held in February 2002.[53] There were two further meetings in 2002 and there have been around three meetings every year since.

The current terms of reference of the 'National Customer Representative Liaison Forum' are as follows.

> 1. To provide a joint national forum between the Appeals Service, the Office of the Social Security and Child Support Commissioner (OSSCSC) and representatives of users who use or rely on our service, in an environment where we can discuss and resolve all issues affecting appellants. This will ensure:
>   - The Appeals Service and OSSCSC can provide updates on performance and Operational Policy and promote awareness of initiatives designed to improve the service provided to appellants
>   - Customer representative groups have the opportunity to provide feedback on current levels of service delivery and new initiatives, and raise any national issues of concern
>   - Customer representatives groups are involved in the development of service improvements and to give advice on the effects on appellants of changes made to the way our service is delivered
>
> 2. To provide a forum for discussion, as and when necessary, of issues related to any area of diversity and equality.

The AS Operations Director, Norman Egan, currently chairs the group and the Chief Commissioner and/or another Commissioner, one of the legal officers and a member of the OSSCSC administrative staff regularly attend meetings. The agenda items include regular performance updates from both AS and OSSCSC, and a range of service delivery issues. The membership of the committee includes representatives from AS, OSSCSC, ACIB, the Council on Tribunals, CPAG, the Disability Alliance and a number of other organisations. The existence of the group has been useful as a means for AS and OSSCSC to flag up initiatives and for representative groups to provide suitable feedback. For example, early meetings of the group signalled concerns about the problems that might be encountered by the transfer of housing benefit review work to AS and the Commissioners.

However, membership of the consultative committee tends to change quite rapidly, in particular in relation to welfare rights' participants. Without greater continuity of membership it is difficult to see how the 'user perspective' is going to be successfully articulated and tested. It would be a missed opportunity if this group were to degrade into an inward-looking forum focused on 'service delivery'

---

[52] National Customer Representative Liaison Forum, *Minutes*, 3/01 NCR, 29 October 2001, 5th floor Whittington House, London, item 4. The Forum minutes are available at: http://www.appeals-service.gov.uk/532.htm

[53] *Ibid*, 1/02 NCR, 28 February 2002.

viewed more or less exclusively from a Departmental viewpoint. There are opportunities here to spread good practice; for example, the Commissioner's observation we referred to earlier[54] about welfare rights groups and departmental staff attending Commissioners' oral hearings as a training event could be further developed in the context of user group activity.

The quality of statistical information

The various forms of scrutiny applied to the Commissioners has frequently revealed difficulties in identifying relevant statistical data for the purposes required by these various bodies. For example, the statistics on caseload provided by the Commissioners to the Select Committee did not sufficiently highlight that the average waiting times were inflated by the stacking up of 'lookalike' cases at that time. The problem is not so much that there is insufficient data available, though there are still real gaps. (For example, *regional* breakdowns of Commissioners' appeals and applications are not available[55]). There are also no statistics collected on the profile of representation in relation to oral and paper appeals.[56] The real problem is that the data are neither sufficiently defined nor coherently collected. Furthermore, the fragmentation in how data are collected, and where and in what manner reported, make it difficult to obtain a clear picture.

The consequence is that too often one set of data does not tie up properly with another. It is not just the difficulty of some reports of work caseload, for example, being by calendar year rather than financial year. The problem is more fundamental.

We were supplied with OSSCSC figures giving the breakdown of appeals and applications by benefit category (see Chapter 3, Table 3.7). However, these figures do not match up with the overall figures for appeals and applications given in the Commissioners' Annual Reports (and see Chapter 3, Tables 3.2 and 3.3). In round figures, the former suggest the total cases disposed of are around 8,000 while the latter suggest 6,000. No doubt in the former category there will be some double counting of cases where these fall into more than one benefit category. But if that is the explanation it should be made clear.

Further interrogation of the headline figures in the Commissioners' Annual Reports has also revealed, in effect, a 'double counting' problem in the *Judicial Statistics* series on the Commissioners collected by the DCA. In Table 6.4 below, the appeals 'received' figure, appearing in the Commissioners' annual reports is in fact made up of a high proportion of cases where the leave has been granted by a Commissioner. In other words, the *leave granted by Commissioners* appeals (see below) were originally counted as 'applications' by OSSCSC. As made clear in

54 See Chapter 3, p 90.

55 National Customer Representative Liaison Forum, *Minutes*, 8 December 2004, Fox Court, London, para 6.3.

56 Personal communication to the authors from OSSCSC, 16 March 2005.

Chapter 3, where a Commissioner grants leave, these applications will be then automatically treated as 'appeals' and processed accordingly.

Table 6.4 The Social Security Commissioners: appeals *received* broken down by leave of chairman/Commissioner, 2001-02 to 2003-04

	2001-02	2002-03	2003-04
*Appeals received	2,878	2,518	2,180
† Leave granted by chairman	585	538	528
† Leave granted by Commissioners	2,293	1,980	1,652

* *Source: Commissioner's Annual Reports (2002-03) and (2003-04)*
† *Source: OSSCSC figures supplied to authors, 16 March 2005.*

However, the figures supplied by DCA's *Judicial Statistics* (2003) are as follows:

Table 6.5 The Social Security Commissioners: applications and appeals *received* and *disposed of* in England and Wales, 2003

	Number of cases received	Cases disposed of		
		Heard or determined	Otherwise disposed of	Total
Applications	4,468	4,208	91	4,299
Appeals	2,227	2,383	39	2,422
Total	**6,695**	**6,591**	**130**	**6,721**

Source: DCA, Judical Statistics (2003: 83, Table 7.4).

The discrepancy between the appeals 'received' of 2,227 (for 2003) and 2,180 (for 2003-04) from the previous Table can be explained no doubt by the differences between the figures for the calendar and financial years. However, the *Judicial Statistics* series conflates all applications and appeals to produce a 'total' figure of 6,695 and 6,721 respectively for cases 'received' and 'disposed of'. Yet we know that in 2003-04, 1,652 of the appeals figure would have originally been counted as an 'application'.[57] In short, the *Judicial Statistics* figure for total cases received appears to be around 25 per cent more than it actually is. When such a basic

[57] It is therefore likely that the total figure for 2003 is *approximately* (4,468 – 1,652) + 2,227 = 5,043, rather than the figure of 6,695 given in the DCA statistics.

headline figure appears to be quite badly inaccurate, there is little reason to be confident in other figures provided.

The mistake appears to be replicated elsewhere. For example, the Council on Tribunals (2004: 67) gives the figure for cases received by the Commissioners as 6,364 for 2003-04. This would appear again to be a conflation of applications and appeals without the recognition that a majority number of 'appeals' were originally also counted as 'applications'. Furthermore, the methodology of collating data for the Council on Tribunals' annual reports appears to change frequently making it almost impossible to compare one year with another.

In the next few years there will be an incremental introduction of a new unified Tribunal Service with various tribunals arriving under the administrative control of the DCA (see Appendix 6 for the timetable of the reforms). It would be an ideal opportunity during this period to plan and operate a more robust and reliable system of data collection in the tribunal sector as a whole. The integrity of such data will be important for the planning of tribunal work generally. In particular, good quality statistical work will be essential to properly inform the matching of judicial resources with what is known to be a volatile workload.

Evaluation: the future of accountability and the Commissioners – the tribunal reform programme

Leggatt made a number of suggestions about the framework for accountability in a reformed tribunal system. The government has accepted some of these, but rejected others. This section examines the White Paper proposals and draws out both the implications for the Commissioners and what the Commissioner system may contribute to these reform processes.

The availability of reasoned, precedent-setting decisions

It is evident that there are different views about how a system of precedent might be better arranged within the new tribunal service (see generally Chapter 5). The government has perhaps sensed the dangers of applying a 'one size fits all' solution. In its White Paper (2004: para 7.20), it has left the details of the problem to be worked out at a later date in the tribunal reform programme. The one short paragraph[58] in the White Paper about this issue leaves the jurisdictional Presidents the task to develop a system over time as the tribunal reforms develop. However, there do seem to be sufficient elements of commonality in the current practice of at least some of the appellate tribunals for a more directed and coherent attempt to achieve Leggatt's more 'systematic arrangements'.

[58] See White Paper (2004: para 7.20), quoted in Chapter 5, p 162.

Curtailing judicial review

In practice, as already discussed above, there are only around 25 applications for judicial review each year against Commissioners' decisions and the vast majority of these are against decisions to refuse applications for leave and do not get past the permission stage of the Administrative Court. Nevertheless, the elimination of judicial review challenge in this context would deprive tribunal users of a useful legal backstop where the appeal route fails or simply does not cover the substance of a particular challenge. Appeal rights are entirely statutory creatures. A sufficiently determined Executive can change the content of law subject to appeal rights.[59] The very *uncertainty* in the way in which judicial review may impact on tribunals remains a useful protection for the citizen and a good discipline for judicial personnel at both the first instance and appellate levels.

The White Paper (2004: 13) points out that, '[j]udicial review proceedings are complex and demanding and invariably require help and representation by solicitors and counsel. This is inevitably costly.'[60] The government's plans include the creation of a unified second-tier, to be named (perhaps unimaginatively) an 'Administrative Appeal Tribunal'. There would be a requirement for permission to appeal from the first-tier to this new second-tier body and from there to the Court of Appeal. As regards the role of judicial review, the White Paper states:

> With this structure the only possible role for judicial review in the High Court would be on a refusal by the first and second tier to grant permission to appeal. It is this possible route to redress which has caused so much difficulty for both the Immigration Appellate Authorities and the Courts. When permission to appeal has been refused by both tiers, and provided that the tribunal appellate judiciary are of appropriate quality, as we intend that they should be, there ought not to be a need for further scrutiny of a case by the courts. However, complete exclusion of the courts from their historic supervisory role is a highly contentious constitutional proposition and so we see merit in providing as a final form of recourse a statutory review on paper by a judge of the Court of Appeal. (White Paper, 2004: 43, para 7.28)

The government would appear to have predicted the possible resistance to the outright exclusion of judicial review in this field. How the remedy of a 'statutory review on paper by a judge of the Court of Appeal' will be expressed in the forthcoming Courts and Tribunal Bill referred to in the White Paper and how such a provision will fare the Parliamentary passage remains highly speculative. Furthermore, even if the government is successful in securing primary legislation which severely cuts down the availability of judicial review, it may in any event meet human rights challenges in the future based on the incompatibility of such

---

[59] See Chapter 3, p 66.

[60] 'In 2002/03 the Administrative Court received 5,123 applications for judicial review in civil and administrative cases, about half of which related to immigration and asylum' (White Paper, 2004: 13).

legislation with article 6 rights in respect of this barely concealed attempt to curtail access to justice.

It seems curious that Leggatt recommended such a clear curtailment of judicial review where the focus elsewhere was on the *users* of the tribunal system. However, as we have already pointed out, the Leggatt review contained an odd mixed message of a bottom-up perspective but without any real attempt to support this with detailed evidence about that perspective.[61] If the recommendations about judicial review are carried forward there will be no fallback remedy against a refusal to grant an application for leave. However, from the user's perspective this remains the gateway into the system of appeal rights without which he or she cannot secure any legal protection. Our detailed examination of Commissioner practice in respect of deciding whether to grant or refuse applications for leave[62] does at least show that the Commissioners and legal officers have a keen sense of the importance of this decision-making, as for most claimants a refusal here will be their final call in a search for justice. A limitation of such access to justice therefore runs counter to the ethos of both Leggatt and the government's White Paper.

Finally, such a limitation is hardly justified by the judicial resource argument. If, as Leggatt contemplates, there is a more coherent and comprehensive system of appellate rights, then it is unlikely that there will be many areas falling outside what Parliament, as defined as statutorily challengeable. Those areas, as in the example of the Commissioners, are likely to generate small numbers of cases, but may well reflect fundamental issues (for example, the access to justice point relevant to the Commissioners' refusal of leave applications) that ought to be tested by the High Court's supervisory jurisdiction. If there is a pathological expansion of judicial review cases then it is likely and appropriate that the pressure on High Court resources comes to Parliament's attention, as has been the case in the past both in relation to immigration (Shah and Menski, 1998) and housing benefit (Partington, 1998). The suggestion of a wholesale exclusion of judicial review from the tribunal sector omits the recognition that this will deprive the new Tribunal system of an important barometer test of the legal environment of administrative justice.

The role of the Department for Constitutional Affairs (DCA) and appointments of tribunal judges

Although the government has accepted the principle of detaching 'sponsoring' government departments from the appointment process it is interesting that it still sees the need to justify the Secretary of State for Constitutional Affairs' role.

> In contrast to many other Ministers, the Secretary of State for Constitutional Affairs does not make the kind of decisions that are subject to appeal. DCA also has a particular mission to protect judicial independence, which will continue to be a key feature of the new organisation, and to improve access to justice. The creation of the

---

[61] Chapter 4, p. 112.

[62] Chapter 3, pp. 75-80.

> new organisation within DCA will, therefore, ensure that the largest tribunals in administrative justice are manifestly independent, and are seen to be independent, from those whose decisions they are reviewing. (White Paper, 2004: 26)

The White Paper (2004) envisages that DCA will be the responsible government department for co-ordinating 'redress policy'. It is argued that the DCA already has responsibility for five of these ten tribunals, including the Commissioners.[63] The other five tribunals, including the AS tribunals,[64] will be transferred in the 'first phase' of reform to take place in 2006 to 2008. Together, these top ten tribunals are responsible for more than 90 per cent of cases (White Paper, 2004: 25). More tribunals will follow into the new structure on dates to be agreed between DCA and the sponsoring Departments. First-tier tribunal chairs will become 'Tribunal Judges' and second-tier appellate tribunals (for example, the Commissioners) will be called 'Tribunal Appellate Judges'.

The White Paper has recommended that it was no longer acceptable that judicial appointments were entirely in the hands of a Minister and pointed out that the Lord Chancellor already appointed around 60 per cent of tribunal panel members. It suggested that responsibility for recommending candidates for appointment to all tribunal panels be placed under the remit of a Judicial Appointments Commission. This body would make recommendations for appointment to the Secretary of State for Constitutional Affairs (White Paper, 2004: 32). The intention is to create a proper judicial career structure within the tribunal sector and the relationship between tribunal and court judges is to be encouraged. Tribunal Judges and Tribunal Appellate Judges will be encouraged to sit in more than one jurisdiction. This process has already started. An increasing number of Commissioners now also have appointments in other jurisdictions. The White Paper claimed that under the present system there were altogether around 20 per cent of tribunal panel appointments that were multi-jurisdictional (White Paper, 2004: 32).

Although the White Paper rejected Leggatt's divisional structure, it has accepted the recommendation that a 'Senior President' heads a system of judicial leadership in the tribunal sector. As already mentioned,[65] Lord Justice Carnwath's appointment as the Senior President-designate of tribunals was announced in November 2004. The government is committed to establish this post by legislation and suggests that this appointment be made by the Lord Chief Justice of England and Wales with the concurrence of the Lord President of the Court of Session and the Lord Chief Justice of Northern Ireland to reflect the UK-wide role of this post

[63] The other four under the DCA are: the General & Special Commissioners of Income Tax, the VAT & Duties Tribunal, the Pensions Appeal Tribunal and the Immigration Appellate Authority (i.e. the Immigration Adjudicators and Immigration Appeal Tribunal).

[64] The other four are: Employment Tribunals Service (Department for Trade and Industry), Special Educational Needs and Disability Tribunal (Department for Education and Skills), Criminal Injuries Compensation Appeals Panel (Home Office), Mental Health Review Tribunal (Department of Health).

[65] Chapter 5, p. 162.

(White Paper, 2004: 33). Individual jurisdictions will continue to have Presidents, though the White Paper notes that 'a number of jurisdictions will be combined for this purpose'. There will also be regional tribunal judges where circumstances warrant it. However, the White Paper gives little information about how the new Tribunal Appellate Judges will be organised. It is not clear, for example, how far regionalisation will be encouraged at this level. The White Paper (2004: 42) notes that the appellate tier will initially be constituted from the jurisdictional Presidents and panel members who sit in appellate tribunals supplemented where appropriate by a mixture of High Court and circuit judges seconded to the tribunal. But it is also anticipated that Tribunal Appellate Judges will additionally sit at first instance. This would not be a problem, for example, with some of the current Commissioners who have had a previous background as tribunal chairs, but might cause some consternation for others.

The role of the Lord Chancellor/Secretary of State for Constitutional Affairs is arguably a too central one in the post-Leggatt vision of the new Tribunal Service. The White Paper does envisage the Secretary of State for Constitutional Affairs at one remove from appointments, with the Judicial Appointments Commission being brought in to provide a more 'professionalised' approach to such appointments. Furthermore, it is difficult to say how the status question of 'Crown appointment' will be handled under the new proposals.

The Council on Tribunals

The Leggatt report had noted that the Council's detailed focus on tribunal work had in the past precluded a more strategic vision about administrative justice generally but nevertheless, it identified a key role for the Council in the tribunal reforms (Leggatt, 2001: para 7.47). The White Paper proposes that the Council be rebranded as an 'Administrative Justice Council'; it would retain its supervisory role over all tribunals (White Paper, 2004: 52-4). However, its current role in commenting on secondary legislation would need to be reviewed given the proposed establishment of a new procedure committee for the tribunal sector. The new Council is primed to evolve into an advisory body for the whole administrative justice sector and would report to the Secretary of State for Constitutional Affairs. It would review the relationship and balance between the various components of the system, for example, the ombudsman schemes, tribunals, courts and alternative dispute resolution (ADR) routes. It is envisaged that the new Administrative Justice Council will be established in April 2006. It is difficult to predict at the time of writing how these proposals will be represented in the Courts and Tribunals Bill that the White Paper envisages being introduced into Parliament in June 2005 with the intention of obtaining Royal Assent in December of that year: see Appendix 6 for the timetable of reform as set out in the White Paper.

Chapter 7

Evaluating the Commissioners

Introduction

This book has examined the work of the Social Security and Child Support Commissioners, a specialist body of judges exercising statutory appellate jurisdiction, principally on paper rather than through oral hearings. This jurisdiction extends throughout Great Britain on a point of law from the decisions of first-tier appeals tribunals in respect of the range of cash transfer payments we know as 'social security' administered by the Department for Work and Pensions (DWP), the Inland Revenue, and by local authorities; and in respect of child support payments administered by the Child Support Agency. It has also examined the comparable work done by the Commissioners' Northern Ireland counterparts.

This chapter synthesises findings from the other chapters to evaluate the role of the Commissioners, their response to the concerns identified by a number of reviews and commentators, and, in the light of an analysis of views of both professional and lay users, considers the Commissioners as a formative model for the second-tier appellate level in a reformed tribunal system.

Commissioners operate in a very different environment from that studied by Micklethwait (1976). They are a heterogeneous body of men and women with diverse legal backgrounds, highly committed to providing a good service for scrutiny by the higher courts, for Appeals Service (AS) tribunals, lawyers and policy-makers, and to producing within the increasingly restrictive limits of complicated legal rules, both a legally correct and, so far as possible within those constraints, a 'just' result for appellants. As Chapter 3 shows, they make determined efforts to give a 'fair hearing' to arguable cases; efforts that were appreciated by some of our interviewees who had an oral hearing (see Chapter 4).

Broadly we conclude that the response to concerns has generally been successful, sometimes not. Notable successes include major reductions in the time needed expeditiously to process cases, improved access to Commissioners' decisions and making good use of modern technology in electronic publishing. Problems still exist, however, in clearly defining the criteria for the selection of decisions to be given the more authoritative 'reported' status and in securing appropriate representation for individuals whose cases are being dealt with by the Commissioners in these complicated areas of law. More fundamentally, but perhaps inevitably, given the Commissioners' more court-like status than first-tier tribunals, there are problems resulting from perceptions of the process as too complex and remote from the needs of lay users as they see them.

Our study firmly rejects the 'do-it-yourself' representation implied by Leggatt and argues that there is a clear and pressing need for the public financing of quality representation for cases at Commissioner level.

Evaluation against a changing context

There have been a number of important changes in the Commissioner system since Micklethwait (1976). A crucial watershed was the change to appeals on law only from 1987. This firmly established the Commissioners as a second-tier appellate body. Such a body is inevitably rather more formal, perhaps 'court-like', than first-tier appellate bodies dealing with the merits of the case, such as the AS tribunals. The skills required at the first-tier, to determine the facts and merits of a case, might often imply a more 'user-friendly' approach. Baldwin *et al* (1992: 179) concluded from their examination of appellants' experiences that 'social security appeal tribunals in the great majority of circumstances operate in an even-handed and humane manner' (1992: 179). Micklethwait (1976: 46) was convinced that the Commissioners, during the time he wrote about, had succeeded in meeting the gold standard in the Franks Report (1957) of a combination of formal procedure with an informal atmosphere.

However, it should be recalled that Micklethwait had in mind a smaller body of Commissioners responsible for a less far-ranging jurisdiction and dealing with a much smaller caseload.[1] Moreover, the 'fact and law' appeals in Micklethwait's time could appear to maintain a closer relationship between Commissioner and claimant. The Commissioners were better positioned to hear evidence and find new facts to assist a claimant's case and produce a direct result rather than remitting a decision back on the basis of an error of law, for the claimant only to find later at the reconvened AS tribunal that the gain at Commissioner level had been merely a pyrrhic victory. It should also be remembered that Micklethwait's views were based upon only his own experience and assertion rather than on any structured canvassing of the views of claimants or their representatives.

Our research on the views of appellants has shown that their perception of an appeal to the Commissioners is one marked out by complexity and remoteness (Chapter 4). Their access to Commissioner justice is viewed as something of a lottery, depending on a number of factors, including in particular their own abilities to persevere and to connect with good quality representation. What appellants are actually looking for from the appeal system is frequently quite different from the statutory role of the Commissioners as arbiters of points of law, a role that finds

---

[1] Micklethwait (1976: 137) refered to a 'surge' of appeals in 1973. In that year he states there were 435 applications for leave (granted in 248 cases), and 287 appeals of which no fewer than 267 were allowed, nearly all of them being appeals by claimants. He clearly thought a more 'normal' caseload profile was in 1974: 94 applications and 32 appeals.

little resonance with appellants. Indeed, the increasing complexity of social security legislation since Micklethwait has become baffling to lawyers. In addition, the majority of appeals to the Commissioners concern disability- or incapacity-related benefits where the dispute with the benefit authorities may often be a proxy for a combination of grievances and wider resentments experienced by an individual. Loss of benefit in these areas may be seen as a reflection on the character and *bona fides* of the claimant and his or her claim of disability or incapacity. The gap between appellants' expectations and what in reality are the limits of what the Commissioners can deliver, constrained as they are within their statutory role, argues strongly for additional resources to fill this gap. In this context, this implies the need for sufficient resources to be arranged to secure proper representation.

Micklethwait addressed his remarks in relation to what we would now regard as a simpler benefits structure containing broader legal tests, and overall, more discretion for the Commissioners to reach a 'just' result. But even Micklethwait (1976: 94) was perplexed by the way social security legislation was hastily conceived and enacted. He approved of the general thrust of the Renton Report (1975), in particular its recommendation that 'in principle the interests of the ultimate users should always have priority over those of the legislators' (Micklethwait, 1976: 80), a message that finds its modern counterpart in the *leit motif* of Leggatt. However, social security legislation has become even more complex over the last 30 years. In part to aid the computerised delivery of benefits, a good example of Mashaw's *bureaucratic rationality*, it has also arguably become much more rigidly rule-bound. Some areas of interpretative discretion are either now fairly well settled in the caselaw or such areas have been withdrawn and replaced with more objective criteria, an example of the latter being 'good cause' for a late claim.

Major improvements in response to criticisms

The Commissioner system has moved on since the trenchant criticisms of the Select Committee (2000) about delay and other matters.[2] The following sections summarise the improvements made and identifies other areas where further improvement could be achieved.

Precedent and availability of decisions

The availability of Commissioners' decisions has improved greatly. The renewed attention to maintaining the bound volumes and the easy availability to Commissioners' decisions now possible through OSSCSC's website provides welfare rights' representatives or unrepresented claimants with the necessary

[2] See pp. 11-14, 147-8, 187-191.

material to pursue an appeal to the Commissioners. The Commissioners and the government department were effectively stung into action by the Select Committee intervention on this issue.

As regards the matter of the *selection* of decisions for 'reporting' status, there is a more mixed review. On the one hand, the discontinuance of 'starred' status has been helpful as this was misunderstood by many users of the system and even the Leggatt review team managed to misconstrue the significance of 'starring'. The transition from the 'Star Chamber' to an 'Editorial Board' has been accompanied by an increased awareness of the defects in the system, in particular the practical difficulties in obtaining the Commissioners' views efficiently and expeditiously in order to apply the consensus test. There have been sustained efforts to rectify these problems. In short, the process now used by the Commissioners is arguably less hit and miss than it has been in the past. It is also more suitable to address the problem of achieving consistency in Commissioner decision-making.

However, there are, in our view two remaining fundamental problems; the lack of clarity in the criteria that are used for selecting decisions for 'reported' status, and the issue of the composition of the body that controls the selection process. We have set out our own recommendations in Chapter 5 for how these two issues might be addressed in the context of a reformed tribunal system.[3] In short, we recommend that 'Decision Boards', established in each jurisdiction with a wider membership to reflect a range of tribunal users, evolve fuller selection criteria guidance. Such boards will be able to amalgamate in parallel with the combination of jurisdictions that are likely to occur in the future.

Better case management and reduced delay

The efforts of the Commissioners to improve case management following the Select Committee and the Leggatt review,[4] have helped immeasurably in meeting the criticisms of delay in waiting times. The Commissioners have started to develop a clearer management structure in their operation. There are distinct committees for particular tasks (Commissioners' Annual Report 2004: 6). The legal officers are being deployed more rationally and the administrative support staff now have the benefit of new technology by which case progression can be more easily tracked and monitored. OSSCSC has produced annual reports since 2002-03 containing headline figures for applications and appeals, waiting times and performance targets. Both the targets of 10 weeks for applications and 20 weeks for appeals are being achieved, a far cry from the 64-week average reported in 1998 and the average of 344 days we observed in our own research.[5]

The Commissioners' Annual Report (2004: 2) noted, however, that 'statistics alone give no indication as to the quality of Commissioners' individual decisions, or the extent to which their decisions have contributed to the development of a

---

[3] See pp. 163-6.
[4] See Chapter 3, pp. 49-50.
[5] See Chapter 4, pp. 120-122.

coherent body of welfare law'. There are however, standard techniques being developed in other jurisdictions to test the quality of decision-making, for example by the Independent Review Service in respect of discretionary social fund payments. Perhaps such procedures can be developed by the Commissioners in order to better appraise their own core 'product'. Care would be required to ensure this kind of monitoring did not introduce a management culture that might jeopardise judicial independence (Buck 2000: 102-105; 2003). In any event, we have argued that greater care needs to be taken to produce quality statistical data in order to better inform the allocation of judicial resources across a reformed tribunal sector.[6]

The changing workload

As we have seen there has been an overall downturn over the past three years in both applications and appeals to the commissioners: see Tables 3.2 and 3.3.[7] The switch in the proportion of appeals and applications handled by the Commissioners from 63 per cent and 37 per cent respectively in 1998, to 34 per cent and 66 per cent respectively in 2003-04 is complex to analyse. On the one hand, it reflects in part a more 'robust approach' to applications of little merit as claimed in the Commissioners' Annual Report (2004: 4). However, without any more sophisticated means of testing the quality of decision making it is impossible to know whether this switch is also curtailing the further consideration of some types of cases that, for a variety of reasons, ought to receive a fuller airing. There is also some truth in the assertion that some of the DMA changes introduced by SSA 1998, in particular the AS tribunal's power to set aside and review their own decisions, have effected the changing profile of the Commissioners' workload. It is certainly the case that the powers to stay 'lookalike' cases have been used, though the number of cases stayed at the Commissioner level (in the London office) has not exceeded more than about 200 cases in all over the past few years.[8]

The profile of Commissioner applications and appeals broken down by benefit (see Table 3.7)[9] has demonstrated that the Commissioners caseload consists of an overwhelming proportion (72 per cent) of cases concerning disability and incapacity-related benefits; DLA, incapacity benefit, industrial injuries disablement benefit and attendance allowance.

However, the profile of Commissioners' decisions that are of greater legal interest by virtue of having been 'highlighted' by the Editorial Board is somewhat different from this overall picture. The decisions concerning the benefits mentioned above amounted to 48 out of a total of 121 decisions highlighted in the 2004-05 period. But income support and housing/council tax benefits cases also figured prominently in this set of decisions. No doubt there are a number of explanations

---

[6] See Chapter 6, pp. 201-3.
[7] Chapter 3, pp. 73 and 81 respectively.
[8] See Chapter 3, p. 71.
[9] Chapter 3, p. 107.

for this. The supply of new or amended legislation tends to increase the demand for more substantive decision making to iron out interpretational gaps or ambiguities. There is frequently a tendency for more cases to be devoted to new benefits entering the jurisdiction, like housing/council tax benefit.

Table 7.1 'Highlighted' Commissioners' decisions (April 2004-February 2005)

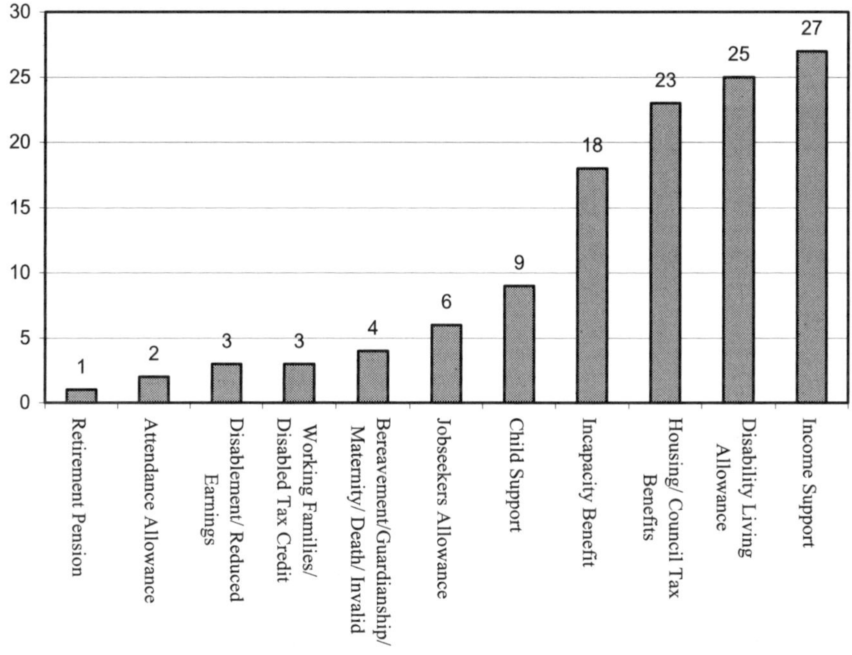

Source: OSSCSC website

Perceptions of the Commissioners by the tribunal users

The perception of any administrative justice system by its users will be a significant indicator of its value. The research we conducted[10] focussed both on the professionals within the Commissioner appeal system and the appellants themselves. The experience within the tribunal sector is that the perception of the appellants matters, even where it is not fully grounded on the facts. That has been the whole basis for the government's position to accept that the 'sponsoring' government departments' links with the administration of tribunals should be severed. It is generally recognised, for example, that AS tribunals are capable of

[10] See Chapter 1, pp. 6-10 for an account of the research methods used for our empirical study of the Commissioners.

acting even-handedly despite this institutional arrangement. However, a continuing body of evidence has continued to suggest that tribunal users see it differently.

This section reviews and summarises the key perceptions referred to in previous chapters of both the professionals connected with the Commissioners and, most importantly, the claimants who appeal.

The professionals' perception of the judicial quality of the commissioners

We have discussed[11] the way in which the higher courts will frequently defer to the specialist expertise of the Commissioners; see the *Cooke* case.[12] The following is fairly representative of the general perception from the House of Lords, for example:

> ... it is, in my view, highly desirable that when the Court of Appeal, or indeed your Lordships' House, are called upon to determine an issue of the kind in question they should have the benefit of the views upon it of one or more of the commissioners, who have great expertise in this somewhat esoteric area of the law. (*Chief Adjudication Officer v Foster*,[13] per Lord Bridge)

The view of a leading barrister, Richard Drabble QC, who has specialised over many years in various areas of social welfare law has also been clearly expressed:

> I have experience of many of the other specialised appellate structures, including, at various stages in my career, the immigration adjudication authorities and employment tribunals and the [Employment Appeal Tribunal]. *The standard of Commissioners' decisions is very high; in terms of the quality of the finished product it is without rival.* (Emphasis added) (Select Committee, 2000, Minutes of Evidence, *Memorandum submitted by Richard Drabble QC (APP 19)*, para 2)

Another barrister, Simon Cox, specialising in social welfare cases, stated in his written evidence to the Select Committee:

> The commissioners are held in high regard by those who work in this field. Generally, their decisions clarify rather than muddle the law, which is especially valuable because of the complexities of the regulations concerned. The commissioners are also generally alive to the social issues underlying benefits claims and child support cases, an attitude and awareness which is essential to the proper and humane administration of these schemes. My view is that the commissioners have played a leading role in developing, refining and humanising social security law. (Select Committee, 2000, Minutes of Evidence, *Memorandum submitted by Simon Cox (APP 16)*, para 2.3)

---

[11] See Chapter 6, pp. 173-77.

[12] *Cooke v Secretary of State for Social Security* [2002] 3 AER 279, reported as *R(DLA) 6/01*.

[13] [1993] AC 754.

Welfare rights groups have also held in high regard the skill and judicial quality of the Commissioners. Indeed, it was noticeable, at the time of the Select Committee (2000) inquiry, how forcibly welfare rights groups praised the Commissioners. The Child Poverty Action Group's (CPAG) verdict was clear:

> Judicially, we would suggest that Commissioners do a very good job, as can be gauged from the limited number of their decisions which are appealed further and the very few successful challenges made on judicial review to Commissioners' decisions refusing to grant leave to appeal. Moreover, they operate in a way which leads to greater fairness, simplicity, consistency and transparency of a very complicated area of law. (Select Committee, 2000, Minutes of Evidence, *Memorandum submitted by the Child Poverty Action Group (CPAG) (APP 11)*, para 2.3)

The Free Representation Unit stated in their written evidence that 'the standard of [Commissioner] decision making is very high'.[14] The welfare rights unit at NACAB stated that they had 'found the Commissioners, as adjudicators, to be fair and extremely knowledgeable on their subject. They therefore command a degree of respect and this is so even where decisions are against our clients.'[15]

The Select Committee, though of course critical about delays, publication arrangements and other matters (see Chapter 6), recognised and valued the independent role the Commissioners played and the esteem in which they were held (Select Committee, 2000: para 8).

There has been nothing in our examination of the Commissioners that has diminished the confidence shown in the *quality* of Commissioners' decisions. Welfare rights groups perceive the Commissioners in practice as the final stopping place in all but a handful of usually exceptional cases. To that extent the Commissioners have been very successful, as a specialised jurisdiction must be, in ensuring that the courts are not inappropriately encumbered with such cases. The greater diversity of legal background of the Commissioners appointed over recent years[16] has probably added to the general perception that the quality of Commissioners' decisions is at the 'very good'/'excellent' end of the spectrum.

The appellants' perceptions of the Commissioners

However, from our analysis of the appellants' perceptions[17] it can be seen that the experience for many of pursuing a Commissioner appeal is that not very much appears to happen for long periods of time, a scenario that poses challenges for meeting the demands of the 'process values' of time, participation, dignity and transparency. There was also some evidence that the process value of participation

---

[14] Select Committee, 2000, Minutes of Evidence, *Memorandum submitted by the Free Representation Unit (FRU) (APP 10)*, para 10.

[15] *Ibid*, *Memorandum submitted by Welfare Rights Unit, the National Association for Citizen Advice Bureaux, London region (APP 12)*, para 4.

[16] See Chapter 2, pp. 51-7.

[17] See Chapter 4, pp. 133-6.

was possible to meet in a largely paper-based jurisdiction such as the Commissioners. For many people, the process of pursuing an appeal, prompts feelings of powerlessness and remoteness. The danger is that such feelings may spill over into a lack of faith in the integrity of the wider framework of administrative justice.

Our analysis in Chapter 4 demonstrated a range of observations relevant for consideration by policy makers in determining the future direction of the new Tribunal Service. For example, only a few of the appellants at Commissioner level had a clear idea that their appeal was constrained to a point of law only. This obviously implies the need for better and timelier information to be made available to tribunal users. The generally low levels of knowledge by appellants about the Commissioners, more fundamentally, also implies a pressing need for more attention to be paid in the reform plans to the question of funded representation, an issue that we explore further at the end of this chapter.

Commissioners and models of justice

Mashaw's three justice models[18] were developed in relation to a disability programme of social security in the United States. The paradigm there of *bureaucratic rationality* is the administrative agency that had responsibility for initial decision-making. The model for *professional treatment* is directed at the role of medical and vocational rehabilitation professionals. The exemplar of *moral judgment* is the appeal to an administrative law judge.

One can apply this tripartite analysis to the British context of social security adjudication. Initial decision makers in the relevant 'departments' have a primary goal to implement the administration of the benefit in question accurately and efficiently within a hierarchical organisation (bureaucratic rationality). The determination of claims for some benefit requires a significant input from, for example, professional specialists such as doctors and accountants (professional treatment). Indeed, it can be recalled that both at the level of AS tribunals and the Commissioners, there was a very high proportion of disability and incapacity related benefits in the total workloads: see Tables 3.6 and 3.7.[19] Where initial decision-making, with or without professional input, has gone wrong, the availability of an appeal ultimately to the Commissioners and courts provides a classic forum that, as pointed out in Chapter 6, stresses conflict resolution by an independent decision-maker in a process ingrained with the legitimating value of fairness (moral judgment). In the sense of procedural fairness, the Commissioners' core function therefore fits most easily, but not exclusively, into Mashaw's *moral judgment* category.

---

[18] See Chapter 1, Table 1.2, p. 25.

[19] Chapter 3, pp. 106 and 107 respectively.

However, in our view, the Mashaw analysis[20] can additionally be usefully applied, not just to the whole end-to-end process of the social security system, but also, for our purposes, to the Commissioner system itself, which has been the central concern of this book. This is especially so when we look at the way in which the three justice models *compete* with each other for primacy in any organisational system.

Finally, in this section we return to a consideration of Legomsky's analysis[21] of 'specialised justice', in particular an attempted application of his proposed criteria for testing whether a jurisdiction ought to become specialised or be accommodated in a generalist environment.

The Commissioners and 'bureaucratic rationality'

Our examination of the way in which OSSCSC has developed, in particular over the last five years, shows various points at which the organisation has attempted to implement the organisational goal of delivering application for leave and appeal decisions accurately and efficiently. The interventions of the Select Committee and other forms of accountability that we reviewed in Chapter 6 have tended to strengthen the dominance of bureaucratic rationality as the organising feature of the Commissioners' operation. The legitimising values of accuracy and efficiency can be seen in the concerted and successful responses to reducing delays and waiting times for the users. The Chief Commissioner and a few other experienced Commissioners have increasingly taken on more obvious 'management' roles in order to meet the legislatively prescribed goal of application and appeal production. Indeed, Judge Harris's 'double appointment' as Chief Commissioner and President of the Appeals Tribunals can be viewed as part of a determined policy initiative to secure bureaucratic rationality within the structure of OSSCSC.

It is difficult to see the possibility of ever reverting to having a Chief Commissioner on the model of a *primus inter pares* merely acting as a spokesperson for a 'college of Commissioners'. But even Micklethwait (1976: 43) understood that the role of the Chief Commissioner was different to the other Commissioners; '[i]n matters of administration ... the difference is very great.' Chief Commissioners will now need to manage *and* judge. It would be imprudent, in the context of a reformed tribunal system to focus only on one of these functions. Indeed, the tribunal reforms envisaged will also require that the Presidents of the individual jurisdictions will increasingly be required to understand and be able to provide leadership in delivering 'bureaucratic rationality' as will be understood throughout the new Tribunal Service. The relevant cognitive technique, 'information processing' (see Table 1.2) in relation to this justice model has also been much improved, for example, the replacement of an out of date system (ERIC)

[20] See Chapter 1, pp. 23-5 for a brief synopsis of Mashaw's 'models of justice'.

[21] See Chapter 1, pp. 21-3.

with new technology and a more determined administrative support staff committed to clearer organisational goals and transparent performance indicators.

The Commissioners and 'professional treatment'

Our analysis of the organisation (OSSCSC) in previous chapters has shown evidence of a growing service culture. The reformed tribunal system is to be called a new Tribunal *Service*. Under Mashaw's professional treatment model, the primary goal is to satisfy the client. Mashaw compares bureaucratic rationality and professional treatment in the following extract:

> The basis for the legitimacy of professional treatment is in one respect similar to that of bureaucratic decision-making: the professional is master of an arcane body of knowledge and supports his judgment by appeals to expertise. But whereas the bureaucrat displays his or her knowledge through instrumentally rational routines designed to render transparent the connection between concrete decisions and legislatively validated policy, the professional's art remains opaque to the layman. The mystery of professional judgment is, nevertheless, acceptable because of the service ideal of professionalism. The element of mystery and charisma in the office of physician, priest, or lawyer is combined with the trusteeship implicit in professional-client relations. Justice lies in having the appropriate professional judgment applied to one's particular situation *in the context of a service relationship*. (Mashaw, 1983: 28-9)

An appellate body, such as the Commissioners, based on professional treatment would therefore be client-oriented. If one supposes that an appellate body has two main clients, individual claimants and representatives of the administering government department, then such a body would be likely to assume the easy availability of, for example, publicly funded lawyers skilled in providing whatever arcane legal knowledge was necessary to best meet the needs of the client's situation. Arguably, this is precisely the role of the Adjudication and Constitutional Issues Branch (ACIB) in Leeds with regard to the Secretary of State's side of the equation. However, as we have seen, in Chapter 4, the arrangements for representation of claimants are fragmented. The ability of appellants to connect with good representation is something of a lottery.

In a narrow sense, the Commissioners themselves provide professional treatment, mainly as a result of the absence from the social security tribunal system of sufficiently skilled lawyers to represent claimants. As we have seen from Chapter 3, their approach to considering applications for leave and appeals is ingrained with a sense of their inquisitorial or enabling function; the pursuit of legal argument not previously raised that may serve the needs of the appellant.[22] The role of the legal officers can also be seen as an extension of these functions. The legal officers, as we have seen,[23] form a small group of highly professional experts in social security law. Arguably the role of the registrar within the Leggatt

[22] See Chapter 3, pp. 72-3, 77.
[23] See Chapter 3, pp. 98-103.

recommendations is an attempt to utilise this kind of valuable resource within the system and re-direct it more to the goals of bureaucratic rationality. The cognitive technique of professional treatment is the 'clinical application of knowledge', in this context, the skilful management of legal materials to support what the client wants. It should be noted however, as Mashaw (1983: 27) reminds us, that there is a difference between 'scientific' and 'clinical' knowledge. In the context of the Commissioners, the need to maintain judicial neutrality between the parties can be seen as an expected quality of the judicial 'product' required to satisfy users. In that sense, Commissioners must therefore apply the 'science' of law without partiality to either side. However, the legal 'clinician' who acts on behalf of either party is, by contrast, expected to utilise his or her specialised knowledge to best advance the client's policy or monetary interests in the dispute.

The Commissioners and 'moral judgment'

Mashaw states that publicly provided benefits by means of a non-adversary hearing process are capable of conforming to his model of moral judgment. He claims that 'the "justice" of this model inheres in its promise of a full and equal opportunity to obtain one's entitlements' (Mashaw, 1983: 31). The issue in this context then is the 'deservingness' (to use Miller's (1976) terminology)[24] of the parties within the matrix of the relevant legal rules. The primary goal is generally to resolve conflict between competing claims. There are different levels at which this might manifest itself in relation to social security appeals. Sometimes the subtext of the dispute is about the competing claims of the state's guardianship of the public purse and an individual's claim to welfare support as an aspect of citizenship. Sometimes, the dispute is more prosaic; a short interpretational point requires resolution in a context where there are neither real policy points nor even any significant resource implications at stake. The legitimising value is always fairness. This is meant both in the sense of 'deservingness' but also, as Mashaw (1983: 30) makes clear this issue 'seems to imply certain things about a just process of proof and decision'. In short, procedural justice can be regarded as integral to 'moral judgment'. As already discussed,[25] Commissioners do not make 'moral' judgments but their 'legal' judgments do imply a responsibility for delivering *procedural* 'fairness'. As Mashaw notes, judicial hearings can also provide an administrative system with an appropriate legitimising piece of symbolism:

> At the hearing … the claimant is provided a 'day in court' that seems to have a substantial impact on acceptance of an ultimate denial. Appeals from hearing decisions occur with much less frequency than do appeals to the hearing stage. This may be due, at least in part, to the symbolic power of the judge or the legal hearing to promote acceptance of the legitimacy of a disappointing judgment. (Mashaw, 1983: 143)

---

[24] See Chapter 1, pp. 25-6 for a brief synopsis of Miller's approach to the concept of social justice.

[25] Chapter 6, p. 167.

Furthermore, moral judgment is premised on the basis of an 'independent' structure. As we have seen, the constitutional understanding of the role of courts and tribunals generally is that they are emanations of a disinterested judicial function separate from executive and legislative functions.

However, as our examination of the Commissioners has shown, the *substantive* 'fairness' of the moral judgment model, which ought theoretically to be most applicable to the Commissioner system, has suffered in the shadow of bureaucratic rationality. Broad discretionary formulations in social security law have tended eventually to give way to detailed and more exact legal rules that tend not to admit broader 'fairness' claims. Such a legal framework is simply easier for the executive to control. As Mashaw points out, bureaucratic rationality tends to compete for dominance more successfully than the other two models. For example, the legislative limitation on the subject matter of appeal rights[26] is such that some of the more interesting conflicts of interests underlying social security provision may never be brought to light, at least by means of litigation strategies. Therefore, the appeal system fails to identify 'deservingness'. It is more likely to identify processing problems, seemingly one of the imperatives of a system dominated by bureaucratic rationality. The evidence discussed in Chapter 4 suggests that users of the system are not sufficiently informed or interested to distinguish between the different 'moral judgment' tasks at the tribunal and Commissioner levels respectively. The 'symbolism' of the Commissioners is only residually evident in the occurrence of oral hearings, but these remain a small minority (4 per cent) of hearings, at least from the London office of Commissioners. Finally, 'independence' will be constantly threatened by the need for a new breed of judicial managers.

Specialised justice and the Commissioners

This book has concerned itself with the highly specialised and complex jurisdiction of social security law. In the words of one of the Commissioners:

> I think that British social security law is actually more complex and more difficult to handle than British tax law, British tax law is regarded the world around as the most complex tax law, it's far more complex than the American or the French or the German system. British social security law, in my view is excessively and obsessively complex, and you've got to have experts who can handle that for claimants who haven't in most cases got a clue what's going on.

Indeed, Micklethwait devoted a whole chapter in his book to the complexity of the legislation and favoured maintaining social security law in a consolidated form. He stressed the user perspective long before Leggatt in his message to those with responsibility for drafting social security legislation:

---

[26] See Chapter 3, pp. 66-8.

> My own view is emphatic. I think the words which all of those concerned in the preparation of legislation should have in the forefront of their minds are: 'Think always of the user'. (Micklethwait, 1976: 80)

Micklethwait also thought that the specialisation of the Commissioners had worked in terms of delivering a remedy to claimants who would otherwise be without one:

> When one takes into account the various advantages to the claimant of an appeal to a Commissioner compared with proceedings in the High Court, I do not believe that anything like one-tenth of the successful appeals [to the Commissioners] would have reached the court at all. (Micklethwait, 1976: 137)

How far has our examination of the Commissioners answered the question of whether the specialisation of the Commissioners is an appropriate one? In applying Legomsky's criteria[27] for determining whether a given class of case should be assigned to specialised adjudicators, the following conclusions are offered.

The Commissioners, as an appellate body, by definition apply a high proportion of exclusively 'law' questions. As we have seen (Chapter 3) the identification of an 'error of law' is easily made at least an 'arguable' entity in relation to most first-tier tribunal decisions. The expertise required to carry out its identification is a well-known administrative law task. Consequently, this feature of the Commissioners' operation points away from specialisation to more generalist treatment. Although it is early days to comment too specifically about the government's reformed tribunal system, it does seem that the concept of the single office of the 'Appellate Tribunal Judge' will be evolved to cover a larger number of individual jurisdictions. That process of rationalisation, the addition of further jurisdictional areas and contemplation of future jurisdictions, has already commenced.[28]

On the other hand, the technical complexity of social security law leans towards specialisation. One of the complaints of Commissioners about representatives, particularly at oral hearings, was that there were few specialists who would have sufficient depth of knowledge to know how a detailed point of interpretation of a regulation was set in relief against the wider policy imperatives of the overall programme of social welfare provision. It is interesting to recall that some of the Commissioners' most significant concerns about the future integrity of a reformed tribunal system was that it would require judges to move from social security to immigration to employment in the space of a working day. Nevertheless, many of the Commissioners had already been, and were in the process of being, encouraged to take on multiple judicial appointments. The Leggatt (2001) recommendations on a divisional structure at least attempted some kind of organisation into coherent legal fields. The rejection of this recommendation in the White Paper (2004) would appear to leave the organisation of this matter to be dealt with in a more *ad hoc* fashion. However, while the Commissioners have the generalist skills to move

[27] See Chapter 1, pp. 21-3..
[28] See Chapter 2, pp. 46-7.

into other jurisdictions, the DCA should nonetheless be chary about the wisdom of moving non-specialists into the social security area on a temporary or *ad hoc* basis.

The degree of isolation of the social security law terrain is arguably a factor in favour of specialisation. However, one needs to carefully examine what is meant by 'isolation' in this context. It is arguable that social security provision has increasingly been used as one element of a more 'joined-up' government policy, for example, efforts to tackle 'social exclusion', the 'Sure Start' programme and other efforts to eliminate child poverty (Lakhani, 2003: 169). Social security has multiple connections with immigration, family, employment law to name but a few cognate areas. There are many issues that go to appeal to the Commissioners, precisely because they concern very difficult matters on the borderline or overlap between two legal regimes that may have rather different overall policy objectives, thus making the interpretative task even more difficult. One of the oral hearings we observed in fact related precisely to this kind of 'overlap' case and required high levels of expertise on immigration and social security law. The Leggatt team also observed an oral hearing (Leggatt, 2001: 184) and drew from this only a sense of the lengthy periods that could occur in such appeals. In fact the Commissioner who sat in this case told us later that the case was:

> …a second time around case, alleged over-payments dating back nine years, the papers were in disarray, …and it involved my considering *R(A) 1/95*, which was a rather unknown decision, and not following it. So it was a completely atypical case.

On the question of internal coherence tending towards specialisation, there are undoubtedly some recurring concepts of social security law that are common to the many different benefits, allowances and credits available, for example, the core concept of 'conditions of entitlement' and the legal definition of a 'family'. However, what makes social security law difficult and complex is probably the fact that there is a bewildering quantity of regulations in relation to each individual benefit, often legislated without proper reference to how it might fit into the overall system of legal protection. Micklethwait supported the idea of simplifying the drafting of social security legislation. In his evidence to the Renton Committee he said:

> A statute should not only be clear and unambiguous, but readable. It ought not to call out for the exercise of a crossword/acrostic mentality which is able to ferret out the meaning from a number of sections, schedules and regulations. (Renton Report, 1975: para 28)

However, the simplification of benefit regulations has since been a persistent problem.[29] In this sense a lack of internal coherence in the law itself may argue for a more generalist approach. Any one piece of social security law may have more coherence with other social welfare law terrains rather than its own internal

[29] The National Audit Office is currently reviewing this subject and is due to publish its report, 'Managing the Complexity of Benefit Regulations' in summer 2005.

consistency. But the arcane specificity and 'non-joined-up' nature of each regime of social security benefit points surely to a need for specialisation.

The degree of repetition of cases is also said to indicate either specialisation or a generalist approach. Where there is a high number of similar cases specialisation could be favoured. The Commissioner may acquire a detailed knowledge of factors that can impact on the final outcome. The knowledge thus acquired will be finely calibrated and built up over a long time. The Commissioner may therefore arguably have a reservoir of experience to draw from when novel situations arise. There will already be a pre-existing framework established into which the next case is positioned for decision-making. Thus, for example, many of the questions arising frequently under DLA appeals about the nature of 'attention to bodily functions' and other issues, were, as we have seen[30] so familiar to the Commissioners that it was thought appropriate to take legal officers off the task of looking at all DLA applications as part of their case management initiatives.

If it is the case that a greater degree of controversy favours a generalist approach to ensure legitimacy then the interface of Commissioners' appeals with the disability lobby ought to indicate a generalist approach according to Legomsky. On the other hand, this criterion does no more than beg the question of whether specialist jurisdictions can be regarded as more or less 'legitimate' than a generalist one. Our examination of the Commissioners has in fact shown that they are highly regarded precisely *because* of their specialist expertise in a complex area.

Legomsky favoured adjudication by legal generalists where one could detect 'clannishness' in a specialised community. Historically, as we have seen, Commissioners used to be drawn exclusively from members of the Bar and often had no knowledge of social security law prior to their appointment. However, the position has changed and they are now drawn from a wider base.

The importance of the need for consistency in law indicates specialised adjudication. Indeed, that issue has been explored in some detail in Chapter 5. Prior to the interventions of Leggatt and the Select Committee there was a certain amount of inattention to this aspect of the Commissioners' work. The reporting system was not utilised proactively to guide a consistent development of the law. Indeed, the Commissioners appeared to disagree amongst themselves about how this system should be further developed to achieve such consistency. There did not appear to be much evidence that this specialised jurisdiction had been acting any better in terms of consistency than could have been achieved by means of a more generalist forum. However, as we have seen, there have been some improvements made here in recent years.

The dynamic nature of the subject matter of social security law indicates, according to Legomsky, the need for specialisation. There is certainly always a great quantity of both primary and secondary social security law to consider. There

[30] Chapter 3, p. 78.

have been no less than eight Acts of Parliament relating to social security from 2001 to 2004, and a great quantity of statutory instruments.[31] See Table 7.2 below.

The number of regulations in social security even outstrips those in the fast-changing area of immigration and asylum.[32] As we have seen,[33] the legal officers at OSSCSC have been used as a research resource specifically to ensure that new regulations are scrutinised and to help make any important changes known to the Commissioners.

Table 7.2 'Social Security' Statutory Instruments, 2001-2004

	2001	2002	2003	2004
Social Security	107	88	92	71
Social Security, England & Wales	0	0	1	0
Social Security, Northern Ireland	12	8	5	2

Source: HMSO website – www.legislation.hmso.gov.uk/si-statistics.htm

Legomsky also claims that a high volume of like cases can be more efficiently dealt with by a specialist body, especially where such cases are time consuming and geographically dispersed. The Commissioners do deal with a (relatively) high volume of cases.[34] If these cases were to be added to a more generalist court forum one would have to look carefully at the effect this might have on the workload of that court.

Another criterion said to favour specialisation is where there is a special need for the prompt resolution of cases. There are obviously many social security appeals where the money values at issue are extremely important to the individuals concerned. The claimants' perspective is frequently focussed on simply obtaining a quick and timely answer from the appeal system. It is argued that specialists will take less time to clear cases and be better equipped to filter out unmeritorious cases. It is perhaps this enhanced expectation that specialists will be capable of clearing caseloads efficiently that fuelled the public concerns about delay and made the Commissioners extremely vulnerable to such criticisms.

Finally, a classic advantage of specialisation is that the procedure can be customised to the attributes of the type of case. In the case of the Commissioners,

[31] Micklethwait (1976: 21) also complained of the 15 statutes enacted between 1971 and 1975 relating to national insurance that contributed, in his view, to the complexity and confusion of the law.

[32] The aggregate number of SIs in the 'Immigration' and 'Immigration and Asylum' categories for the same years were, respectively 20, 27, 43 and 34.

[33] Chapter 3, p. 100.

[34] Chapter 3, Tables 3.2 and 3.3, pp. 73 and 81 respectively.

we have seen how in fact most appellants have to represent themselves, though statistical data on representation is surprisingly lacking.[35] This has prompted the development of an inquisitorial element to the social security jurisdiction to mitigate the adverse effects of such a lack of representation.

As already seen from Chapter 1, Legomsky preferred the model of 'multiple-speciality adjudication' in particular at the appellate stage. He assumed that all members of this type of adjudicative unit would have multiple specialities, and identified the following advantages. Firstly, the model provided an opportunity for 'collegial interchange' with other judges conversant in the various specialities. As the quote[36] in Chapter 1 makes clear, the important benefit of a generalist perspective lies in the value of analogy. The hope is that the combinations of jurisdictions envisaged by the government can equally provide a multiple speciality framework capable of delivering similar or better opportunities of such 'productive analogies'. However, as Legomsky points out, the introduction of an interesting mix of subjects in this framework reduces the potential tedium of a single speciality and increases the likelihood of recruiting more able individuals. Moreover, the combination of specialities is capable of being 'an efficient way to absorb fluctuations in the volume of cases filed in a single specialized subject area' (1990: 41). He also claimed other advantages for this model.

> Since the members' exposure to specific areas will be more dispersed, there is not the same likelihood as in a single-speciality unit of developing improper sympathy for a single agency or another frequent litigant. For the same reason, the members are appreciably less likely to become over-confident and unduly assertive in substituting their own policy views for those of legislators or other government officials. Finally, the combination of more adjudicators and less intensively involved adjudicators tempers the biases sometimes associated with single-speciality bodies. In all these ways, the multiple-speciality unit can, in appropriate settings, optimize the quality of the end-product by combining the positive attributes of specialists and generalists. (Legomsky, 1990: 41)

In our interview work with the Commissioners, their responses to Leggatt in respect of the tribunal reforms (see Chapter 6)[37] and the likely impact on their own specialised jurisdiction to some extent reflected a desire, at least amongst some of them, to enter the wider world of combined specialist jurisdictions. There were concerns too about the future prospect, but on balance many of the Commissioners saw this as an opportunity to be involved in a more varied and interesting caseload and that it would inevitably enhance their own judicial status if they could offer more than one specialism. With the prospect of new legislation setting out a reformed tribunal system, the current Chief Commissioner is clearly actively encouraging the multiple 'ticketing' of Commissioners in readiness for such changes. But the complexity and often-arcane nature of the social security system

---

[35] See Chapter 6, p. 201.
[36] Legomsky (1990: 40); cited in Chapter 1, p. 22.
[37] See Chapter 6, pp. 191-7.

should make the DCA pause before moving non-specialists on an *ad hoc* or temporary basis into the social security jurisdiction. Fortunately, given the reduction in the Commissioners' workload and a pool of Deputies available for present and future specialist appointment, this is unlikely to be a problem in the foreseeable future.

Future prospects

Finally, this section briefly summarises the future challenges that lie ahead for the Commissioners in terms of additional jurisdictions, the impact of the tribunal reform programme and lastly, but by no means least, the need for justice to be improved by means of a proper provision for legal representation in this field.

Additional jurisdictions

The history of the Commissioners has seen a development from a narrow jurisdiction to a much wider one, or to use Legomsky's terminology from a single to a multiple speciality. These developments have also involved the Commissioners considering appeals based on the initial decision-making not only of the DWP but also a number of other governmental authorities. Up until 1998 the Commissioners dealt only with appeals concerning decisions made by the then Department of Social Security. In 2003 the Commissioners, for the first time, took on appeal work based on the decision making from *local authorities* in respect of housing and council tax benefit. The Commissioners also now hear appeals in respect of a number of benefits and credits, shortly to include certain decisions under the Child Trust Fund Act 2004, derived from initial decision making by the Inland Revenue (see Wikeley, 2004). In due course, they will also take on appeals from decisions emanating from the Department of Health in relation to the recovery of compensation for NHS costs in respect of traffic accidents.[38] The Commissioners will also take on war pension appeals based on decisions of the Ministry of Defence. The current appeal available from the Pensions Appeal Tribunal (PAT) to the High Court will be replaced by an appeal from PAT to the Commissioners.[39] As the next section explains, the future prospects of the Commissioners will depend on how the reforms to the tribunal system are delivered by the DCA over the next five years.

---

[38] Health and Social Care (Community Health and Standards) Act 2003, Part 3, section 159. At the time of writing the regulations bringing this Part of the Act into force had not been made.

[39] See the Armed Forces (Pension and Compensation) Act 2004, Schedule 1, para 4.

Commissioners and the tribunal reform programme

The timetable for reform (see Appendix 6) has already seen the formation of a 'shadow' Tribunal Service in April 2005 in advance of its formal launch planned for April 2006. The senior 'virtual management team' is already planning the better use of hearing centres and piloting new ways of resolving disputes.[40] According to the White Paper (2004), a new second-tier appellate body with the working title of 'Administrative Appeals Tribunal' will come into operation in April 2007. It is likely that the collective experience of the Commissioners, some of whom are already 'multiple-ticketed' judges in other jurisdictions, will make a major contribution to the formation of the new judicial body. Their reputation and high regard in terms of judicial quality ought to be capable of extension into this new appellate body. It is likely too that their practice on reporting decisions will be carefully scrutinised with a view to eventually devising a more uniform approach to suit the challenges this new body will have to meet.

The (virtual) Tribunal Service is conscious that bringing together specialised jurisdictions will not be effectively achieved by a 'one size fits all' solution. It is expected that the new Service will 'have a "federal" structure that recognises individuality.'[41] At the judicial level, a Tribunals Presidents' Group (including the Chief Commissioner), originally established by Brooke LJ, is chaired by the Senior President designate, and meets regularly to further develop the reform plans (Carnwath, 2004). There are also a number of smaller groups examining legislation, training and appraisal, appointments and deployment, appeal routes and information technology. The new Senior President designate is, not unsurprisingly, taking a cautious public approach in circumstances where it is clear that the planned combination of jurisdictions will eventually eliminate some of the individual Presidents from their current roles:

> What is already clear to me, and I am very grateful for it, is that all the major tribunals have their own well-established Presidents (under whatever name), who are already providing 'strong and vigorous' leadership [a reference to the White Paper's description of the Senior President's role]. The last thing they need is me treading 'strongly and vigorously' on their toes. What I hope we can do together is to co-ordinate our efforts, and to build on the firm base which they and you have all created. (Carnwath, 2004)

In order to avoid confusion between the two tiers in the new system, Carnwath LJ's has suggested that the first- and second-tiers should be called respectively the 'Administrative and Civil Tribunal' and the 'Tribunal Appeal Court'. The latter, in his view, should be known as a 'court' 'to emphasise that its functions are more formal and concerned principally with issues of law' (Carnwath, 2004). For the same reason he urges consideration of reserving the name 'judge' for the second-

[40] DCA *Press Notice*, 4 April 2005.

[41] www.tribunalservice.gov.uk, accessed April 2005. But the White Paper (2004: 5) points out that 'we see this new body as much more than a federation of existing tribunals.'

tier and finding another name for the first-tier to better express the less formal role to be performed at that level. As we have seen in Chapter 2, concerning the debates over the original 'Commissioner' title, these matters of nomenclature frequently reflect significant differences of views about how such bodies are located in the overall judicial hierarchy.[42] Clearly, the way in which the amalgamation of a number of tribunal jurisdictions is handled and the level of resources committed to it will be important developments to watch for the future. There are some interesting lessons to be drawn from research evidence now appearing from other jurisdictions, for example, in Australia, where such amalgamation has been attempted, sometimes successfully, sometimes not: see generally, Bacon (2005).

Representation and the need for public funding

Our analysis of the Commissioner system and in particular of the appellant sample and the Commissioners' own views about representation discussed earlier indicates strong concerns about the Leggatt-style world of mass self-representation in relation to a second-tier appellate authority.[43] This is consistent with much previous evidence in the social security field that good representation is required for the proper exercise of appeal rights (Genn and Genn, 1989; Baldwin *et al*, 1992, Adler and Gulland, 2003). The discrepancy between the appellants' experience of the appeal process and the legal forensic task of identifying and assessing whether there is an adequate flaw in a tribunal's decision for the 'error of law' switch to be turned on provides a strong argument for addressing users' needs for good quality representation at the second-tier in a reformed tribunal system. Although ours was only a small qualitative study of appellants, these individuals had by definition already overcome a number of obstacles to become engaged in a Commissioner appeal. Even the small group comprising articulate, assertive and confident individuals, usually with professional backgrounds, experienced real difficulties in representing themselves at Commissioner level.

The Commissioners too gave voice to their concerns in this area. Only a few had had any experience of cases where the Lord Chancellor's exceptional power to award legal aid had been used. One Commissioner mentioned a child support case but 'it took ages and ages but they did eventually fund it. But it is just so cumbersome and not suitable, unless in exceptional circumstances'. Some Commissioners told us that they had suggested for many years that they ought to have a power to certify a case fit for publicly funded legal representation. Another Commissioner thought either the Commissioners should have such a power or the legal aid board should make the decision. One Commissioner thought the Lord

[42] It would seem the Commissioner title may not last much longer. Lord Justice Carnwath (2004: 8) has stated in a recent speech '(I hope at least that we can improve on names like the "Office of Social Security and Child Support Commissioners", which is indigestible and inaccurate, and does not even have a pronounceable acronym).'

[43] See Chapter 4, pp. 126-133.

Chancellor was right in wanting to go down the road of block grants to specialist organisations.

> Because this is a specialised jurisdiction and I would want to see more public funding going to bodies or firms of solicitors so to speak having accreditation in this particular field. Rather than a generalised entitlement to legal aid for individual solicitors or even worse, claims consultants, who really don't know what they are doing.

One of the Chief Commissioners interviewed commented that in difficult cases, particularly in Tribunal of Commissioners' hearings, an absence of good representation would present real problems. 'They only get that representation through the good offices of welfare rights groups who do a quite tremendous job, but it would be a huge worry if they didn't do it in these cases'.

Disappointingly, Lord Justice Carnwath, the Senior President designate, appears to place much reliance on the Leggatt view that self-representation is the way forward:

> … we might wish that all parties had the help of professional advocates to present their cases before every type of Tribunal. But in the real world it is not going to happen. Within the constraints of the system as it is, a well-informed and sympathetic tribunal, with specialised experience of similar cases, offers the best available means of arriving at a fair and principled result. (Carnwath, 2004)

However, the logic of the plans for a reformed tribunal system is to focus on getting initial decision making right in the first place, but if a dispute does arise, to ensure that alternative methods of dealing with it are pursued. Failing these efforts, the formal processes of appeal are to be further developed to ensure that the types of 'filtering tools' we have surveyed in Chapter 3[44] are harnessed to deal with appellants at the earliest possible stages of the process. Two consequences ought to follow. Firstly, if this policy is successful there ought to be less cases going to full appeal, a point that has implications for the possible resources needed to fund representation. Secondly, the diminished caseload that does manage to persist through to the formal procedures at the second-tier level will be cases more likely to contain a substantial sense of grievance. In our view it is short-sighted to expect justice to be properly maintained without providing proper resources to support such appellants. The Leggatt argument that a representation 'deficit' is compensated by a tribunal's inquisitorial function[45] will need serious examination if and when the framework legislation is debated later this year.

We hope that our examination of the Commissioners in this book can better inform this and other debates on administrative justice for the future.

---

[44] Chapter 3, Figure 3.2, p. 64.

[45] See Chapter 1, p. 16.

Appendix 1

Interview Topic Guide for Commissioners[1]

A Professional background

(<u>Note</u>: We understand that the Commissioners are drawn from the following three groups: (i) practitioners at the Bar, (ii) academics, (iii) former tribunal chairs)

Q Can you tell me which of the three professional groups (i)-(iii) you belonged to before your appointment as a Commissioner?

Q Can you tell me, in your own words, how you view your professional background as a preparation for your work as a Social Security and Child Support Commissioner? Do you have any particular specialisms within the range of Commissioners' work?

B The Work of the Commissioners

Q What are the characteristic reasons for granting or refusing leave to appeal:

1. to the Commissioner, and
2. to the Court of Appeal/Court of Session?

Q What difficulties do you identify with the leave stage(s) of proceedings?

Q How do you regard the direction making powers of a Commissioner?

Q How do you see the value and future use of *oral* hearings?

Q How would you assess the role and contribution of the legal officers at OSSCSC?

Q What is your assessment of the quality of legal representation for:-

1. the appellant, and
2. the Secretary of State?

Q If you had to identify one thing to be remembered for in your judicial career as a Commissioner what would you choose?

C The Development of Social Security/Child Support Law

Q Which particular aspects of social security/child support law have been significantly affected by the Commissioners' intervention?

Q How would you assess the collective contribution made by the Commissioners to the development of social security/child support law?

Q Do you regard the current/proposed reporting arrangements for Commissioners' decisions as satisfactory?

Q Is there anything you have observed from the appeal process that, in your opinion, could reduce the delay in the disposal of cases?

Q Which areas of social security/child support law do you consider the most difficult and why?

---

1 In addition, the Commissioners were asked a range of questions about The Select Committee (2000), Leggatt (2001) and Commissioner 'collegiality'.

Appendix 2

Interview Topic Guide for Appellants[1]

Introduction

Introduce yourself ☐
Remind appellant of his/her opting-in to the research ☐
Arrange convenient time/date for telephone interview ☐
Give instructions about the interview:

1. It will last about 30 minutes; ☐
2. I am tape-recording the interview – is that OK with you? ☐

A Basic Data

Date of Birth? ☐
Which ethnic group would you describe yourself as belonging to? ☐
Employment and/or benefit status now? ☐

B General Questions

1 THE MAIN ISSUE(S) IN THE APPEAL ☐

'Can you identify the main issue(s) relating to your appeal to the Commissioners?'

2 INDEPENDENCE of COMMISSIONERS ☐

'Do you think the local tribunal is independent?'
'Do you think the Commissioner is independent?'
'Do you think your case was heard fairly by the Commissioner?'

3 REPRESENTATION ☐

'Are you represented in the Commissioner's appeal?'
(confirm contact details of rep)
'Do you think it is necessary to be represented?'
'What views do you have, if any, about the quality of representation?'
'Could you represent yourself before the Commissioners?'

---

[1] This document was the *aide memoire* used by the telephone interviewer. Telephone conversations would not necessarily follow the order here; the boxes on the right were ticked by the interviewer when the relevant headings had been answered by a respondent in whatever order they arose.

4 TIMESCALE of APPEAL □

'I have seen from your case file that the local tribunal hearing was on [date]………………. And your application for leave/appeal to the Commissioners was received in their office on [date] ……………….. What was happening during this period?'

'I have seen from your case file that your application for leave/appeal to the Commissioners was received in their office on [date] ……….. and the Commissioner's decision was issued on [date]……………… What was happening during this period?'

5 ORAL or PAPER HEARING □

'Did you ask for an oral hearing'?
'Did you get an oral hearing?'
'Do you consider that your case would have been treated any differently if it had been heard orally?'

6 OUTCOMES □

'What do you think was the outcome of your appeal'?
'Has/have the outcome(s) of your appeal to the Commissioner had any effect on your confidence in the social security appeals system?'

7 FINAL POINTS

(i) 'Have you any other points you would like to make about your experience of the going through the appeal process to the Commissioners?' □

(ii) The tape will be wiped after transcription and contents will remain confidential. Any material eventually used in our research publications will be suitably anonymised. □

(iii) The research project will pay the appellant £15 for the interview – payable by cheque from the University – cheque will arrive within 5 or 6 weeks. (Confirm postal address.) □

End

Appendix 3

List of Commissioners[1]

Commissioners for Great Britain

Chief Commissioner:
*HH Judge G R Hickinbottom *(appointed September 2003)*

Commissioners

Edinburgh:
*Mr D J May QC *(appointed 1993)*
*Mrs L T Parker *(appointed 2000)*

London:
*Mr M Rowland *(appointed 1993)*
*Mr J Mesher *(appointed 1993) (Chairman, Pensions Appeal Tribunals)*
*Mr J M Henty *(appointed 1993)*
*Mr P L Howell QC *(appointed 1994) (Judge, Employment Appeal Tribunal)*
*Mr R J C Angus *(appointed 1995)*
*Mr S J Pacey *(appointed 1996) (Immigration Adjudicator)*
*Mr J P Powell *(appointed 1996)*
*Mr H Levenson *(appointed 1997)*
*Dr D Williams *(appointed 1998)*
*Mr E Jacobs *(appointed 1998)*
*Mr A Lloyd-Davies *(appointed 1998)*
*Miss C Fellner *(appointed 1999) (Chairman, Pensions Appeal Tribunals)*
*Mr A Bano *(appointed 2000) (Chairman, Pensions Appeal Tribunals)*
*Mr C E L Turnbull *(appointed 2000)*
*Mrs E A Jupp *(appointed 2001) (Chairman, Pensions Appeal Tribunals)*

Past Commissioners

*H H Judge M Harris *(appointed 2001) retired as Chief Commissioner September 2003*
*Mr W M Walker QC *(appointed 1988) retired August 2003*
*Mrs R F M Heggs *(appointed 1981) retired 30 August 2002*
*Mr M Heald QC *(appointed 1988) retired 30 June 2002*

---

[1] *Source:* The unofficial website of Commissioner Howell QC, see www.hywels.clara.co.uk/commrs/list.htm; and the Commissioners' 'official' website, see www.osscsc.gov.uk/

* H H Judge K A Machin QC *(appointed 1990) retired as Chief Commissioner July 2001*
Mr R A Sanders *(appointed 1986) retired on 31 October 1999*
Mr J G Mitchell QC *(appointed 1979) retired on 31 May 1999*
Dr M J Goodman *(appointed 1979) retired on 31 December 1998*
Dr D G Rice *(appointed 1979) retired on 30 May 1998*
Mr A T Hoolahan QC *(appointed 1986) retired on 1 September 1997*
Mr A W E Wheeler CBE *(appointed 1992) retired on 1 September 1997*
Mr J B Morcom *(appointed 1981) died on 23 January 1997*

Commissioners for Northern Ireland

Chief Commissioner

*H H Judge J A H Martin QC *(appointed 1997)*

Commissioner
*Mrs M F Brown *(appointed 1997)*

Mr C McNally *(appointed 1981) retired on 31 July 1999*

(*) = Interviewed by research team

Deputy Commissioners

Alan Gamble *(appointed 1994)*
Alison Green *(appointed 1995)*
Christopher Whybrow QC *(appointed 1996)*
Ann Humphrey *(appointed 1996)*
*John Wright QC *(appointed 1997)*
Michael Mark *(appointed 1997)*
Elisabeth Ovey *(appointed 1997)*
Robin White *(appointed 1997)*
David Burns QC *(appointed 1998)*
Anne McGavin *(appointed 1998)*
Harcourt Concannon *(appointed 1999)*
Jeremy Thomas *(appointed 2000)*
Sir Crispin Agnew of Lochnaw Bt QC *(appointed 2000)*
Nicholas Paines QC *(appointed 2000)*
Richard Poynter *(appointed 2000)*
Alison Rowley *(appointed 2000)*
Nick Wikeley (appointed 2000)

Appendix 4

Prefix Definition of OSSCSC Case Reference Numbers[1]

CA	Attendance Allowance
CDLA	Disability Living Allowance
CDWA	Disability Working Allowance
CF	Child Benefit
CFC	Family Credit
CFIS	Family Income Support
CG	Bereavement/Guardianship/ Maternity/ Death/ Invalid
CI	Disablement/ Reduced Earnings
CIB	Incapacity Benefit
CIS	Income Support
CJSA	Jobseekers Allowance
CM	Mobility Allowance
CP	Retirement Pension
CS	Invalidity/ Severe Disablement/ Sickness
CSB	Supplementary Benefit
CSSP	Statutory Sick Pay
CTC	Working Families/ Disabled Tax Credit
CU	Unemployment Benefit
CFG	Forfeiture – Widows/ Bereavement Benefit
CFP	Forfeiture – Retirement Pension
CPC	State Pension Credit
CHR	Home Responsibilities
CCS	Child Support
CH	Housing/ Council Tax Benefits
CCR	Compensation Recovery
UK	Unknown (only used when OSSCSC cannot identify what type of benefit the claimant is appealing, it is changed to a proper benefit category when identified at a later stage)

[1] Supplied to the authors by OSSCSC in March 2005. The OSSCSC website also carries a category of benefit index at: www.osscsc.gov.uk/practiceproc/ncd5.htm

Appendix 5[1]

The Publication and Citation of Commissioners' Decisions

The Social Security and Child Support Commissioners of Great Britain Practice Memorandum No 2

1. Decisions of Commissioners are available on notice for inspection and for the purchase of copies either at the London Office or the Edinburgh Office of the Commissioners. They are also available electronically (further details of which can be found on the Office website, at www.osscsc.gov.uk/decisions/subscriptions.htm).

2. Selected decisions of Commissioners are published on the website of the Commissioners' Office (www.osscsc.gov.uk). Decisions of more general importance that have been issued in the last 12 months are highlighted on the website under "What's New?", and will also be sent by e-mail or in hard copy to subscribers. Details of the subscription service are available from either of the Commissioners' Offices.

3. Decisions are selected for reporting in the official series of reports by an Editorial Board of Commissioners, after consultation with all other Commissioners. Relevant decisions of the higher courts are published in the same series of reports. Decisions are selected for reporting because they are considered to be of general significance and to contribute to the orderly development and operation of the law. They will usually be decisions that deal with points of construction of legislation or with questions of legal principle but, where experience has shown a particular need for guidance in some area of practice, may be decisions that illustrate the application of legislation or established legal principle in that area.

4. Reported decisions of individual Commissioners may be taken to command the broad assent of at least a majority of Commissioners.

5. Suggestions as to, or comments on, the suitability of any decision for reporting and/or publication on the website may be sent to the Secretary to the Editorial Board at the London Office of the Commissioners.

---

[1] All the current *Practice Memoranda* are available on the OSSCSC website: www.osscsc.gov.uk.

6. In whatever form Commissioners' decisions are published or made available for public inspection, the anonymity of parties to decisions will be preserved so far as reasonably practicable.

7. Any decision of a Commissioner may be cited to the Commissioners in written submissions or at an oral hearing. However, reported decisions should be cited in preference to unreported decisions and, in general, unreported cases should be cited only if they decide some point of relevant principle. Citation of numerous unreported decisions that are merely illustrative of the application of a principle to similar facts is unlikely to be of assistance.

8. Where an unreported decision is relied upon by a party in proceedings before a Commissioner, a copy of that decision should be sent by that party to the relevant Commissioners' Office.

9. At least 14 days before an oral hearing, each party should send to the appropriate Commissioners' Office (i) a list of authorities that will be relied upon at the hearing and (ii) a copy of any unreported decision that will be relied upon, unless a copy has already been sent.

10. When citing a reported Commissioner's decision, the report number should be used (e.g. R(CS)1/05). When citing a decision that is not reported, the Commissioners' file number should be given in full (e.g. CIS/1234/2005). The former "starred decision" numbers should not be used. For higher court decisions, the usual citation should be used but, in addition, if the case is also reported in the Commissioners' series of reports, that report number should also be used.

11. For the avoidance of doubt, the Chief Commissioner's Practice Memorandum of 25 March 2002 in respect of the publication and citation of Commissioners' decisions is revoked.

His Honour Judge Gary Hickinbottom
Chief Commissioner
31 December 2004

Appendix 6[1]

The Timetable for Tribunal Reform in the Government's White Paper

2001	August	Leggatt Review published and public consultation started
2003	March	Lord Irvine announces Government's intention to establish new Tribunals Service
	Nov	Lord Filkin in his speech to the Council on Tribunals' Conference, sets out a broader vision for reform
2004	Feb	DCA tribunals separate from the Court Service to form the nucleus of the new system
	June	Administration of General Commissioners of Income Tax transferred to DCA Tribunals Group Law Commission housing adjudication project starts
	July	**White Paper published**
	Sept	Chief Executive of the new Tribunals Service agency appointed
	Oct	Better Information Project starts
2005	Jan	Pilots of PDR and enhanced advice schemes commence
	April	Tribunals Service executive agency launched on a shadow basis, taking over the administration of the DCA tribunals
	June	Law Commission consultation paper on housing adjudication *Courts and Tribunals Bill introduced*
	Oct	Better Information Project reports
	Dec	*Royal Assent for Courts and Tribunals Bill*
2006	Jan	Review of role of different types of members starts
	March	Evaluation of enhanced advice and PDR schemes published
	April	Formal launch of Tribunals Service agency *Tribunal Procedure Committee established* SENDIST and Employment Tribunals Service join new service *Council on Tribunals becomes Administrative Justice Council*
	Dec	Review of roles reports
2007	Jan	Review of local government tribunals starts
	April	Appeals Service joins new service *Single judicial office implemented* *Administrative appeals tribunal operational*
	May	Law Commission final report on housing adjudication
2008	Jan	Review of local government tribunals reports
	April	CICAP and Mental Health tribunals join new service
2009	April	Remaining central government tribunals join new service

[1] *Source*: White Paper (2004: 55). The White Paper states that some changes will require legislation – these are set out in italics.

Bibliography

Adler M (2002) 'Who is Afraid of Sir Andrew Leggatt?' (2002) 9 *Journal of Social Security Law*, 177.

Adler M and Bradley A (1975), *Justice, Discretion and Poverty*, Abingdon: Professional Books.

Adler, M and Gulland J (2003) *Tribunal Users' Experiences, Perceptions and Expectations: A Literature Review*, London: Council on Tribunals.

Akehurst M (1970) 'Statements of Reasons for Judicial and Administrative Decisions (1970) 33 *Modern Law Review* 154.

Altbeker A (2003) 'Justice Through Specialisation? The Case of the Specialised Commercial Crime Court', *Monograph 76*, Institute for Security Studies, Pretoria. http://www.iss.co.za/Publications/Monographindex.html

Appeals Service (2004) *The Appeals Service: Annual Report and Accounts 2003-04,* (HC 785), Appeal Service Agency, London: The Stationery Office.

Appeals Service Agency (2005) *Business Plan 2004-05*, Appeal Service Agency, London: The Stationery Office.

Bacon R (2005) 'A Study in Tribunal Amalgamation: The Importance of a Principled Approach' 12 *Journal of Social Security Law* 81.

Baldwin J and McConville M (1977) *Negotiated Justice: pressures to plead guilty*, London : Martin Robertson.

Baldwin J, Wikeley N and Young R (1992) *Judging Social Security: the adjudication of claims for benefit in Britain*, Oxford: Clarendon Press.

Berthoud R (1995) 'The medical assessment of incapacity: a case study of research and policy' (1995) 2 *Journal of Social Security Law* 61.

Beveridge Report (1942) *Social Insurance and Allied Services* (Cmd 6404), London: HMSO.

Beveridge W (1953) *Power and Influence: an Autobiography*, London: Hodder and Stoughton.

Bonner D (1995) 'Incapacity for work: a new benefit and new tests' (1995) 2 *Journal of Social Security Law* 86.

Bonner D (2002) 'From whence the Social Security Commissioners? The creation of the national insurance commissioner and the industrial injuries commissioner' (2002) 9 *Journal of Social Security Law* 11-42.

Bonner D and Buck T (2004) 'Reflections on the appointment of a new Chief Social Security Commissioner' (editorial) (2004) 11 *Journal of Social Security Law* 1-5.

Bonner D, Buck T and Sainsbury R (2001) 'Researching the Role and Work of the Social Security and Child Support Commissioner' (2001) 8 *Journal of Social Security Law* 9-34.

Bruce M (1968) *The Coming of the Welfare State* (4th ed) London: Batsford.

Buck T (1987) 'Unemployment Benefit: The "Full Extent Normal" Rule' [1987] *Journal of Social Welfare Law* 23-36.

Buck T (1989) 'Part-time workers and Unemployment Benefit: Chief Adjudication Officer *v* Brunt and another' (1989) 52 *Modern Law Review* 93-104.

Buck T (1993) 'The Disabled Citizen' in Blackburn R (ed) *Citizenship Rights,* London: Mansell, pp 179-200.

Buck T (2000) *The Social Fund: Law and Practice* (2nd ed) Sweet & Maxwell, London.

Buck T (2001) 'A Model of Independent Review?' in Partington M (ed) *The Leggatt Review of Tribunals: Academic Seminar Papers*, Bristol Centre for the Study of Administrative Justice, Working Paper Series No 3, pp 127-140.

Buck T (ed) (1998) *Judicial Review and Social Welfare*, London and Washington: Pinter.

Buck T and Smith R (2003) *Poor Relief or Poor Deal? The social fund, safety nets and social security,* Ashgate, London.

Bull D (1980) The Anti-Discretion Movement in Britain: Fact or Phantom?' [1980] *Journal of Social Welfare Law* 65.

Carnwath R (2004) 'Tribunal Justice – Building on Strength', Lord Justice Carnwath's speech to the Council on Tribunals' annual conference, 25 November 2004.

Cazalet E (2001) 'Specialized Courts: Are they a "Quick Fix" or a Long Term Improvement in the Quality of Judges?' A World Bank Conference: *Empowerment, Security and Opportunity Through Law and Justice*, July 8-12 2001, Saint Petersburg,

Commission for Judicial Appointments (2004) *Annual Report 2004*, London: Stationery Office.

Commissioners' Annual Report (2003) *The Office of the Social Security and Child Support Commissioners of Great Britain: Annual Report 2002-03*, London: OSSCSC.

Commissioners' Annual Report (2004) *The Office of the Social Security and Child Support Commissioners of Great Britain: Annual Report 2003-04*, London: OSSCSC.

Commissioners' Annual Report (2005) *The Office of the Social Security and Child Support Commissioners of Great Britain: Annual Report 2004-05*, London: OSSCSC.

Committee of Justice (1988) *Administrative Justice: some necessary reforms*, Committee of Justice/All Souls Review of Administrative law in the United Kingdom, (Chairman: Patrick Neill), Oxford: Clarendon Press.

Cornish W and Clark G (1989) *Law and Society in England 1750-1950*, London: Sweet and Maxwell.

Council on Tribunals (1999) *Annual Report 1998-1999* (HC 00), London: TSO.

Council on Tribunals (2000) *Annual Report 1999-2000* (HC 23), London: TSO.

Council on Tribunals (2001) *Annual Report 2000-2001* (HC343), London: TSO.

Council on Tribunals (2002) *Annual Report 2001-2002* (HC 14), London: TSO.

Council on Tribunals (2003) *Annual Report 2002-2003* (HC 1163), London: TSO.

Council on Tribunals (2004) *Annual Report 2003-2004* (HC 750), London: TSO.

CPAG (1985) *Burying Beveridge*, London: Child Poverty Action Group.

Dicey (1914) *Law and Public Opinion in England during the Nineteenth Century* (2nd ed) republished with a Preface by ECS Wade as a Macmillan Student Edition (1963), London: Macmillan.

Donoghue B and Jones G (1973) *Herbert Morrison Portrait of a Politician,* London: Weidenfeld and Nicholson.

Donoughmore Committee (1932) *Report of the Committee on Ministers' Powers* (Cmd 4060), London: HMSO.

Dworkin R (1986) *Law's Empire*, Fontana, London.

DWP (2004) *Departmental Report: Department for Work and Pensions*, Cm 6211, The Stationery Office.

DWP SA4 (2003) Social security agreement between the UK and Jersey and Guernsey, (leaflet) DWP (Communications), Leeds, October 2003.

Eardley, T. and Sainsbury, R. (1993) 'Managing Appeals: The Control of Housing Benefit Internal Reviews by Local Authority Officers' in *Journal of Social Policy*, 4, 461-485.

Franks Report (1957) *Report of the Committee of Administrative Tribunals and Enquiries* (Chairman, Rt Hon Sir Oliver Franks), (Cmnd 218), London: HMSO.

Fraser D (1984), *The Evolution of the British Welfare State*, (2nd ed) London. and Basingstoke: Macmillan.

Fulbrook J (1978) *Administrative Justice and the Unemployed*, London: Mansell.

Fuller L (1978) 'The Forms and Limits of Adjudication' 92 *Harvard Law Review* 353-409.

Genn H and Genn Y (1989) *The Effectiveness of Representation at Tribunals*, London: Lord Chancellor's Department.

Gilbert M (1986) *Road to Victory: Winston S Churchill 1941-1945*, London: Heinemann.

Government Response (2000) Select Committee on Social Security, Fourth Special Report (1999-2000) Government Response to the 4th Report of the Social Security Committee, (HC 868), August, 2000. (See also 'Select Committee (2000) below.)

Greer S (1999) 'A Guide to the Human Rights Act 1998' [1999] *European Law Review* 3.

Griffiths J (1969) *Pages From Memory*, London: Dent & Sons.

Harris J (1997) *William Beveridge: a Biography* (2nd ed) Oxford: Clarendon Press.

Harris N (1995) 'The Social Security Commissioners' (1995) 22 *Industrial Law Journal* 222.

Harris N (ed) (2000) *Social Security Law in Context*, Oxford: Oxford University Press.

Hartfree,Y, Stafford B and Beach J (2001) *Housing Benefit and the Appeals Service*, (DSS Research Report No.129) Leeds: CDS.

Hervey T (1999) 'Social Security: the European Union Dimension' in Harris N (ed) *Social Security Law in Context*, Oxford: Oxford University Press, pp. 231-256.

Hewart G (1929) *The New Despotism*, London: Benn.

Judicial Statistics (2004) *Judicial Statistics for the year 2004*, (Cm 6565), London: The Stationery Office.

Kemmis S and McTaggert R (1990) *The Action Research Planner*, Geelong (Australia): Deakin University Press.

Lakhani, B (2003) 'Achieving Policy Goals' in Buck T and Smith R (eds) *Poor Relief or Poor Deal? The social fund, safety nets and social security*' Aldershot: Ashgate.

Larkin P (2004) 'The Rule of Forfeiture and Bereavement Benefits' (2004) 11 *Journal of Social Security Law*, 59.

Law Reporting Committee (1940) Lord Chancellor's Department, *Report of the Law Reporting Committee*, March 1940, London: HMSO.

Leggatt, A (2001) *Tribunals for Users: one system, one service: report of the review of tribunals*, London: The Stationery Office.

Legomsky S (1990) *Specialized Justice: Courts, Administrative Tribunals, and a Cross-national Theory of Specialization*, Oxford: Clarendon Press.

Lewis G (1983) *Lord Atkin*, London: Butterworths.

Lindley N (1885) 'The History of the Law Reports', 1 *Law Quarterly Review* 137.

Lynes T (1976) 'Unemployment Assistance Tribunals in the 1930s', in Adler M and Bradley A (eds) *Justice, Discretion and Poverty: Supplementary Benefit Appeal Tribunals in Britain*, pp 5-31, Abingdon: Professional Books.

Machin K (2001) *Tribunals for Users: Response to the Lord Chancellor's Consultation Paper on the Leggatt Report*, London, 2001. This response and the Scottish and Northern Ireland responses – Walker, 2001 and Martin 2001 – are available on the Commissioners' 'unofficial' website. See http://www.hywels.clara.co.uk/commrs/leggatt.htm

Machin K (1992) 'Error of Law' (1992) 34 *Adviser* 15-16.

Magrath P (2001) *135 Years of The Law Reports and The Weekly Law Reports,* Special Issue, London: Incorporated Council of Law Reporting. http://www.justis.com/titles/iclr_si.html

Martin J (2001) Commissioners Martin, Brown and Powell, *Response to Leggatt Report*, Belfast, 8 October 2001.

Mashaw J L (1983) *Bureaucratic Justice: Managing Social Security Disability Claims*, Yale University Press.

Mesher J (1987) *CPAG's Supplementary Benefit and Family Income Supplement: The Legislation*, (4th ed) London: Sweet and Maxwell.

Micklethwait R, (1976) *The National Insurance Commissioners*, London: Stevens & Sons.

Miller, D (1976) *Social Justice*, Oxford: Clarendon Press.

Nabatchi T and Bingham L B (2002) 'Expanding Our Models of Justice in Dispute Resolution: A Field Test of the Contribution of Interactional Justice'.

International Association for Conflict Management *15th Annual Conference*, June 2002, Utah, USA. http://ssrn.com/abstract=305205

National Audit Office (2003) *Getting it Right, Putting it Right: improving decision-making and appeals in social security benefits*, (HC 1142), 7 November 2003, London: The Stationery Office.

NI Judicial Statistics (1999-2003) *The Northern Ireland Court Service Judicial Statistics 1999, 2000, 2001, 2002, 2003*, London: National Statistics.

Ogus A and Barendt E (1978) *The Law of Social Security*, London: Butterworths.

Ogus A, Barendt E and Wikeley N (1995), *The Law of Social Security* (4th ed) London: Butterworths.

OSSCSC Explanatory Leaflet (2004) 'Appealing to a Social Security or Child Support Commissioner, England and Wales', OSSCSC 'official' website. http://www.osscsc.gov.uk/

Partington M (1989) *Claim in Time: time limits in social security law* (2nd ed) Rochdale: Legal Action Group.

Partington M (1998) 'Judicial Review and Housing Benefit' in Buck T (ed) *Judicial Review and Social Welfare*, London and Washington: Pinter, pp 182-201.

Paterson A (1982) *The Law Lords*, London: Macmillan.

Pennings, F (2001) *Introduction to European Social Security Law*, Studies in Employment and Social Policy, The Hague: Kluwer Law International.

Posner R (1993) *The Problems of Jurisprudence*, Cambridge: Harvard University Press.

Prosser T (1983) *Test Cases for the Poor: legal techniques in the politics of social welfare*, London: Child Poverty Action Group.

Rabin R (1976) 'Job Security and Due Process: Monitoring Administrative Discretion Through a Reasons Requirement' (1976) 44 *University of Chicago Law Review* 60.

Renton Report (1975) *Preparation of Legislation*, report of a committee appointed by the Lord President of the Council (Chairman, Sir David Renton) (Cmnd 6053), London: HMSO.

Resnick D (1977) 'Due Process and Procedural Justice' in Pennock J and Chapman J (eds), *Due Process*, Oxford: Oxford University Press.

Robson P (1998) 'Judicial Review and Social Security' in Buck T (ed) *Judicial Review and Social Welfare*, London: Pinter.

Robson W (1951), *Justice and Administrative Law* (3rd ed) London: Stevens.

Roe G (1996) 'Managing Delay: Perceptions of the Time Taken to Pursue an Appeal via the Social Security Commissioner and its Effects' (unpublished MA dissertation, University of York, 1996).

Rowland M and White R (2004) *Social Security Legislation 2004, vol III, Administration, Adjudication and the European Dimension*, London: Sweet and Maxwell.

Royal Commission on Unemployment Insurance (1932) *Report of the Royal Commission on Unemployment Insurance* (Cmd. 4135), London: HMSO.

Sainsbury R and Eardley T (1991) *Housing Benefit Reviews* (DSS Research Report No. 3) London: HMSO.

Sainsbury R and Eardley T (1992) 'Housing Benefit review boards: a case for slum clearance?' [1992] *Public Law*, 551-559.

Sainsbury R (1992a) 'Administrative justice: discretion and procedure in social security decision-making' in Hawkins K (ed) *The Uses of Discretion,* Oxford: Clarendon Press.

Sainsbury R (1992b) *Survey and Report into the Working of the Medical Appeal Tribunals*, London: HMSO.

Sainsbury R (1999) 'The Reform of Social Security Adjudication' in Harris, M and Partington, M (eds) *Administrative Justice in the 21st Century*, Oxford: Hart Publishing.

Sainsbury R (2000) 'Social Security Decision Making and Appeals' in Harris, N. (ed.) *Social Security Law in Context*, Oxford: Oxford University Press.

Sainsbury R and Corden A (2004) *Medical Evidence and Incapacity Benefit Appeals: Evaluation of a pilot study*, DWP In-house Report no. 129, London: DWP.

Select Committee (1999) *The Modernisation of Social Security Appeals: Eighth Report of Session 1998-99*, (HC 581), 2 November 1999.

Select Committee (2000) *Social Security and Child Support Commissioners: Fourth Report of session 1999-2000*, (HC 263), 24 May 2000. (See also 'Government Response, 2000' above.)

Select Committee (2000a), *The Modernisation of Social Security Appeals: The Government's Response to the Committee's Eighth Report of Session 1998-99*, (HC 182), 27 January 2000.

Select Committee (2001) *Minutes of Evidence: Session 2000-01*, (HC 435-i), 13 June 2001.

Select Committee (2004) *Work of the Committee in 2004: First Report of Session 2004-05* , (HC 133), 12 January, 2005.

Shah P and Menski W (1998) Immigration and Judicial Review' in Buck T (ed) *Judicial Review and Social Welfare*, pp 202-19, London and Washington: Pinter.

Smith P, Bailey S and Gunn M (2002) *Modern English System* (4th ed), London: Sweet & Maxwell.

Star Chamber (2001) 'The Reporting of Commissioners' Decisions', OSSCSC position paper discussing future options in reporting practice (unpublished), 7 November 2001.

Wade H W R and Forsyth C F (2000) *Administrative Law* (8th ed) Oxford: Oxford University Press.

Walker W (2001) Commissioners Walker, May and Parker, *Tribunals for Users: Quality and Judicial Independence Comes First: Response by the Social Security and Child Support Commissioners in Scotland to the Report of the Review of Tribunals by Sir Andrew Leggatt*, Edinburgh, 31 August 2001.

Wallington P and McBride J (1976) *Civil Liberties and a Bill of Rights*, London: Cobden Trust.

White Paper (2004) *Transforming Public Services: Complaints, Redress and Tribunals* (Cm 6243), July 2004, Stationery Office, London.

White, R (1999) *EC Social Security Law*, Longman, London.

Widdison R (2001) 'Some current issues in Legal Information Retrieval', conference paper *16th BILETA Annual Conference* (April 9th – 10th, 2001), University of Edinburgh. http://www.bileta.ac.uk/01papers/widdison.html

Wikeley N (2004) 'Child Trust Funds – asset-based welfare or a recipe for increased inequality?' 11 *Journal of Social Security Law* 189.

Wikeley N, Ogus A and Barendt E (2002) *The Law of Social Security*, London: Butterworths.

Wood P, Poynter R, Wikeley N and Bonner D (2001) *Social Security Legislation 2001: Vol. II: Income Support, Jobseeker's Allowance, Tax Credits and the Social Fund*, Wood P, Poynter R, Wikeley N and Bonner D, London: Sweet and Maxwell.

Index